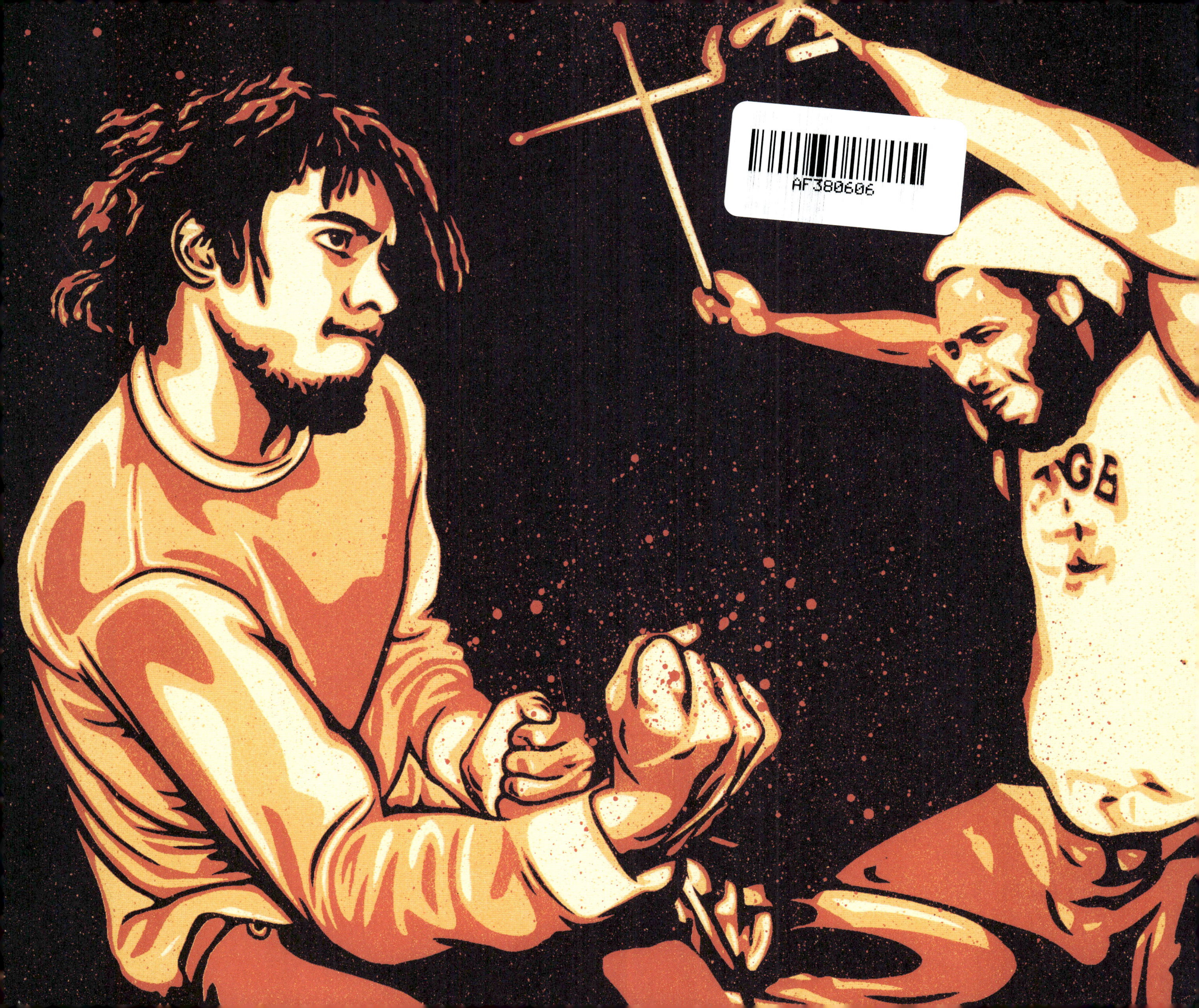

AF380606

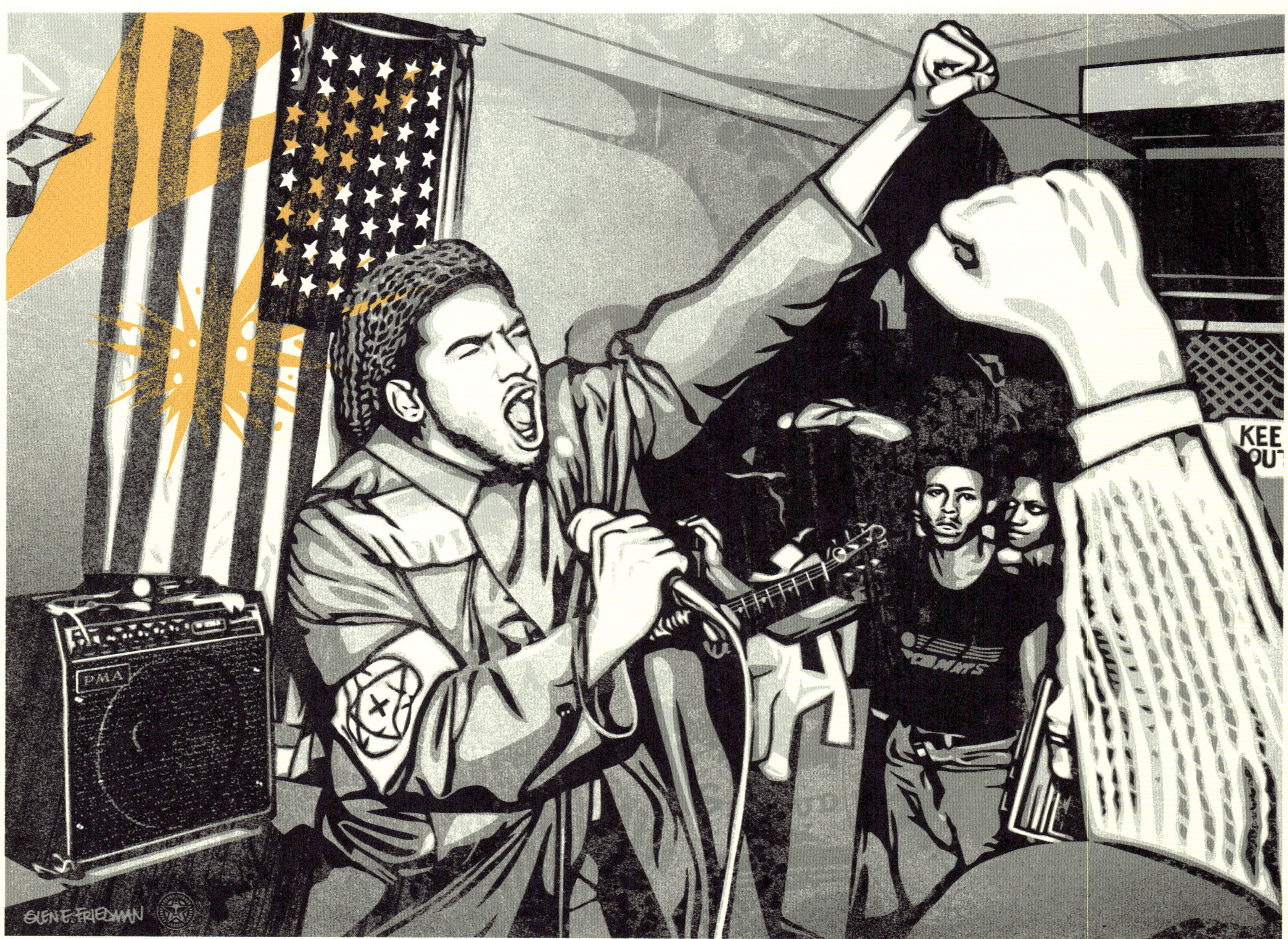

PMA
KEEP
OUT
GLEN E. FRIEDMAN

# FEARLESS VAMPIRE KILLERS

## THE BAD BRAINS PHOTOGRAPHS

## GLEN E. FRIEDMAN

# FEARLESS VAMPIRE KILLERS
## THE BAD BRAINS PHOTOGRAPHS
### GLEN E. FRIEDMAN

FIRST EDITION

Published by Akashic Books
Copyright © 2025 Glen E. Friedman
ISBN: 978-1-63614-208-1
Library of Congress Control Number: 2024940611
Printed in China



All photographs by Glen E. Friedman
preface by H.R., essay by Darryl Jenifer, and afterword by Zack de la Rocha

This book was edited and designed by Glen E. Friedman, with Sohrab Habibion

Special thanks for technical photographic assistance to Michael Vorrasi, Astrida Valigorsky
Endsheet illustrations by Shepard Fairey

Akashic Books, Brooklyn, New York, USA
Facebook, Instagram, Twitter: AkashicBooks
info@akashicbooks.com, www.akashicbooks.com

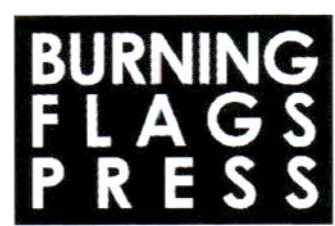

Burning Flags Press
PO Box 69, New York, NY 10003
www.BurningFlags.com

# Preface by H.R.

The song "Fearless Vampire Killers" was a warning to the kids, to let them know what to look out for; we explained what we could. We wanted to encourage kids as they encouraged us, with our attitude that was different—that's what I was singing about . . . just to be more positive and refreshing compared to a lot of other bands. I would say we weren't into politics, yet we wanted to recognize and withstand the problems of the world.

Bad Brains were into having fun. I always wanted to have fun—we did it for the love of the music. We had an attitude about us, and punk rockers had an attitude that was peculiar and different from others at that time. There was nothing but positivity at our shows. We may have been considered a little outrageous and fast at first, but the punk rockers really liked us and were inspired by our shows.

I got a chance to meet cool people from a lot of different places. Good people who loved us and cared about our band and wanted to be loyal to us—that was a beautiful thing and I will always be grateful. The act of getting together and the unity of call-and-response with the audience was always encouraging to us. The fury we had often transferred into the audience, and even got me in trouble sometimes.

I remember meeting Glen when he was a little youth, and I would ask him to please not take these photographs, because I was a shy person, but he would start from the back and move his way to the front and shoot. We were shy, and wanted to do things on our own, but Glen was relentless and just kept on trying to capture our music as outbursts of energy that inspired him, and in return his pictures, being so positive, became receptors for people to see and understand us deeper.

# Introduction by glen E. friedman

It's obvious that the Bad Brains were one of the great bands in all of punk, if not rock and roll in general. I am not here as a historian or a documentarian. My work is just here to excite and inspire others. My work is sharing images that I made of folks who inspire me.

I saw the Bad Brains play at least four or five times before I eventually made my way to photographing them. The shows were phenomenal; they played like no one else and astonished people everywhere they went, all before they had nothing more than one 7" record. Those first times I saw them, the attendance was usually between ten and thirty people, no more. But that didn't stop anyone from experiencing the incredible force they were. Singing and shouting along to "Right Brigade" was probably the highlight of those shows for me among all the blasting incredible songs.

I can tell you with 100 percent certainty that it was a show at the Botany Talk Lounge (aka Botany Rocks), a combination bar and plant shop in New York City's Botany district on Sixth Avenue in the upper 20s, just a few days after Christmas in 1980, when I brought "slam dancing" to New York for the first time. I had been back in Los Angeles where I started college that fall. I'd seen Michael "X-Head" Marine slowly strutting around the dance floor of the Starwood nightclub in West Hollywood, at an X show. He would speed up as the tempo of the music sped up; it was scary, totally threatening, and exciting all at the same time, as many things are. Within weeks, everyone was moving to faster music like this; the tempo of the original "pogoing" up and down just could not keep up with it. So when I saw the Bad Brains again at the show in NYC, I was going off, bashing other dancers in this small 15'-by-15' area in front of the stage, knocking people over like I was a bowling ball and they were all pins. Harley Flanagan (of the Stimulators at that time) was there, as well as my high school friend Robbie CryptCrasher, fanzine creator Jack Rabid, and a few other people I knew. They all took note. Some guy came up to me after the show and asked if I wanted to fight him and why I was being so belligerent on the dance floor. I replied, "It's just the music, I kinda had to!" Seed was planted. History tells us that two of the original Beastie Boys met there at the Bad Brains show the following night. When I came back to the city at the end of the school year, what I introduced had morphed into something way different—New Yorkers had turned it into a "moshing" circle of sorts, the antithesis of the chaotic, out-of-control free-for-all of the original style. Disappointing . . .

but I digress. Just had to get that story out! Let's get back to the Bad Brains.

I don't know why it took me so long to shoot the Bad Brains, but the truth was, I hadn't shot live shows more than a few times at that point, and I didn't yet know the band members personally. I was probably intimidated by this, and that they were a bit older. I had made photos of a Stimulators gig because I knew Harley and he was just a little kid, eleven or twelve years old when I first met the rambunctious rascal he was at the time, ha ha. We all loved the Bad Brains, these incredible musicians from Washington, DC, who started frequenting New York more and more as the 1980s began, eventually relocating here. When I first met them, they had a de facto manager who gave me a copy of their first single when I told him I was working with *SkateBoarder's Action Now* magazine, and he gave me a second copy when I told him I was also friendly with Rodney Bingenheimer (who probably had more people listening to his punk radio show in LA than anyone else in the entire country at that time, an "influencer" extraordinaire before that word was ever used). When I went back to school after the holiday, I brought Rodney the first single, "Pay to Cum" . . . He put it on the air during his next show and played it every week for a long time to come—the Bad Brains fire was spreading across the country!

The Bad Brains were all Black. The Bad Brains showed other punk musicians that in fact you could be an incredible musician and be PUNK at the same time.

They were outsiders in the scenes they infiltrated and soon thereafter influenced. I hate to bring it up, but the band is really proud that so many current, famous and infamous—some real, some corny—rock stars claim them as their own, and as a major influence.

Those years that I saw them in early 1980 through 1982 had to be their creative peak. Indeed, they put out much music afterward, but that first "Pay to Cum" single, the ROIR cassette (their first full-length album), and the earlier recordings released years after they were made—including the *Black Dots* album recorded in 1979 (which replicated those first shows I had seen the closest) and the 1980 *Omega Sessions* EP—cannot be topped in my evaluation, in terms of their integrity and hardcore punk mastery. The song "Coptic Times" that was released late in 1982 was the last and hardest incredible blast I heard from them that truly kicked my ass. You can read in various periodicals and histories about the established producers and record labels that tried to make a great, definitive album with them, but in my opinion none of those records came close to the earlier recordings. I remember one time in 1983 standing next to Gary Miller (aka Dr. Know) as we watched the very first Suicidal Tendencies show in New York, at Great Gildersleeves on the Bowery, just up the block from CBGB; I had just produced the debut Suicidal LP and it was getting good reviews all around—it did sound great, and Gary told me he liked it too. I was feeling a bit cocky, and I told Gary that they should've let me produce their album with them. He politely nodded.

There was a show in the summer of 1981 where the Bad Brains set was supposed to start at three a.m., at a club I remember being called the 2+2 (since it was located at #2 Second Avenue) or also the A7 Annex, and more recently I found a flyer where the same spot was called the Warehouse (the building collapsed to rubble in the late eighties). We had to take a freight elevator up a couple of floors to get to the area where the band would play on a stage mere inches above the ground. They had a crazy PA system, and I remember almost no one there and even fewer lights. As promised, they came on around three a.m.—the club didn't even open its doors until midnight. I guess it was because by this point I'd probably met them and had gotten that record played in Los Angeles that I felt comfortable making some photos; I shot less than half a roll of film that night/morning . . . I've included every one of the fourteen photographs on the following pages to start off this book.

Rather than printing everyone's name on each photo over and over again, I'm going to let you know here, just like they did on that cassette-only first album released by ROIR:

H.R.—THROAT
DARRYL—BASSES, BACKING VOCALS
EARL HUDSON—DRUMS, BACKING VOCALS
DR. KNOW—GITS, BACKING VOCALS

In total, I only made around ninety B&W pictures of the Bad Brains, all shot in New York City, and a small handful of color images I made in Los Angeles. (I assume I shot more color at those two LA shows, but they've been lost in the tidal waves of history somewhere, along with one strip of film from the show on December 26, 1981, at CBGB.) This book has almost every photo I made of them that hasn't been lost. I think Bad Brains fanatics will appreciate this, and perhaps photography buffs as well. I also include photos of some of the other bands that were shot on the same rolls of film that I shot the Bad Brains with—a few iconic but lesser-known ones, for sure.

As we age and look back on the special moments we witnessed and survived, seeing this band play at the time I did ranks up there for me. Shooting film, one exposure at a time, waiting for the flash to charge after each exposure, focusing every time after framing the shots, finishing the roll eventually, stashing it in an ultra-safe place until I got it to the lab, since it was the only evidence left of the evening, certainly from my perspective . . . then getting the film developed, seeing what came out and how, days or sometimes weeks after the roll of film was begun. In these mostly tiny venues where sweat dripped not only off our bodies, but off the walls. Where the volume and energy did not give you a choice, other than to go off and get off as intensely as you could. Comfortable or not, angst-ridden or calmed by the storm, most of us went absolutely wild. Hence this book. We got that attitude—the positive mental attitude.

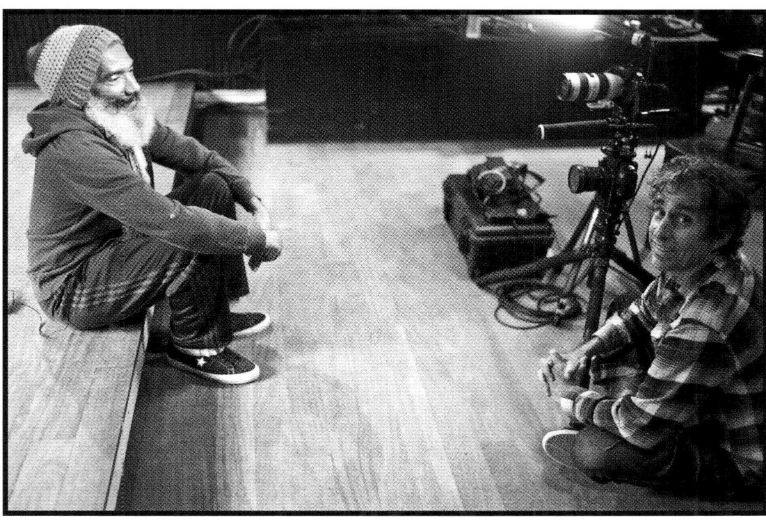

*Interviewing H.R. at the former A7 club at the end of 2018. Photo by Eric Matthies.*

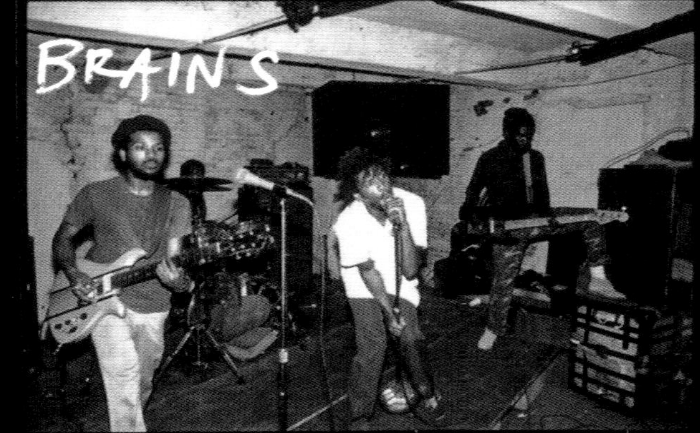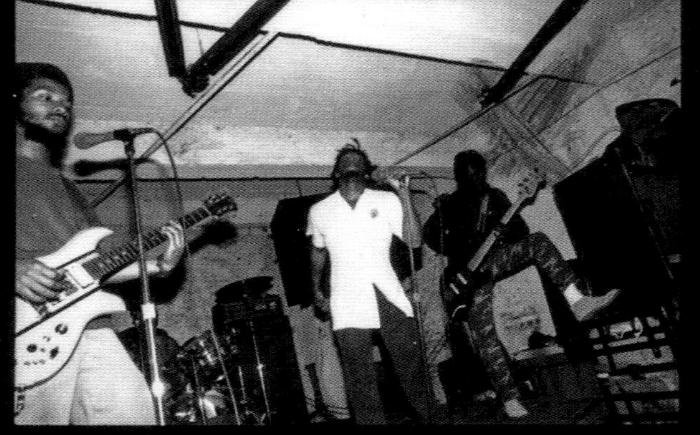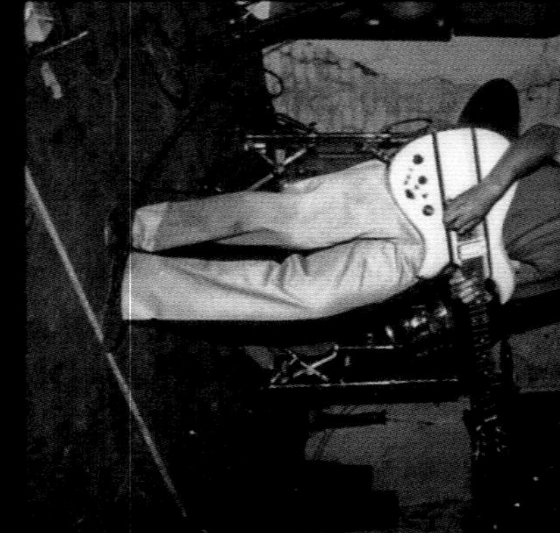

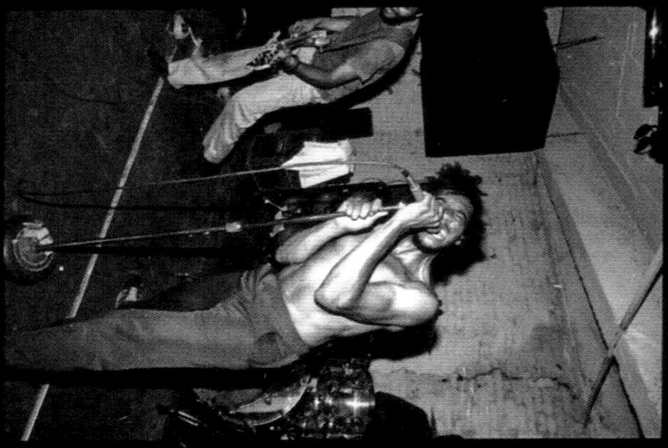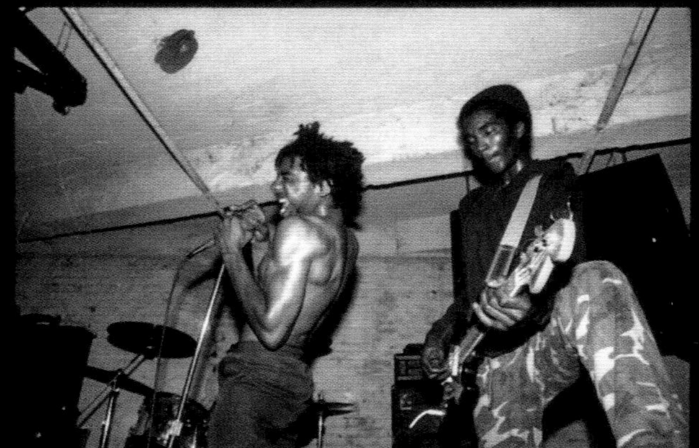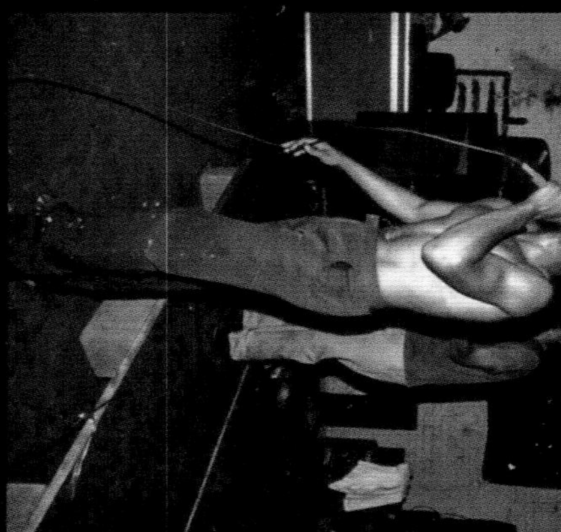

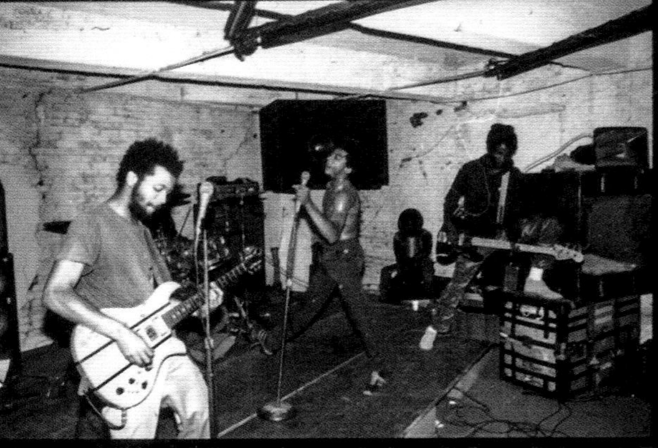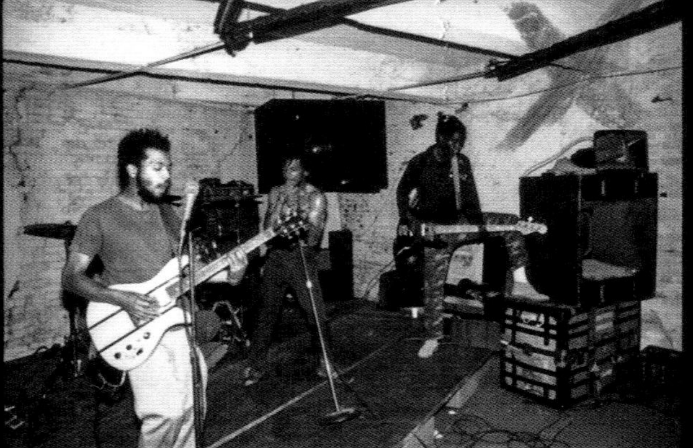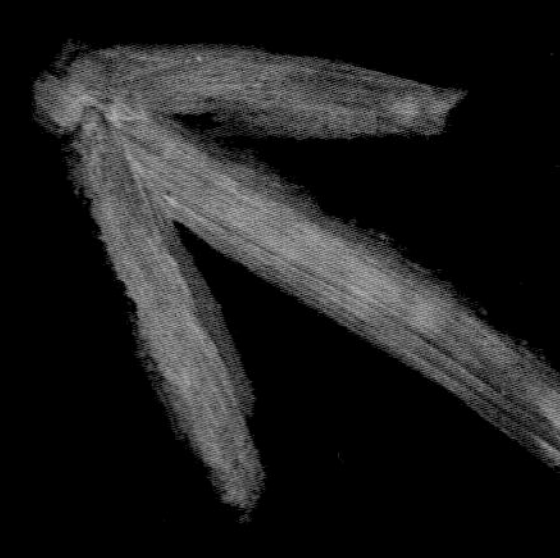

BAD BRAINS

2+2 A.K.A. the WAREHOUSE
NYC 3AM JUNE 12th 1981

→1A →2 →2A →3 →3A
KODAK SAFETY FILM 5063     KODAK SAFETY FILM 5063

SAFETY FILM 5063 →8     KODAK SAFETY FILM 5063 →9A KODAK S

→13A KODAK SAFETY FILM 5063 14A →1 KODAK SAFETY FILM 5063

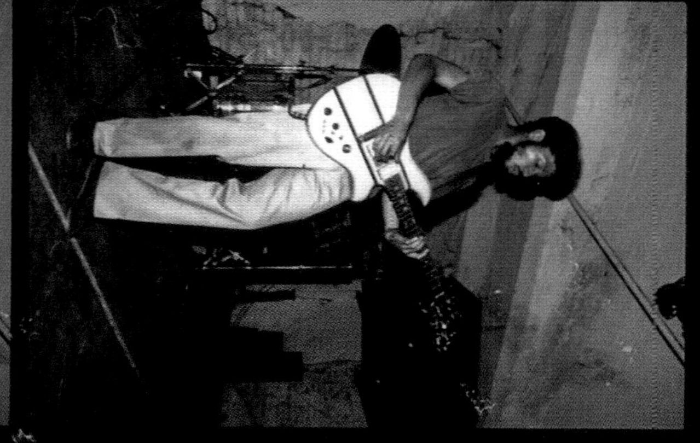
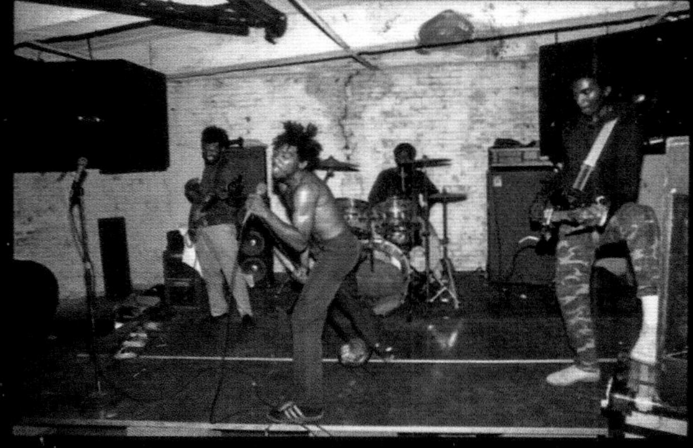
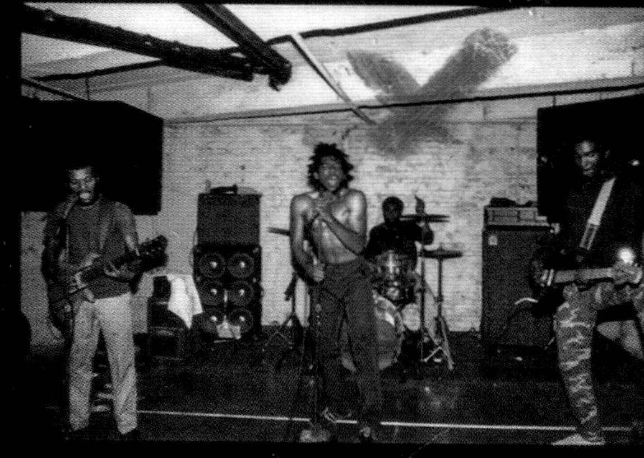

→4A →5 KODAK SAFETY FILM 5063 →5A →6 KODAK SAFETY FILM 5063 →6A →7 KODAK

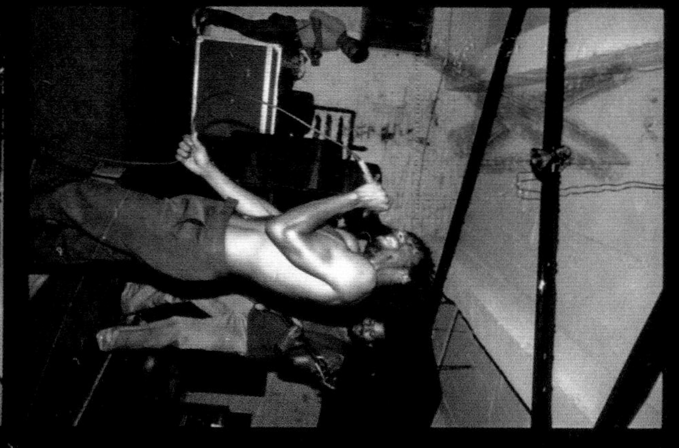
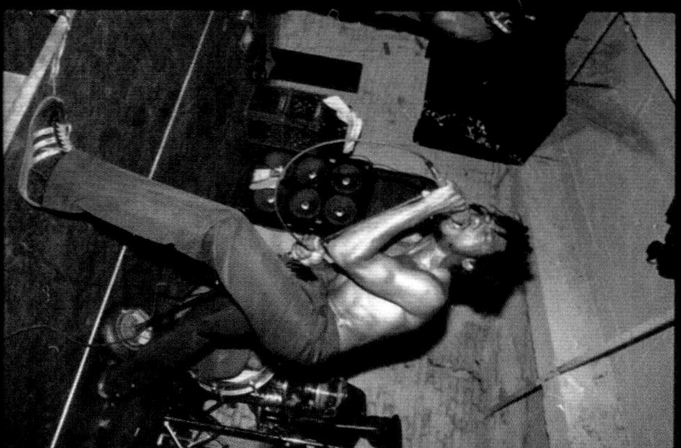
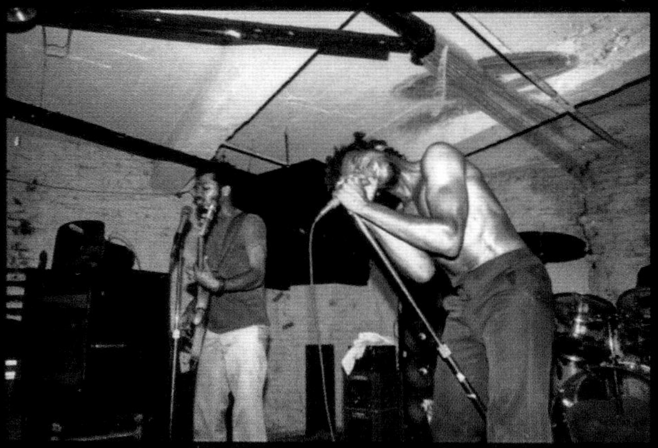

FILM 5063 →10A →11 KODAK SAFETY FILM 5063 →11A →12 KODAK SAFETY FILM 5063 →12A →13

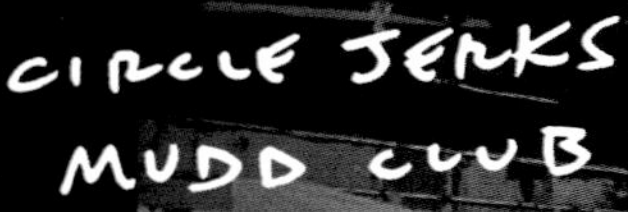
CIRCLE JERKS
MUDD CLUB

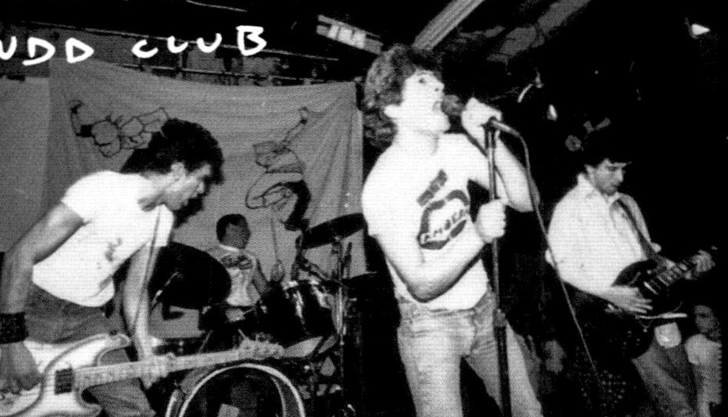
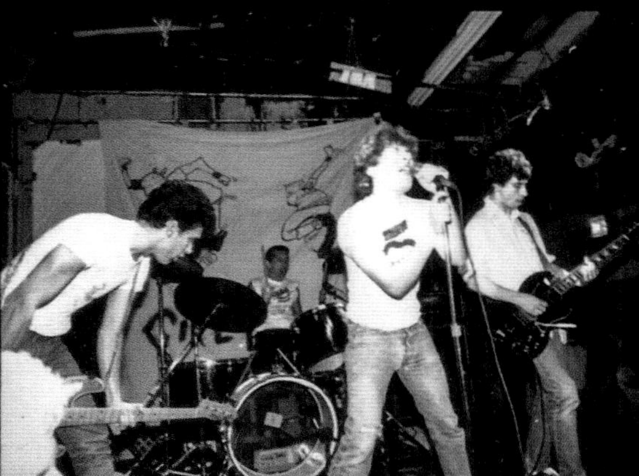
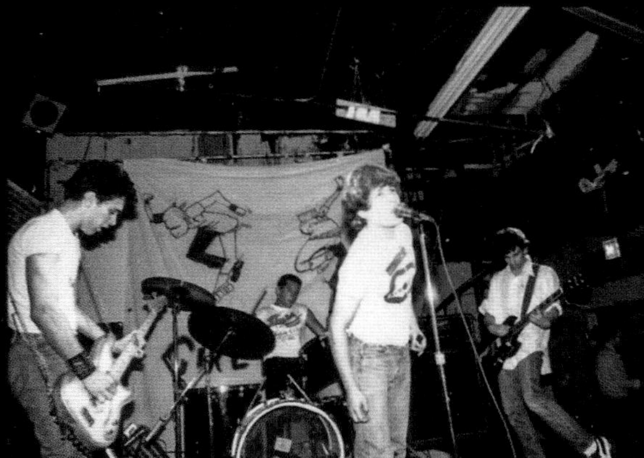

KODAK SAFETY FILM 5063 →17A KODAK SAFETY FILM 5063 →18A →19 KOD

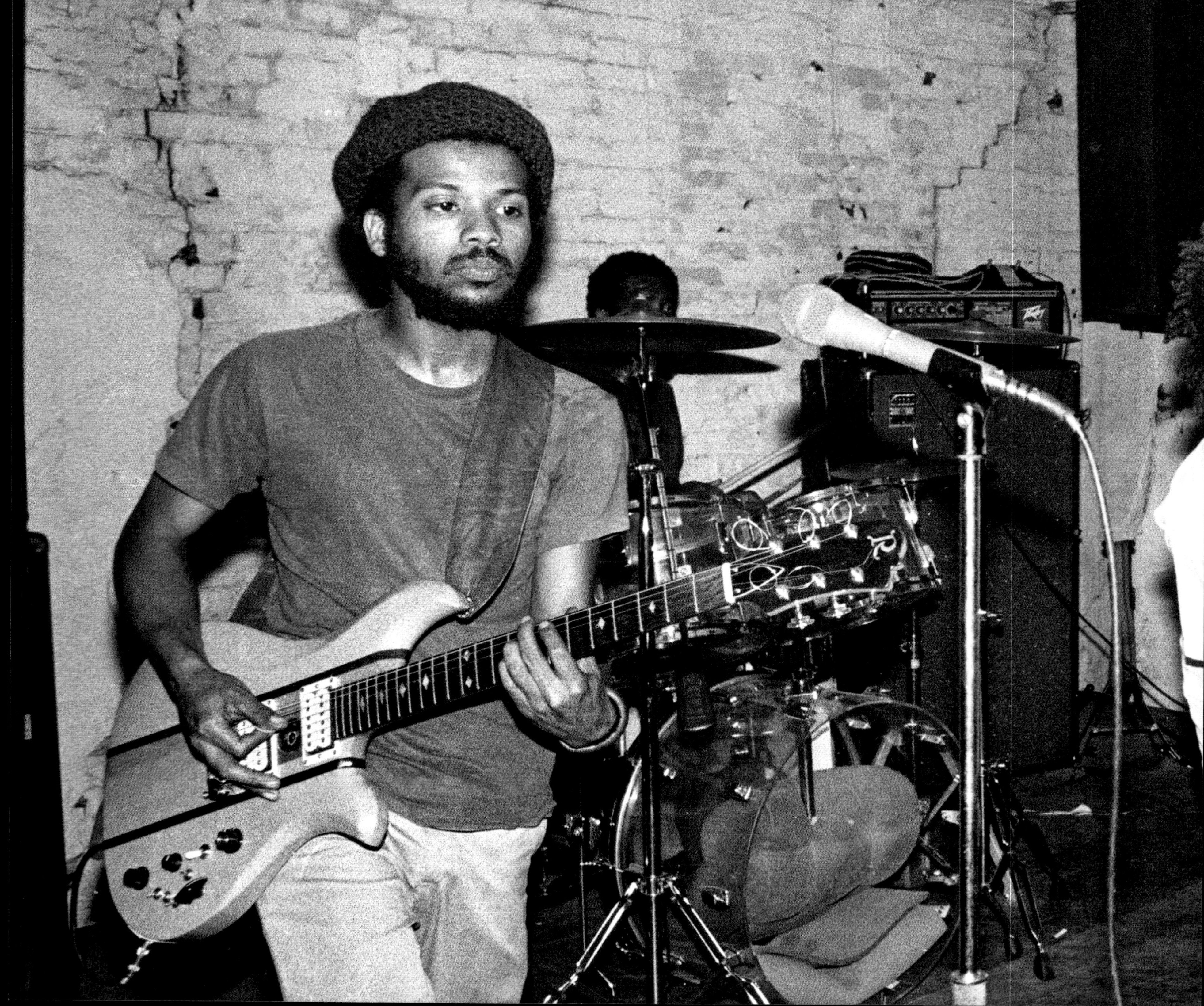

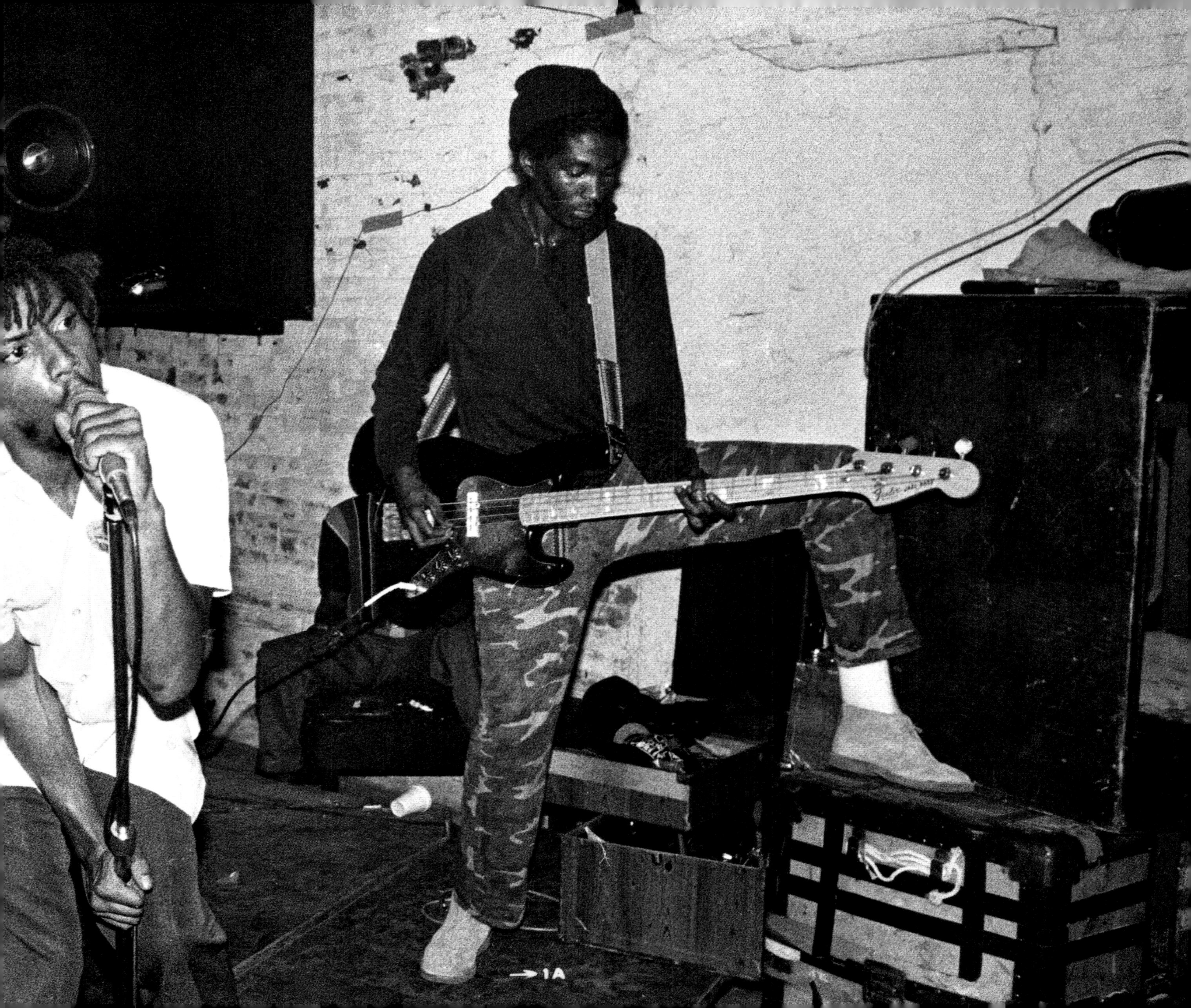
→ 1A

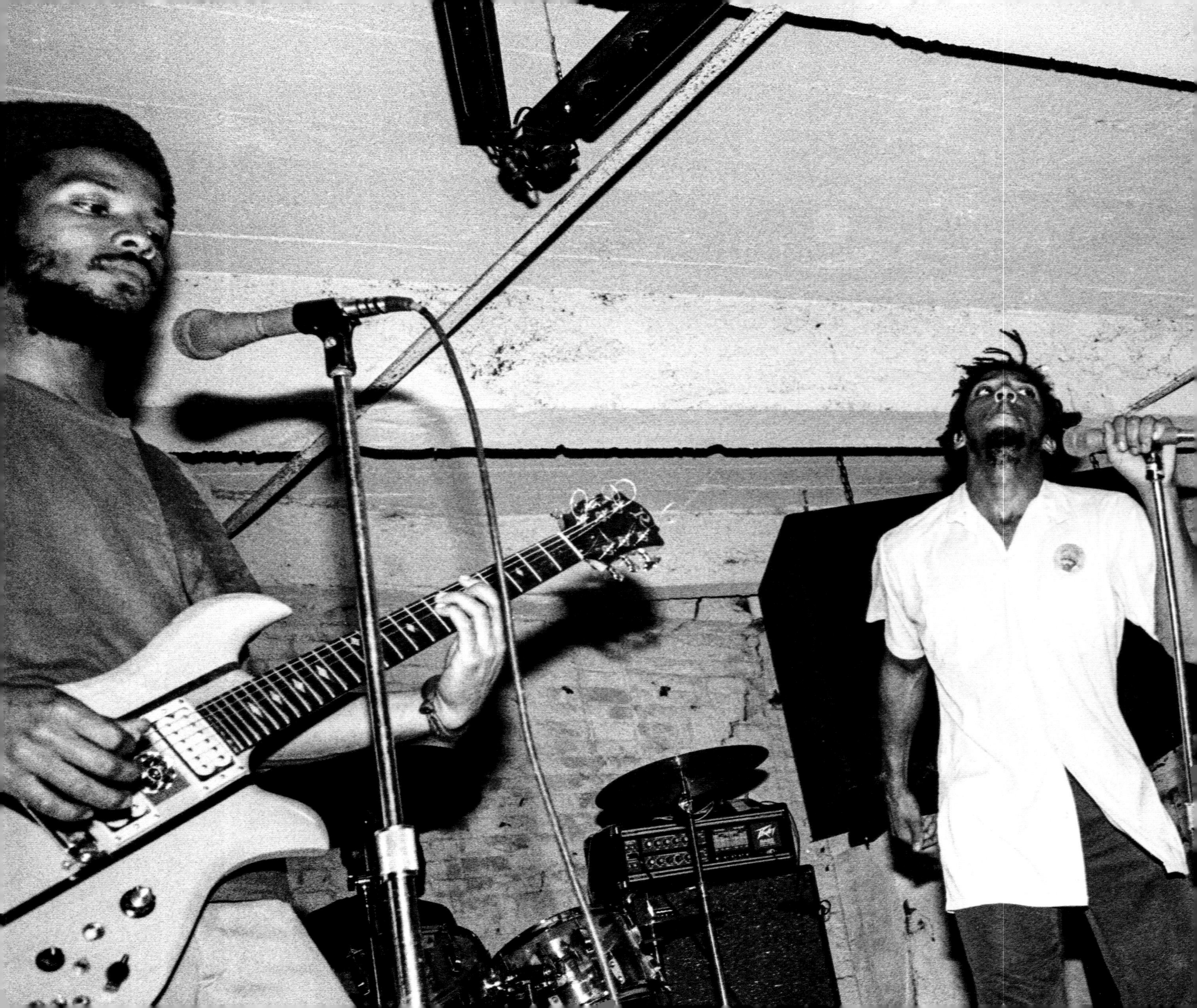

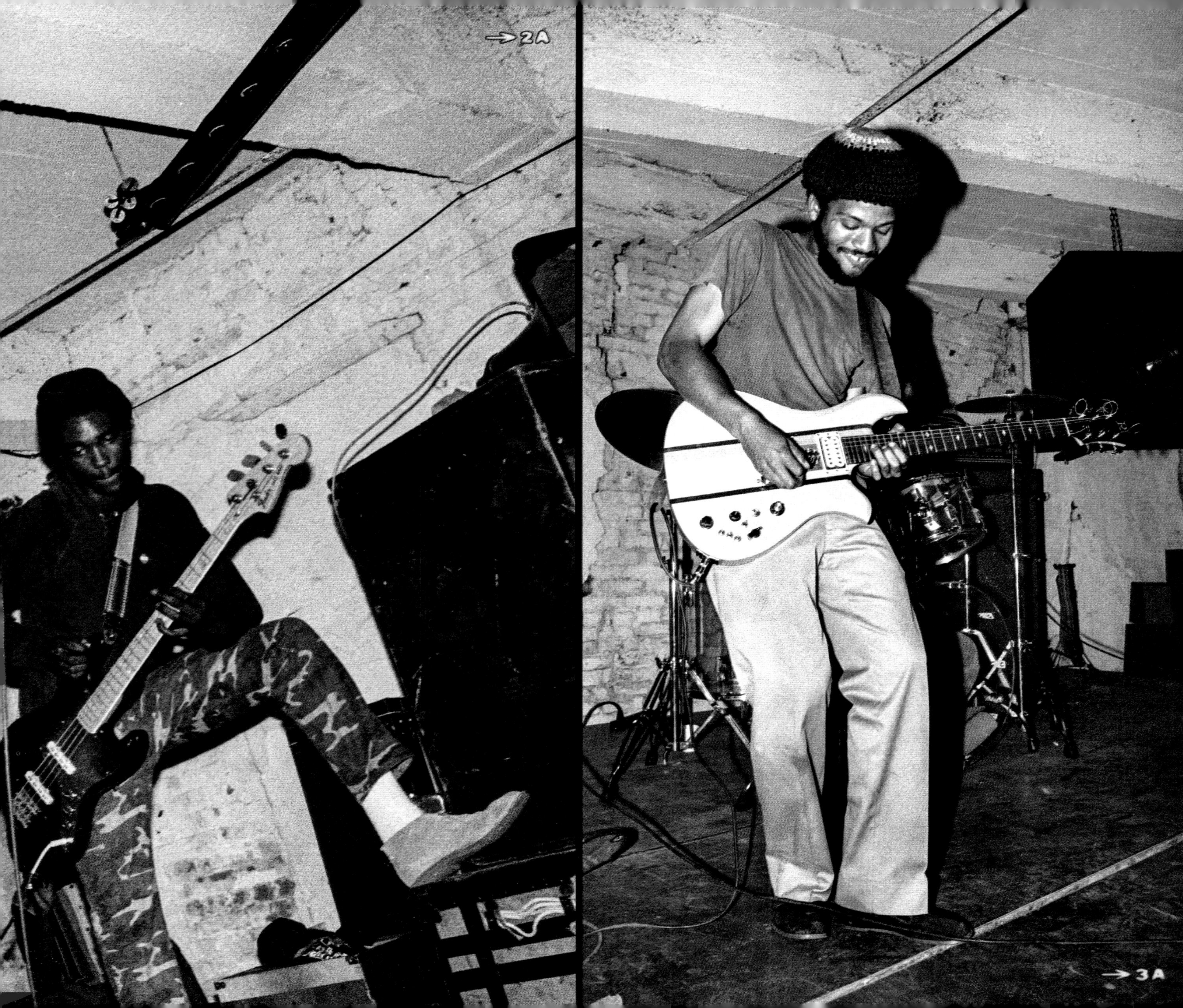
→2A
→3A

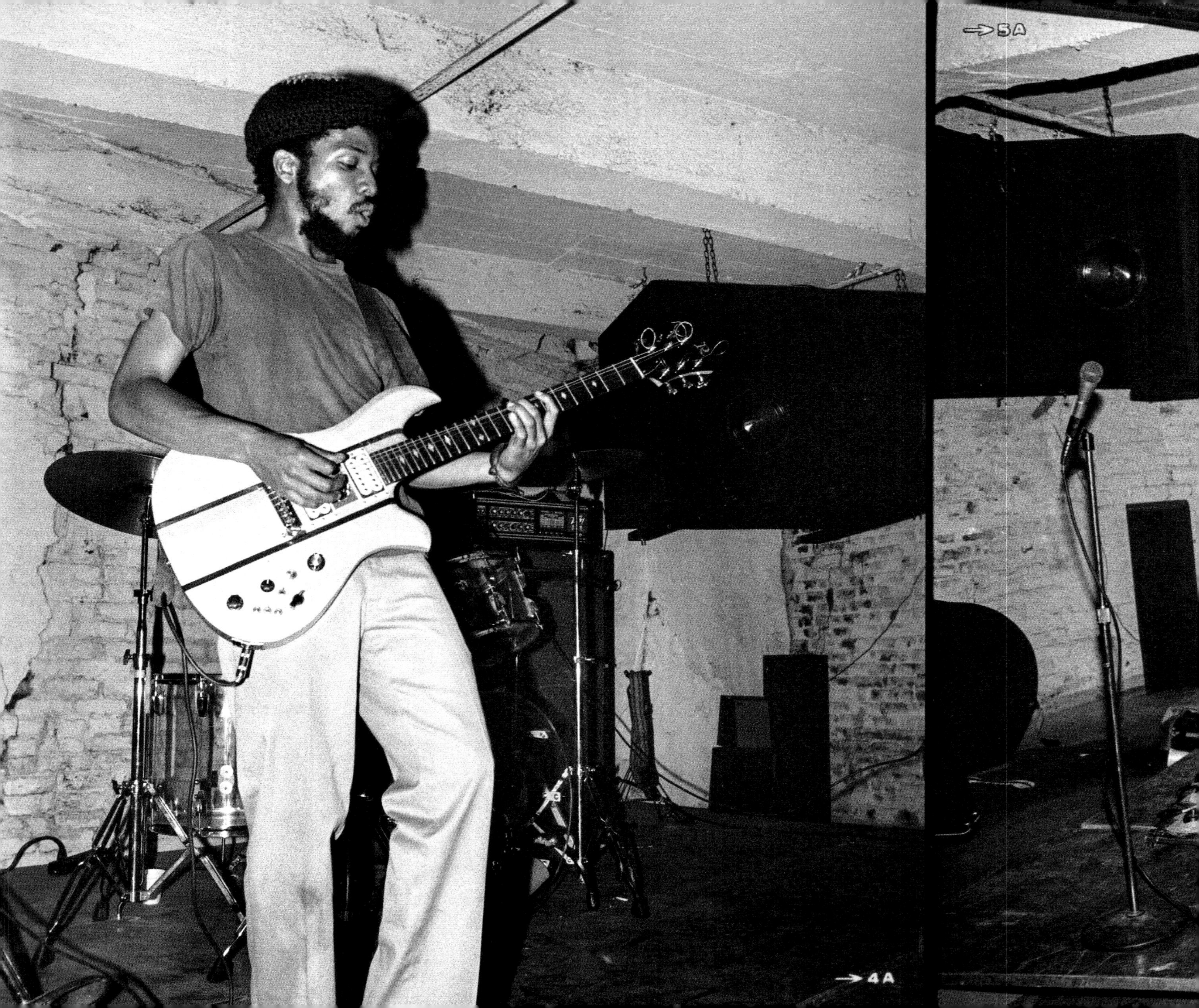

5A
4A

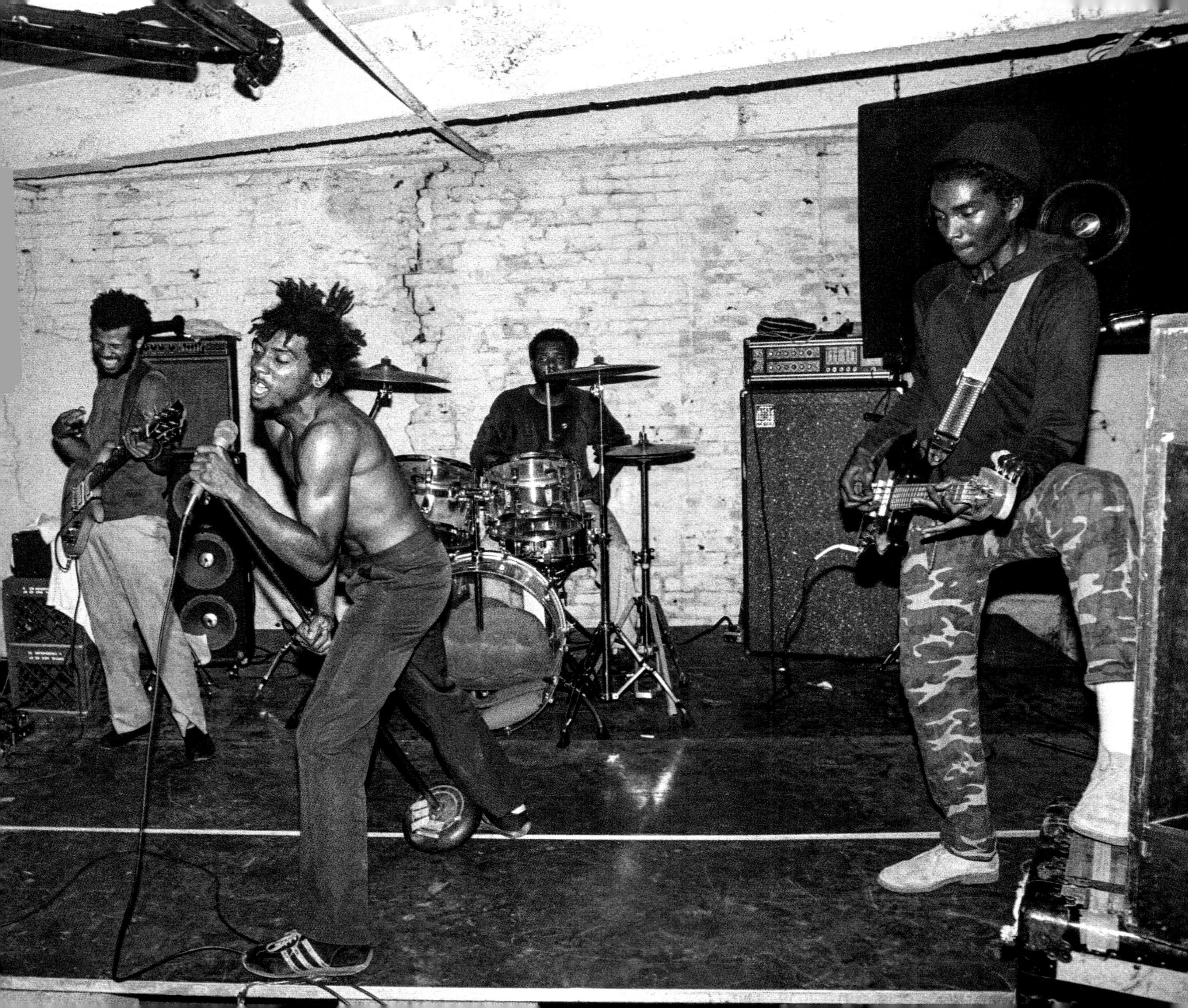

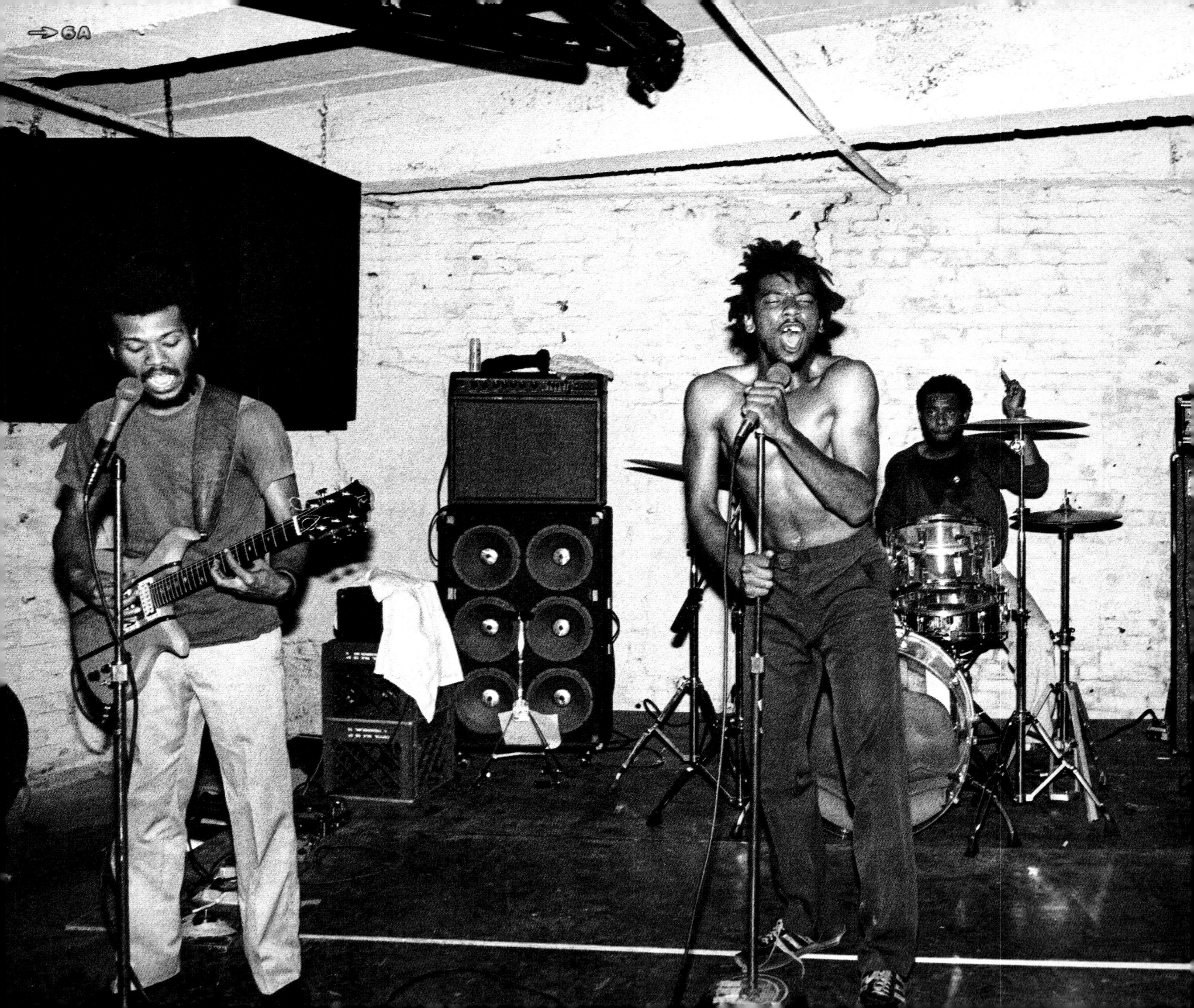
→ 6A

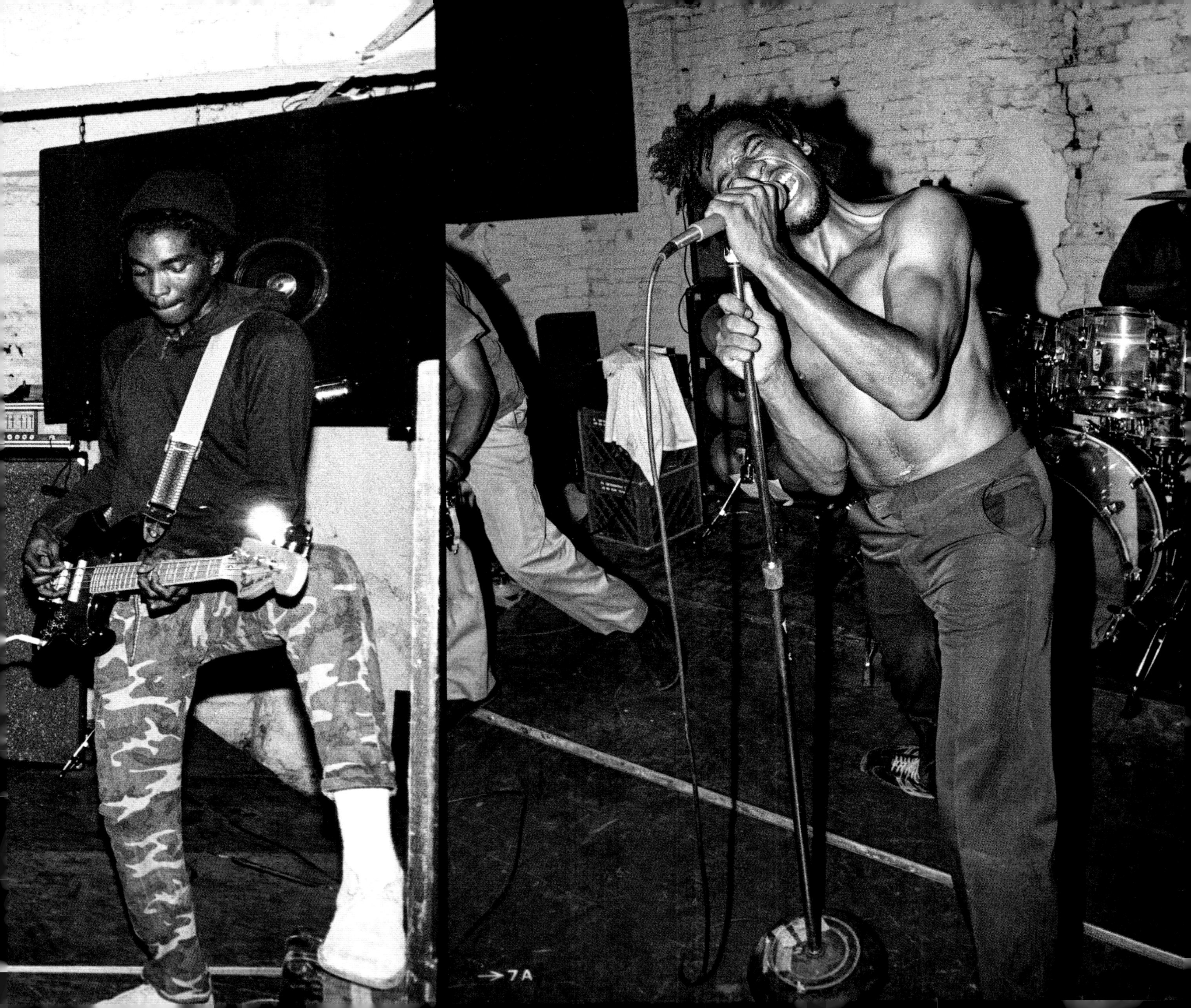
→7A

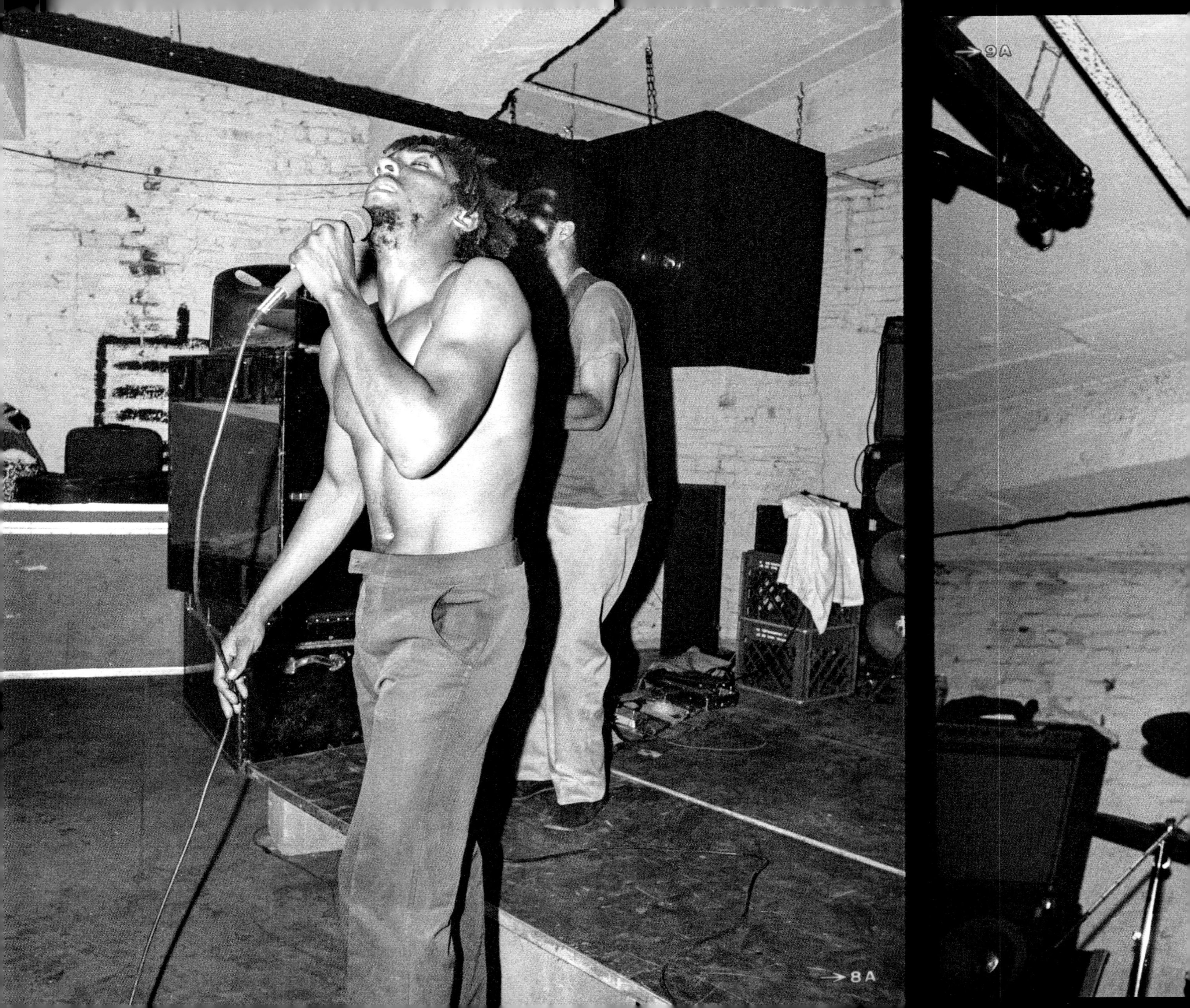
9A
8A

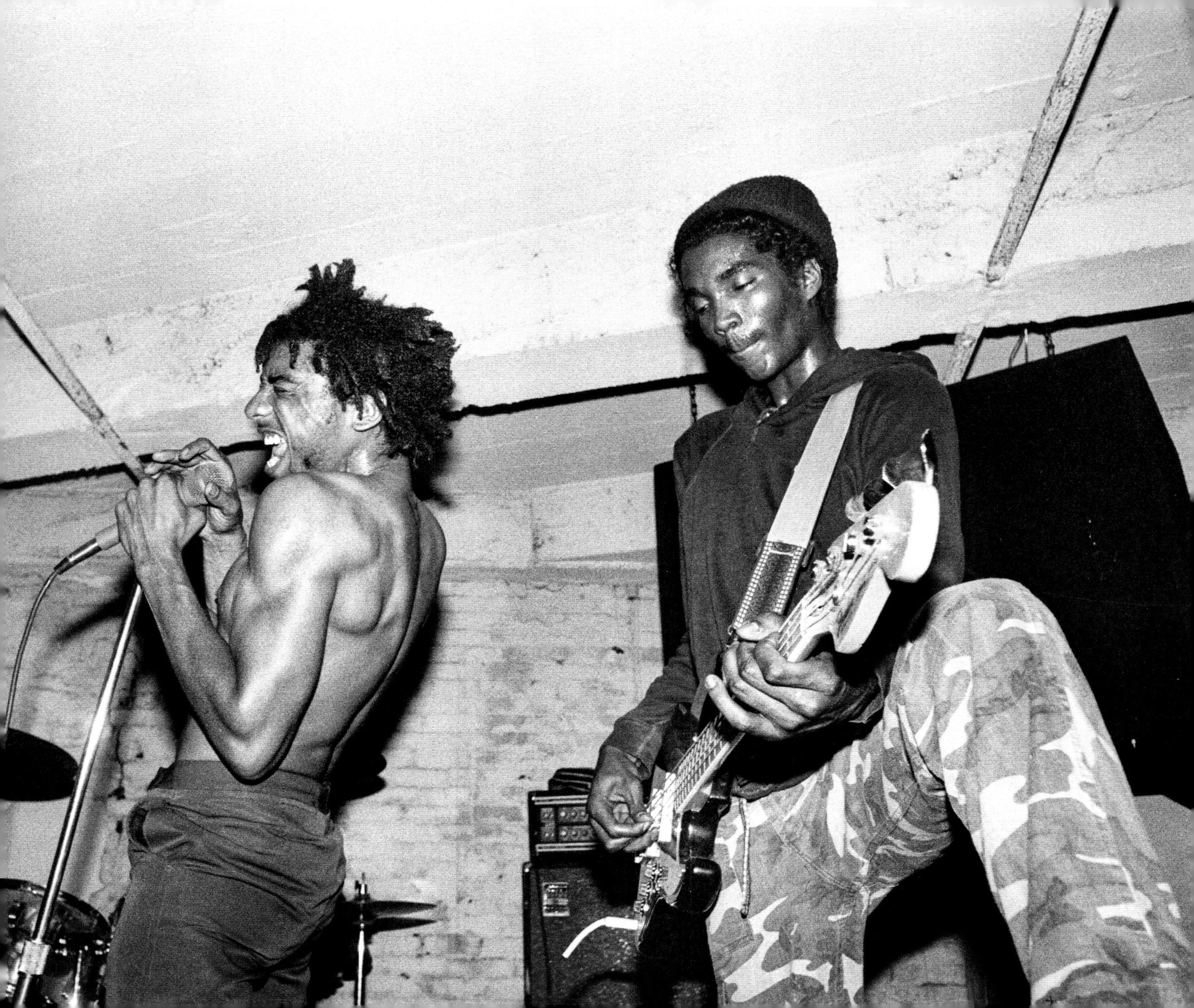

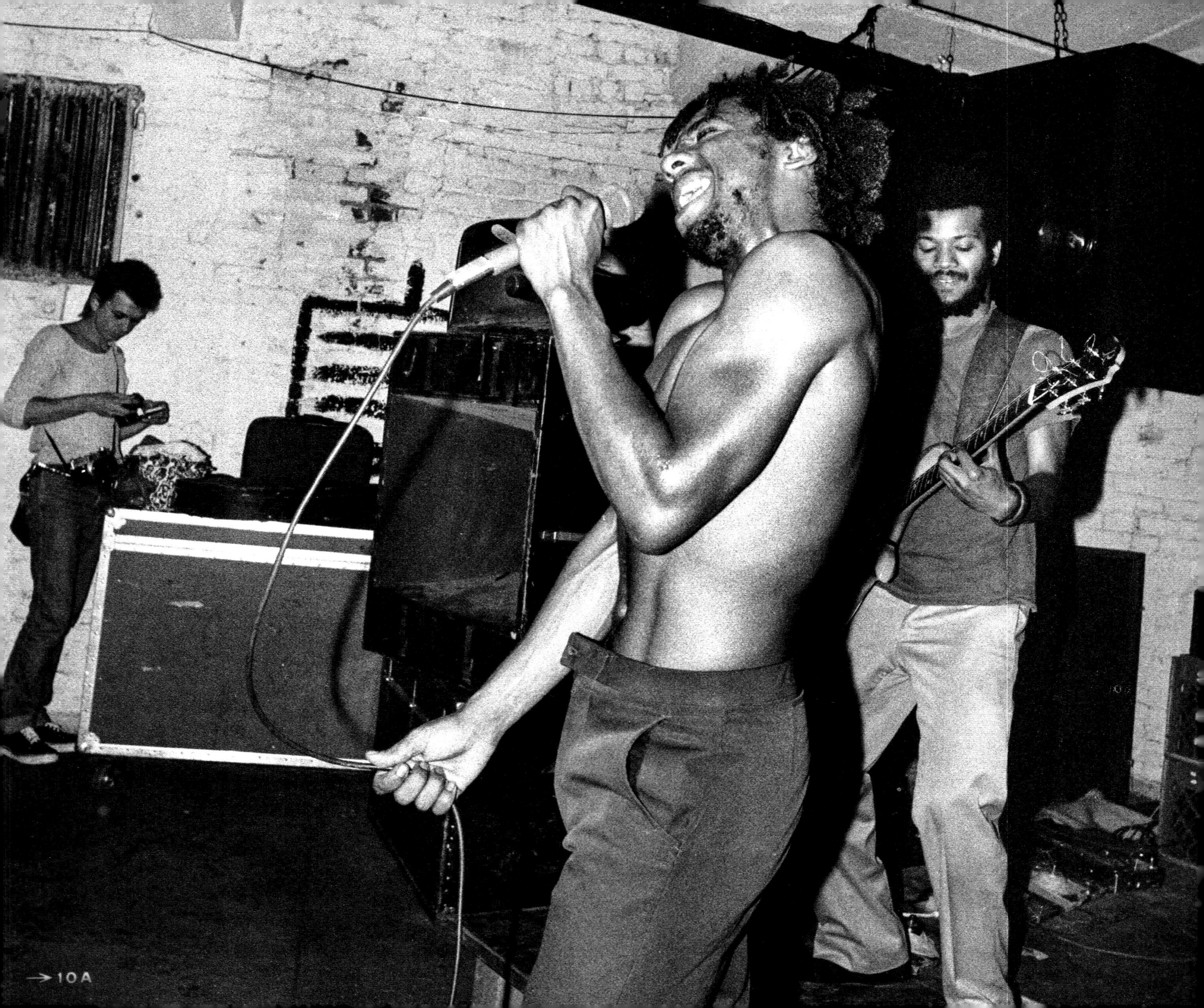

→10A

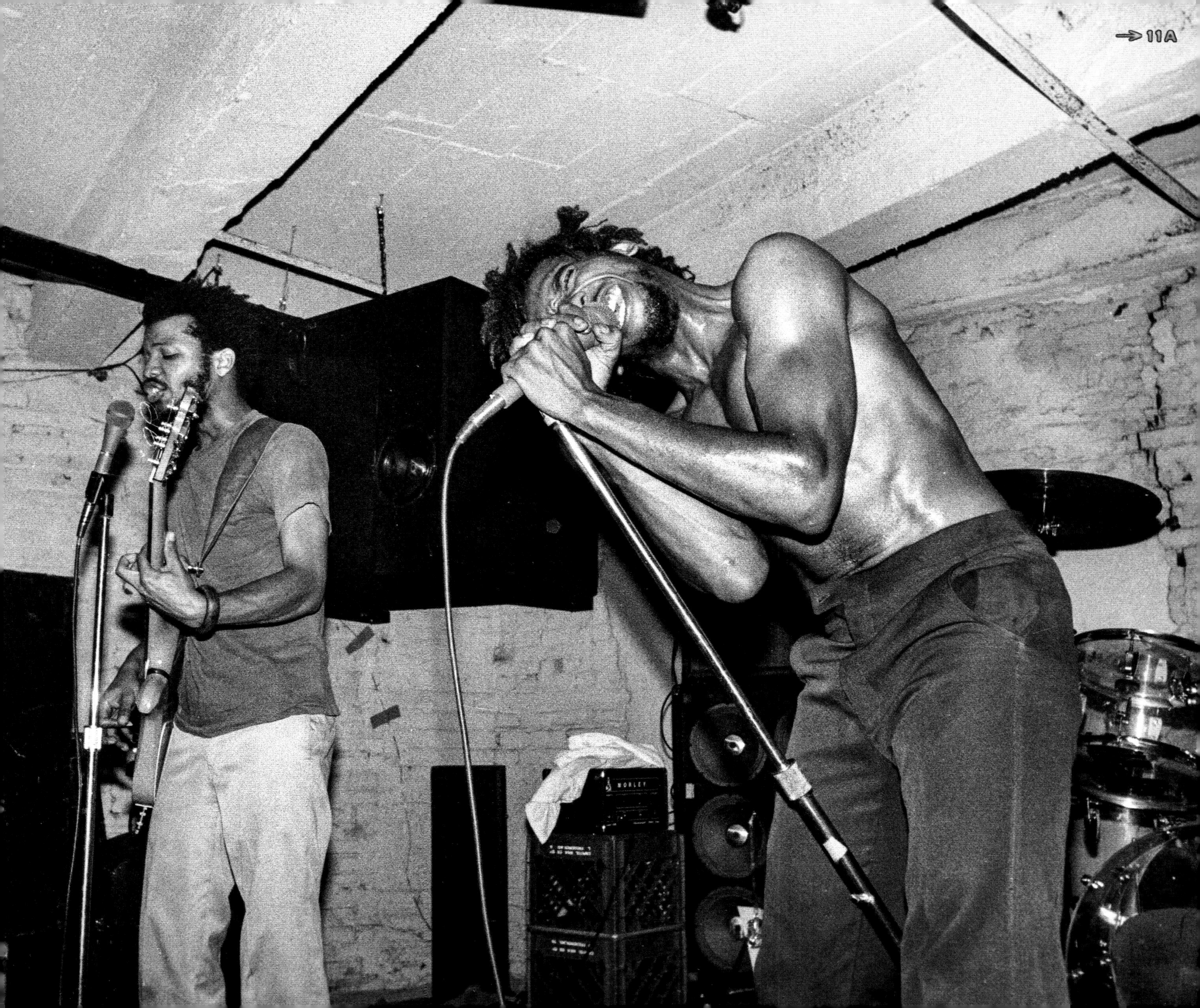
→ 11A

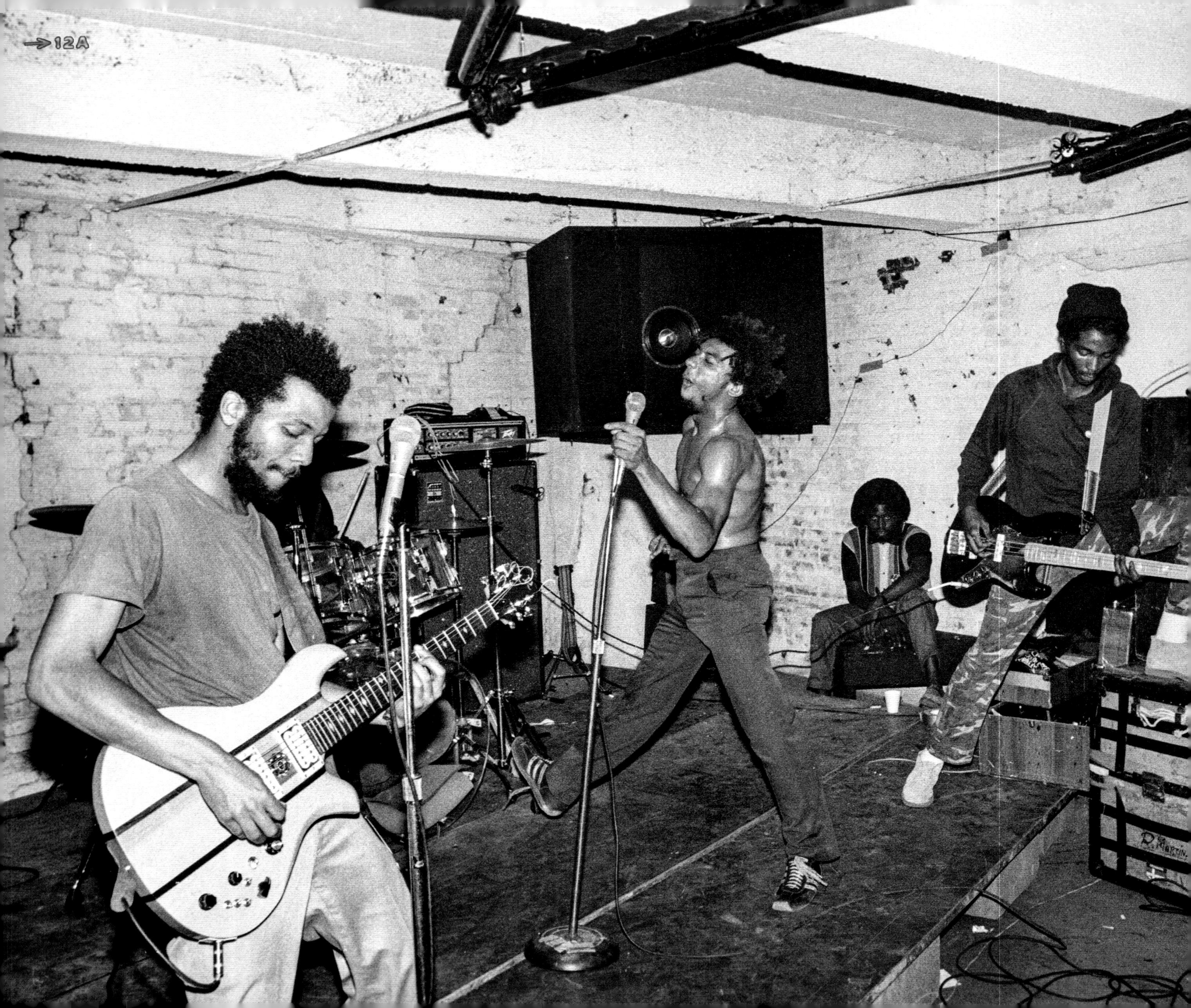
12A

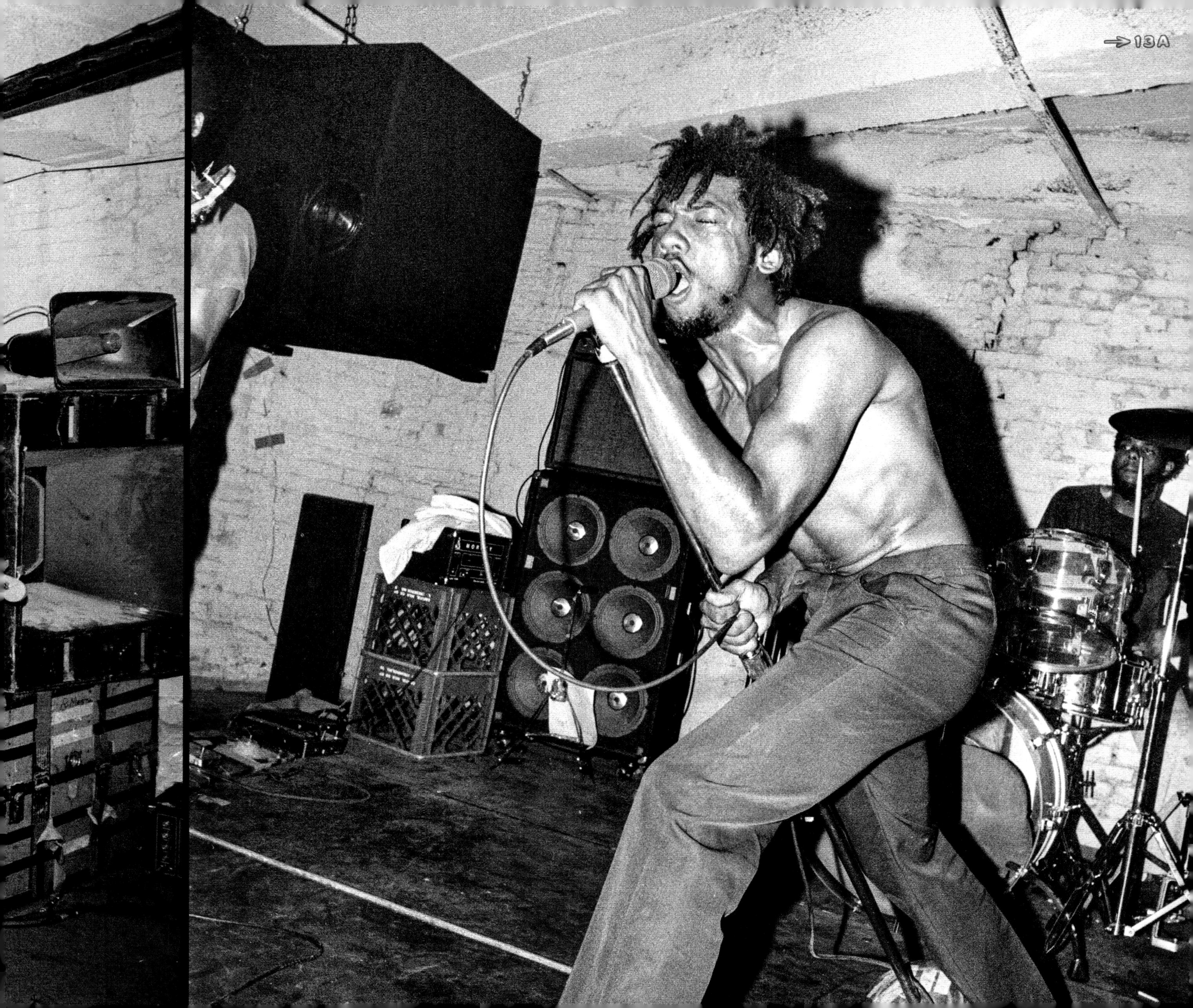
→13A

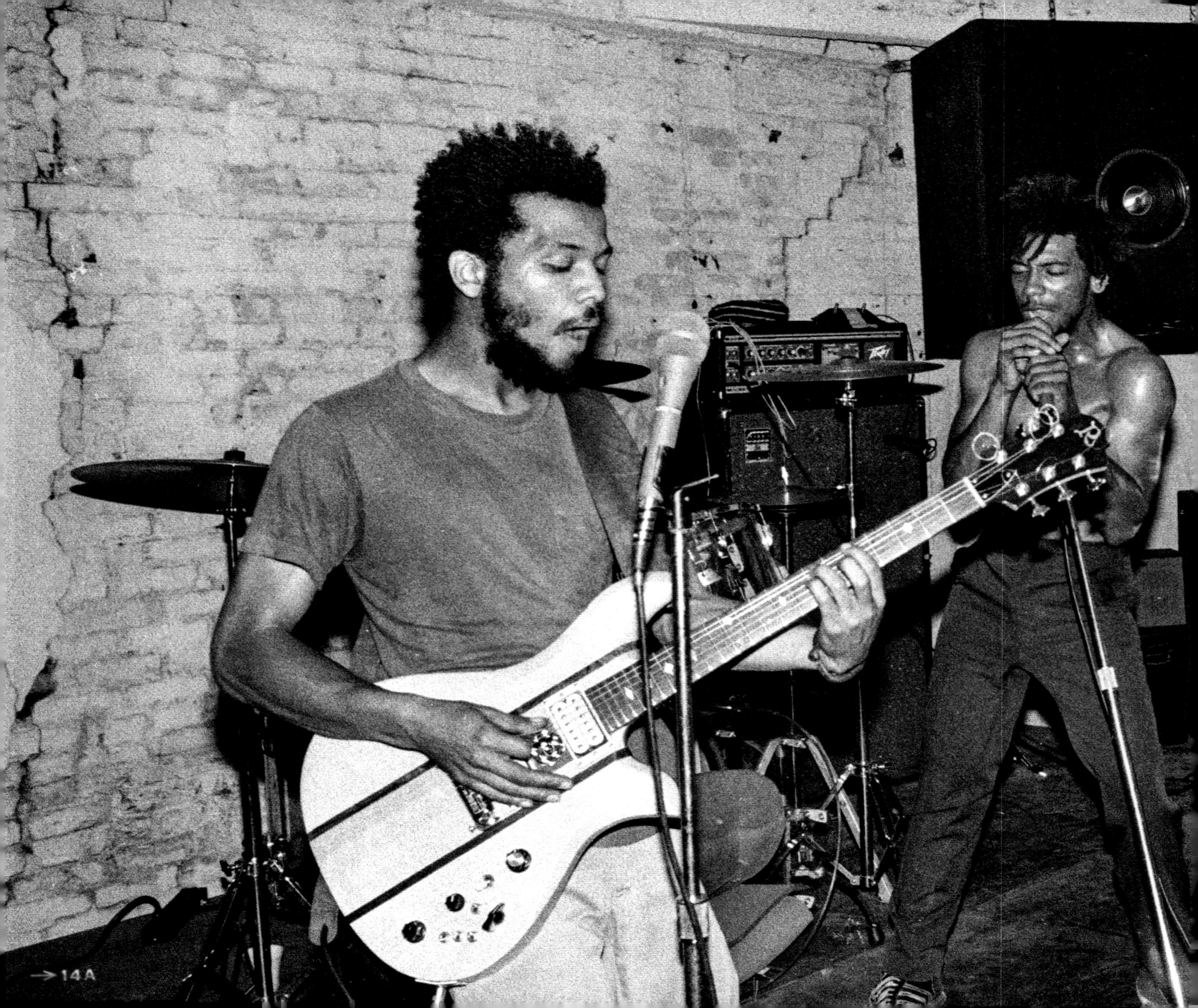

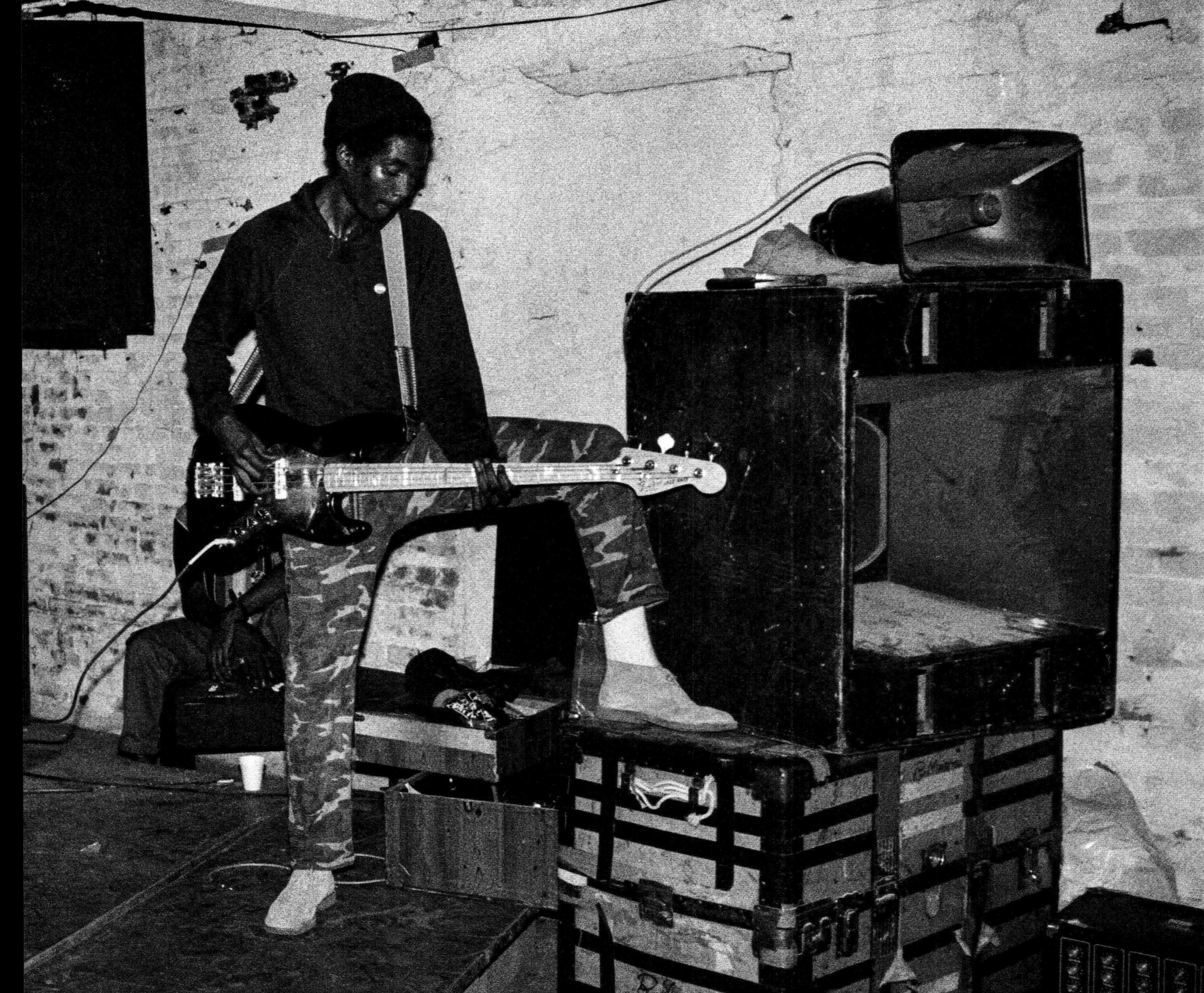

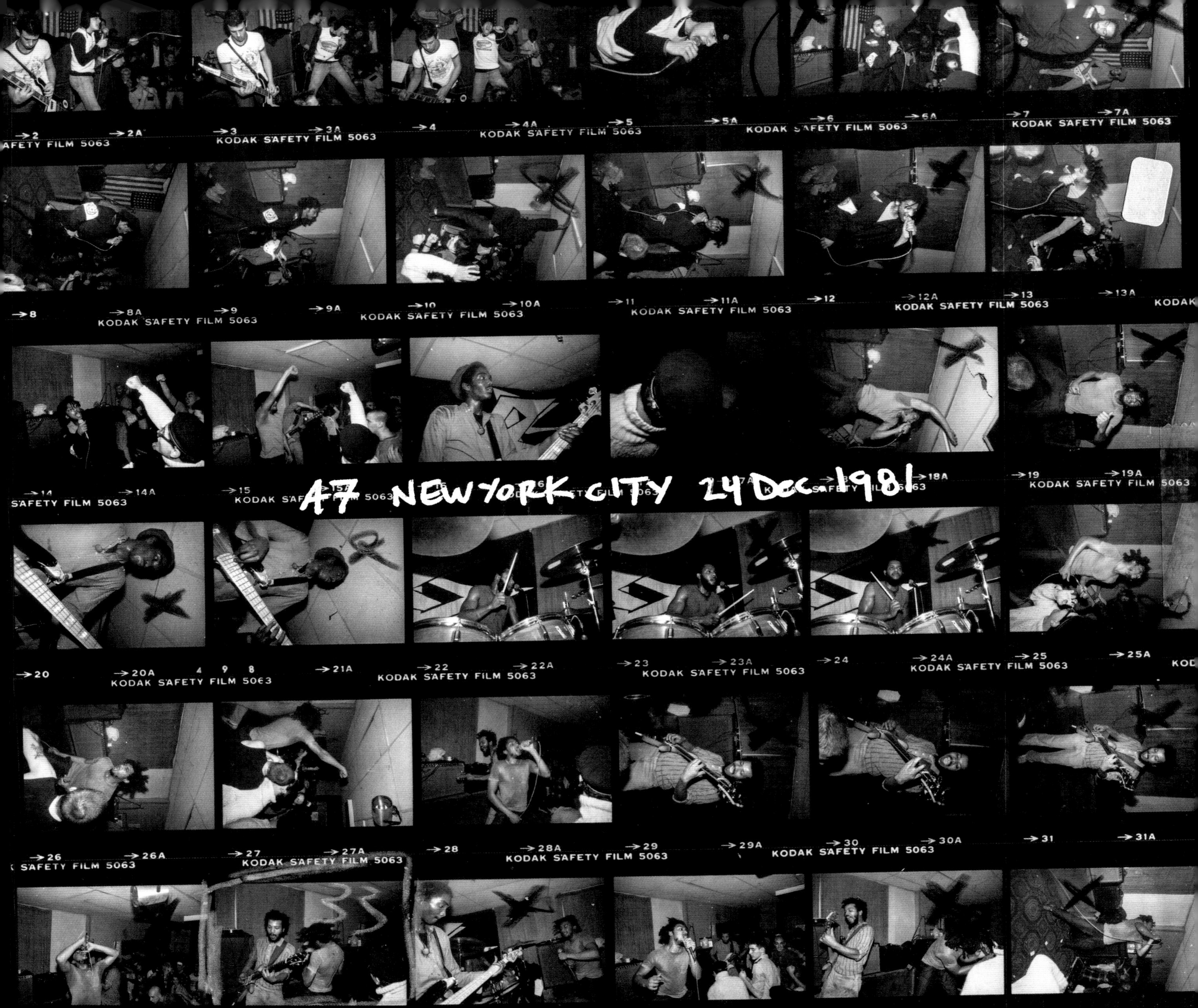
A7 NEW YORK CITY 24 Dec 1981

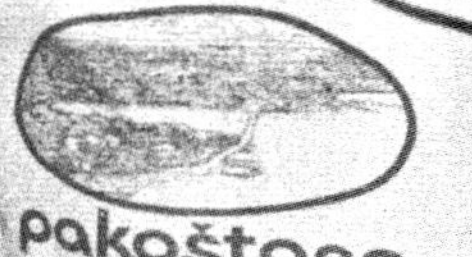
REAGAN YOUTH
pakoštane
BLACK FLAG
4

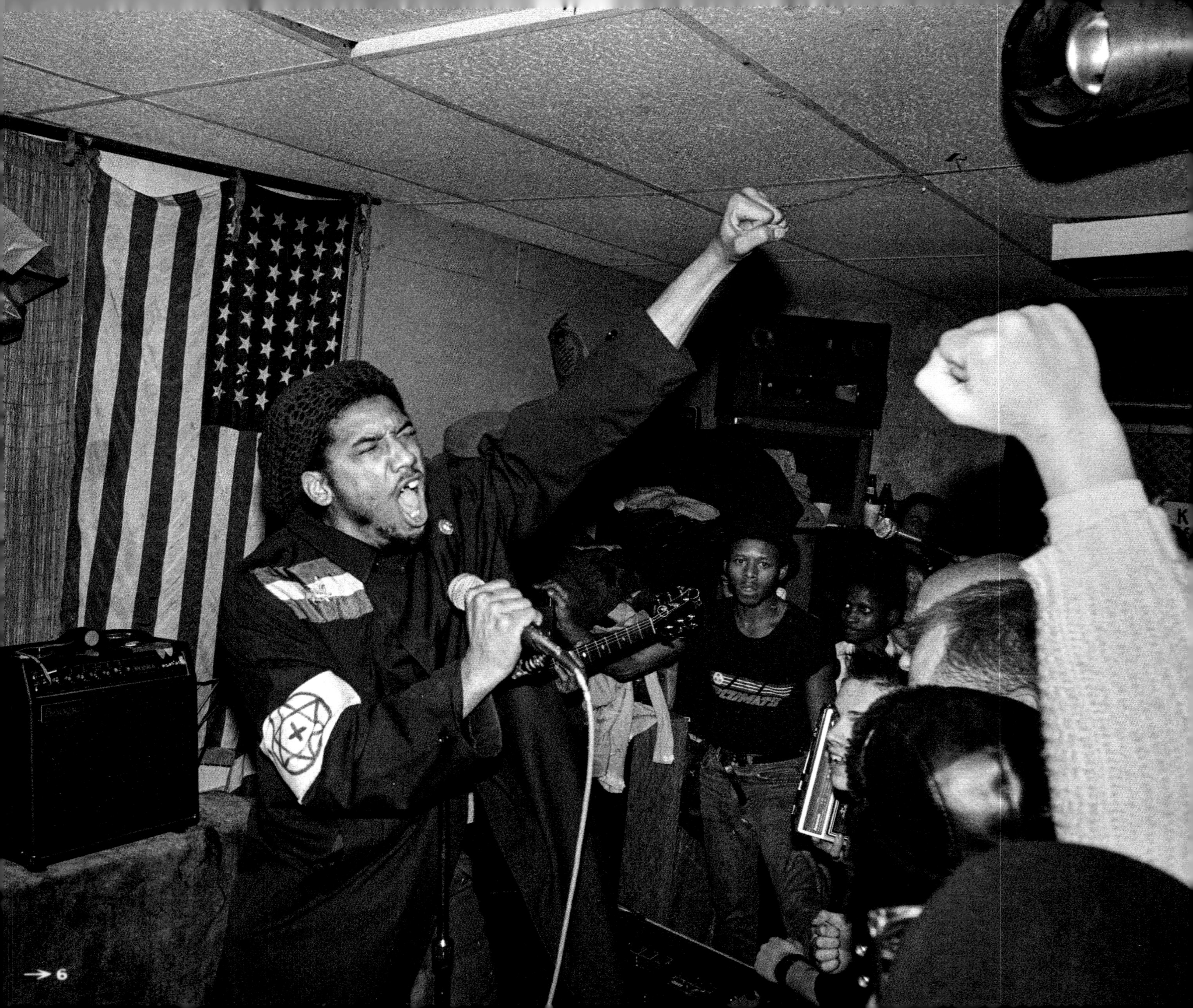

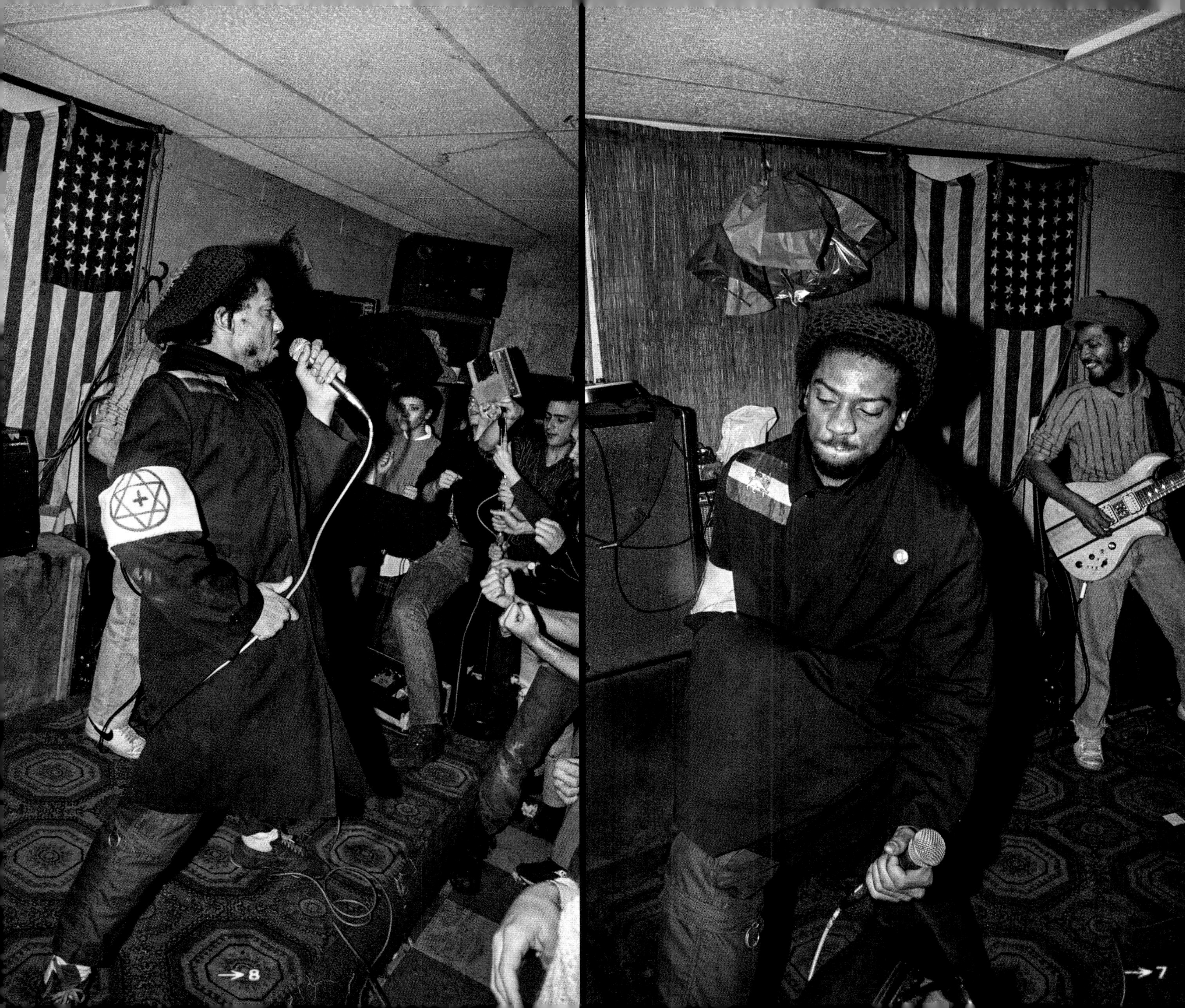

→ 8
→ 7

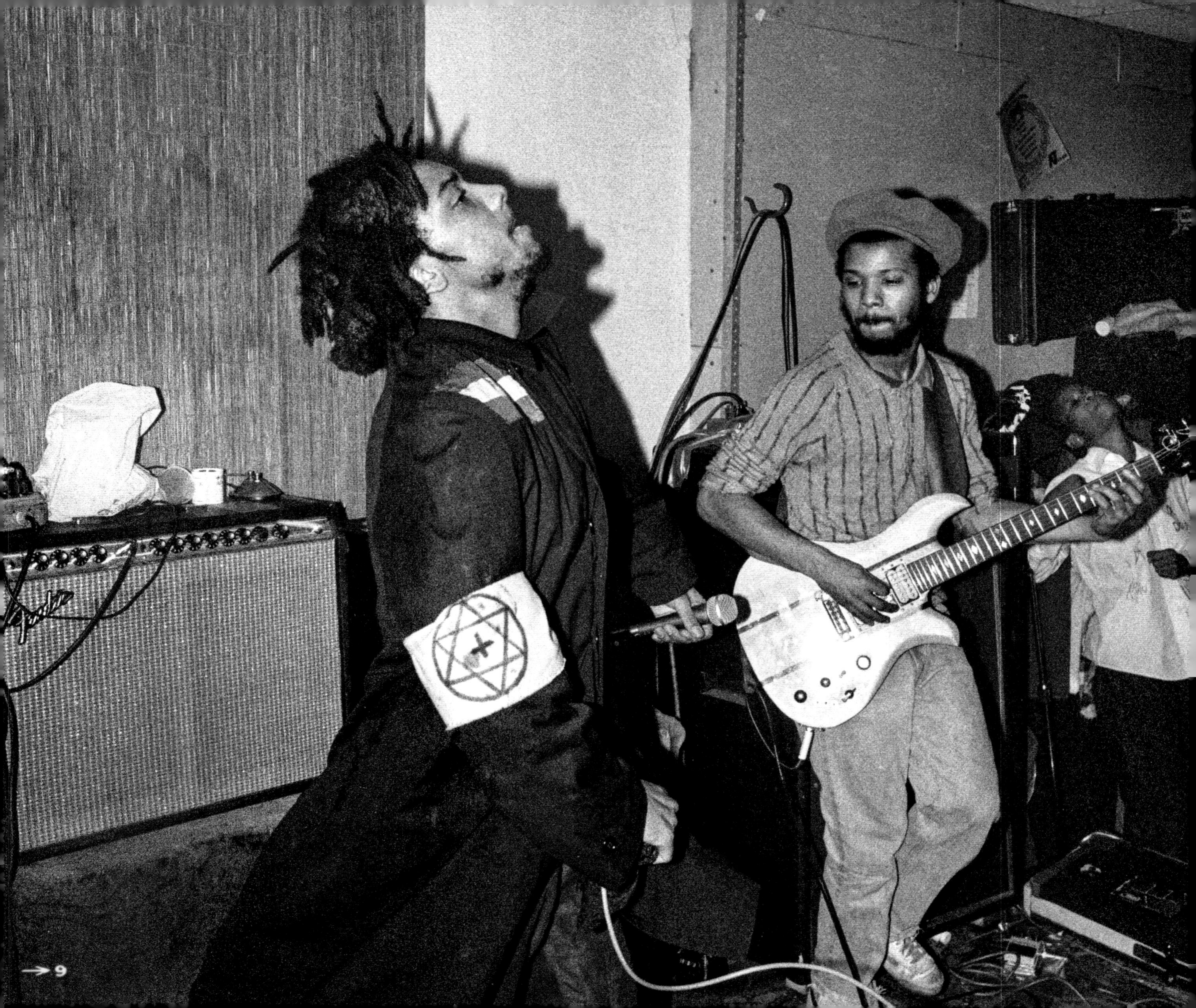
→9

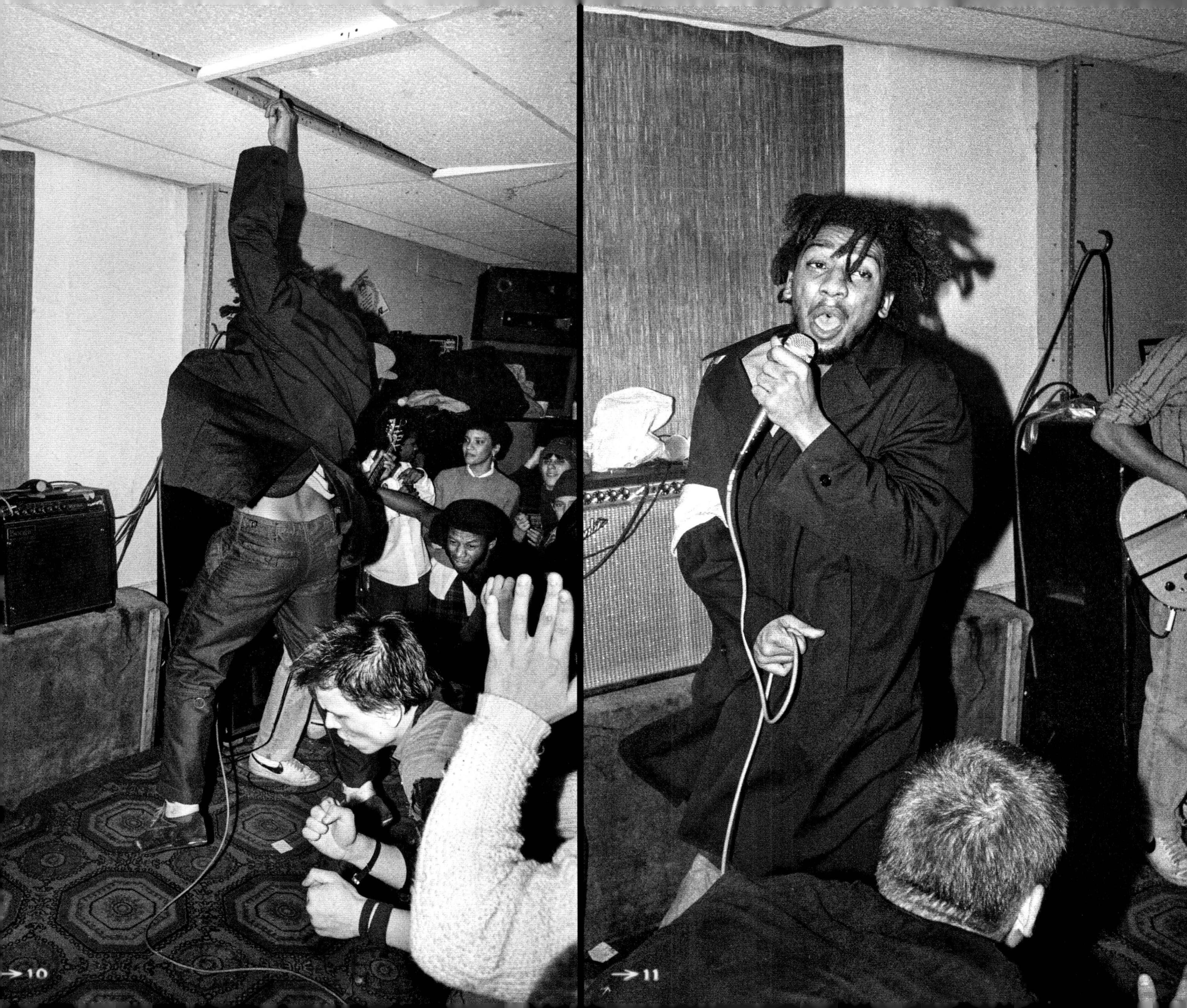

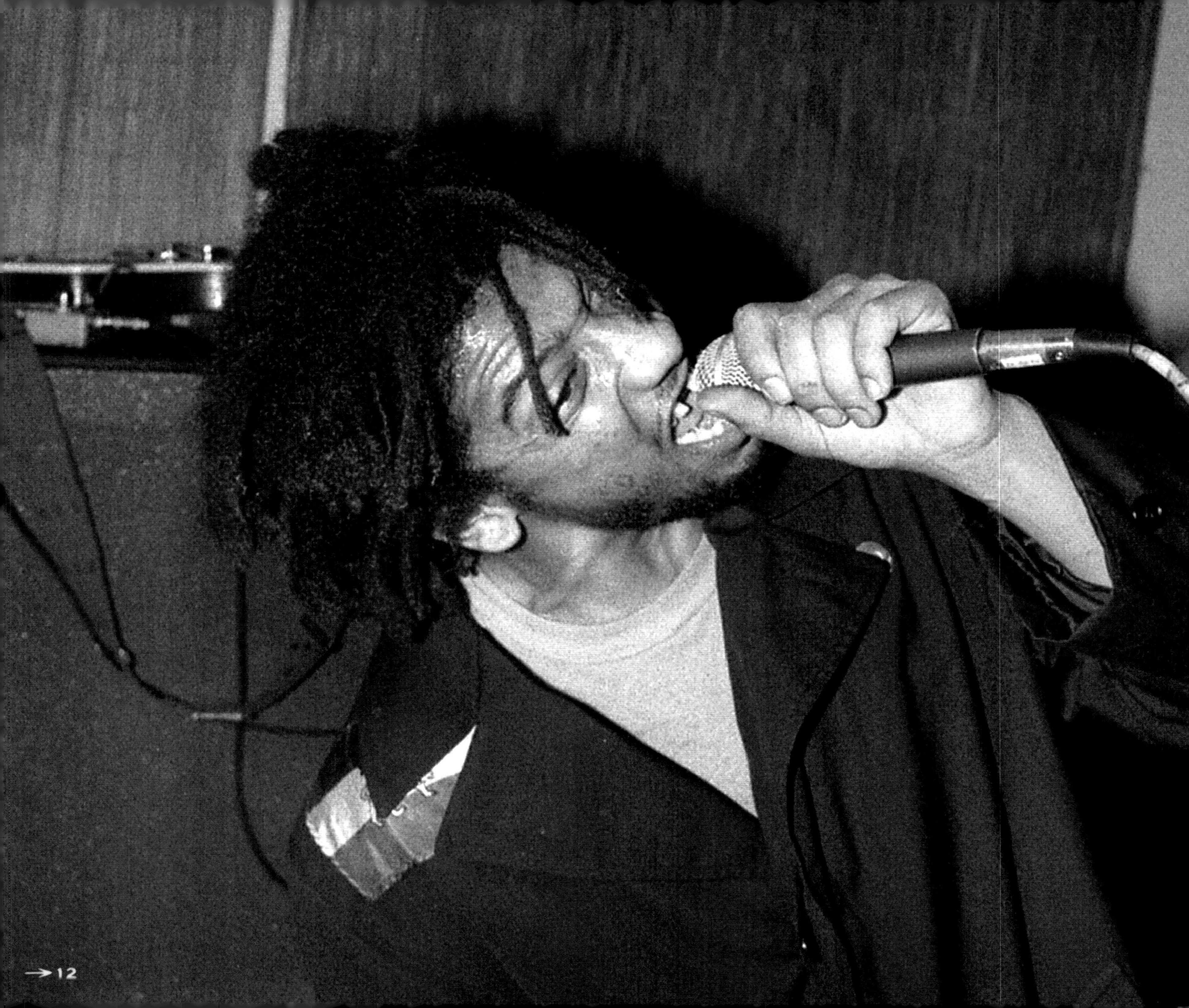
12

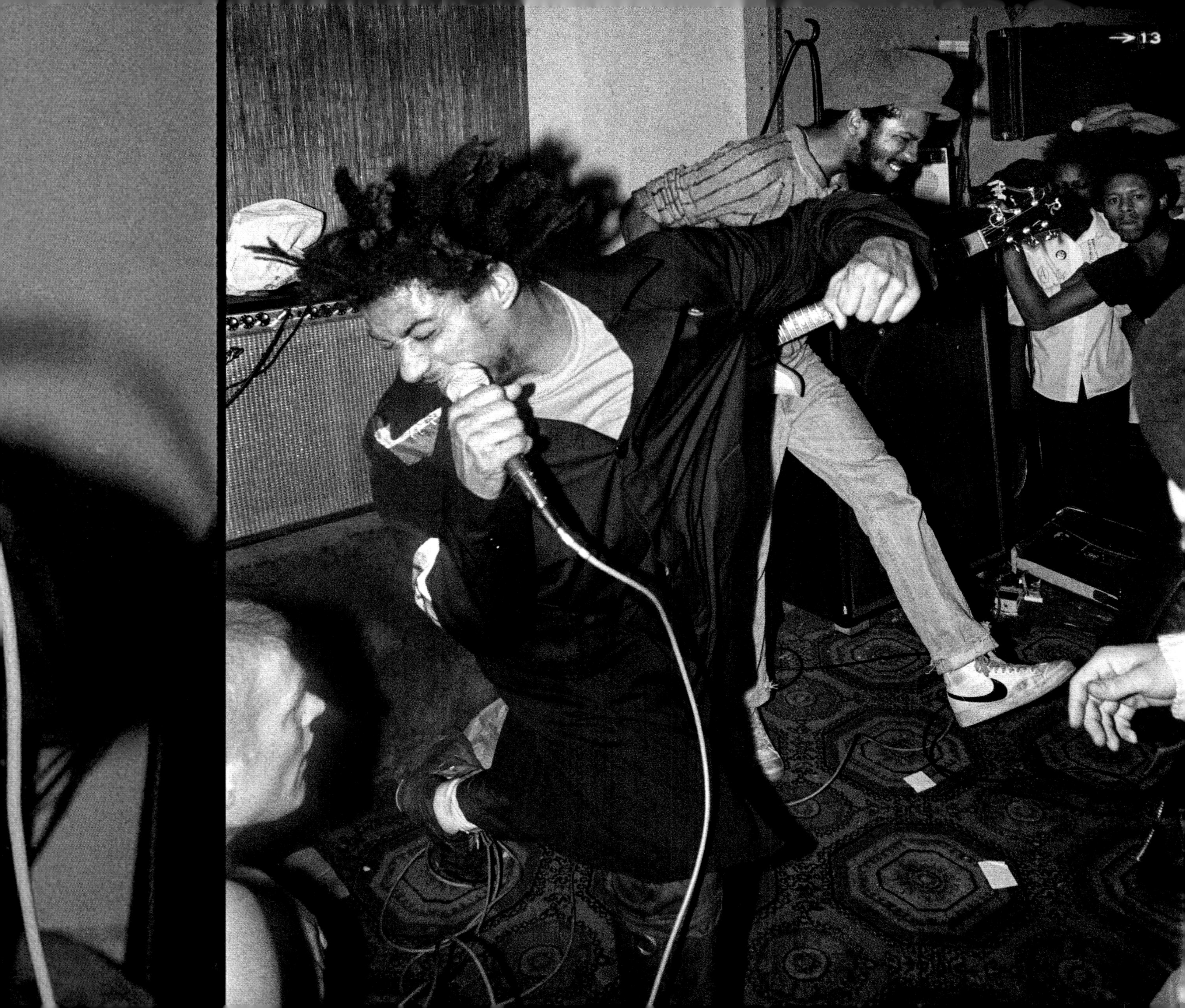

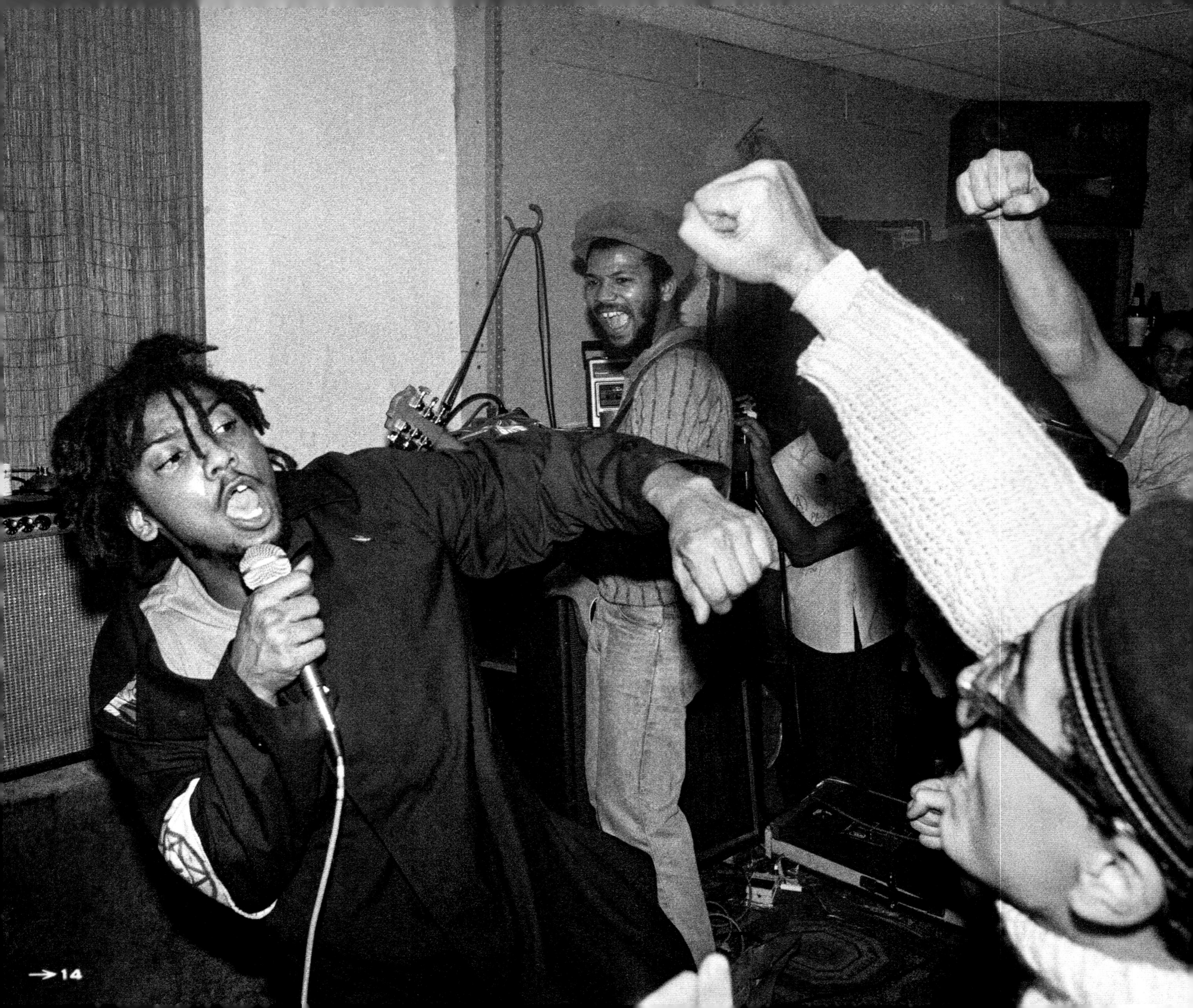
14

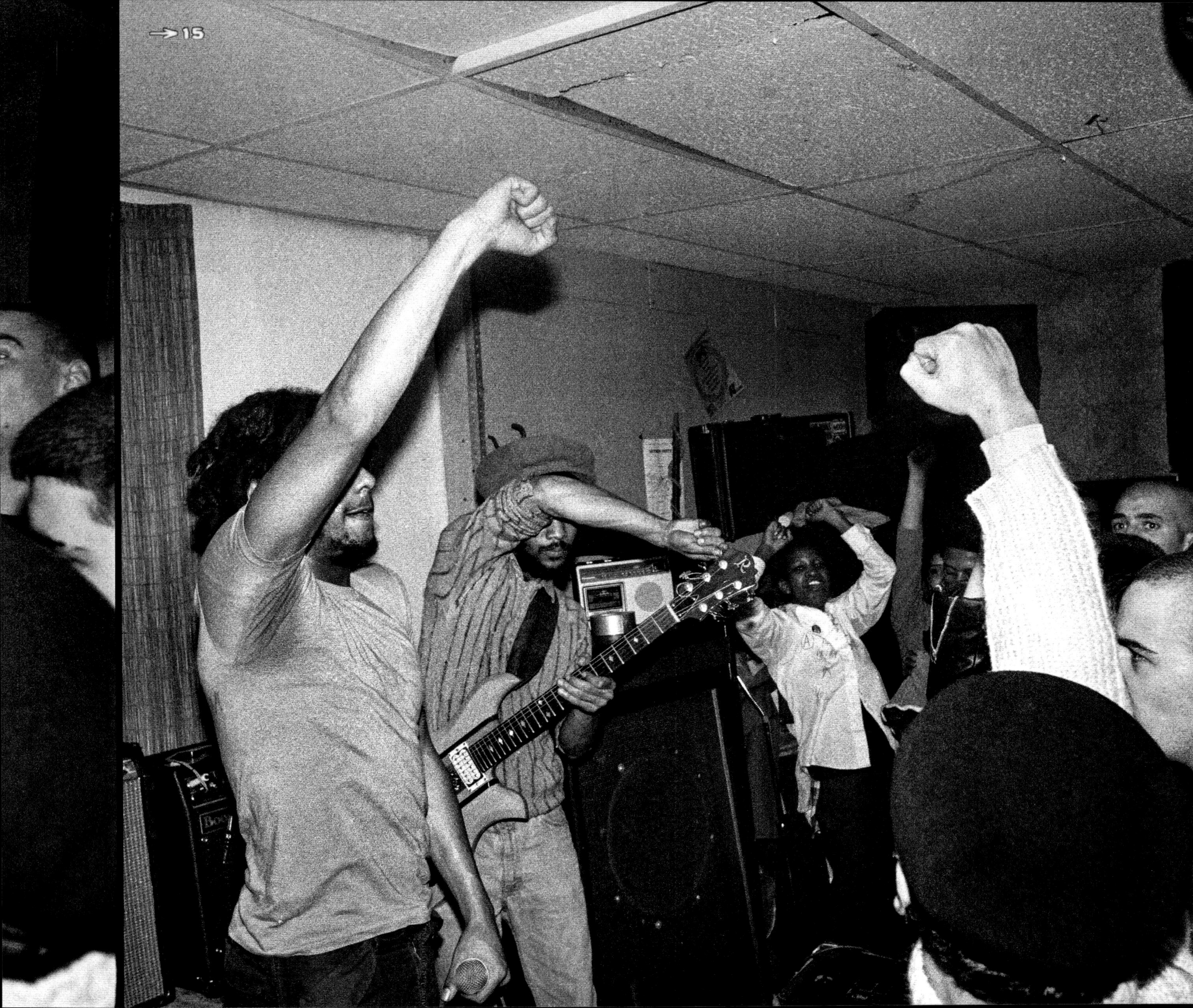

15

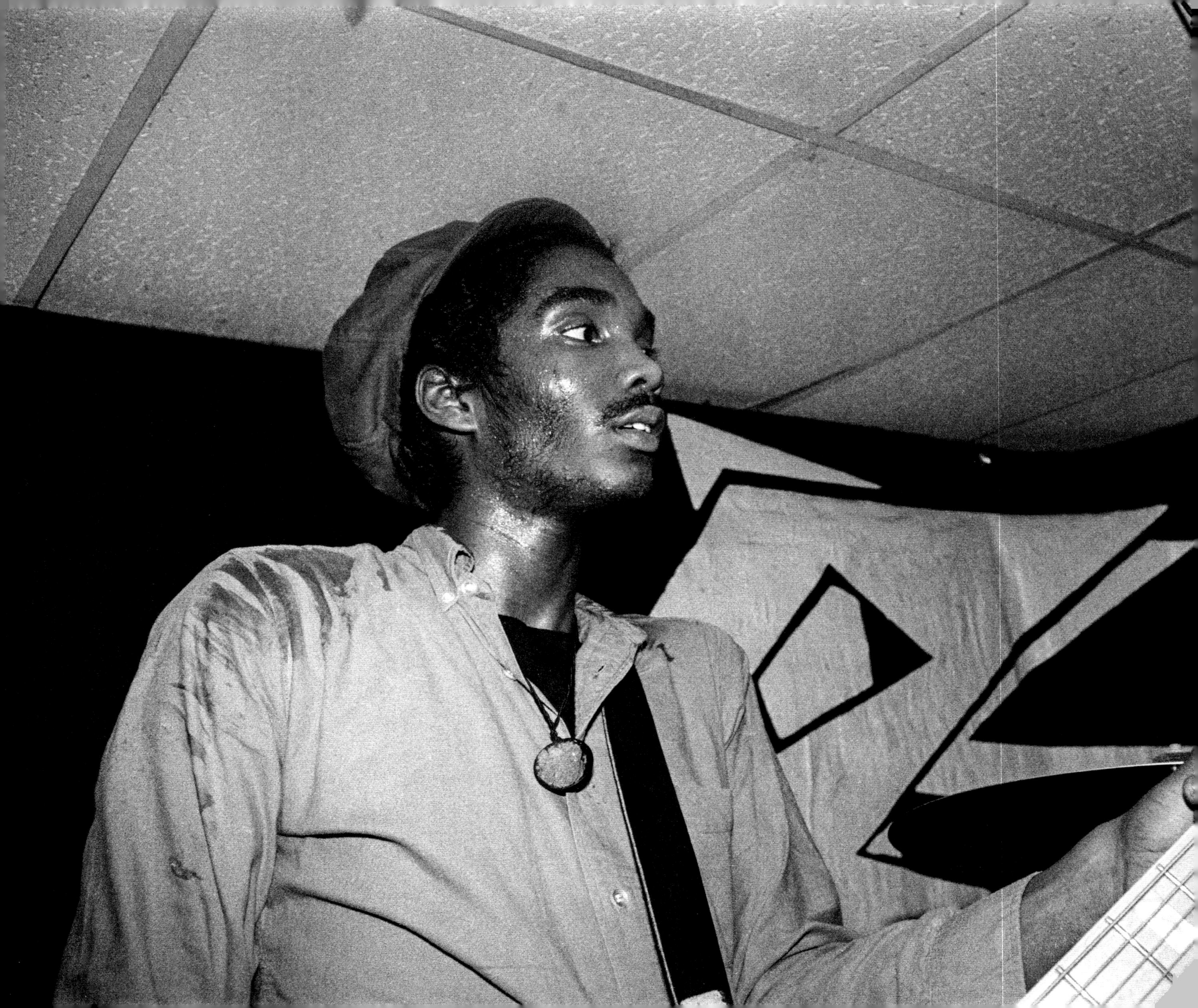

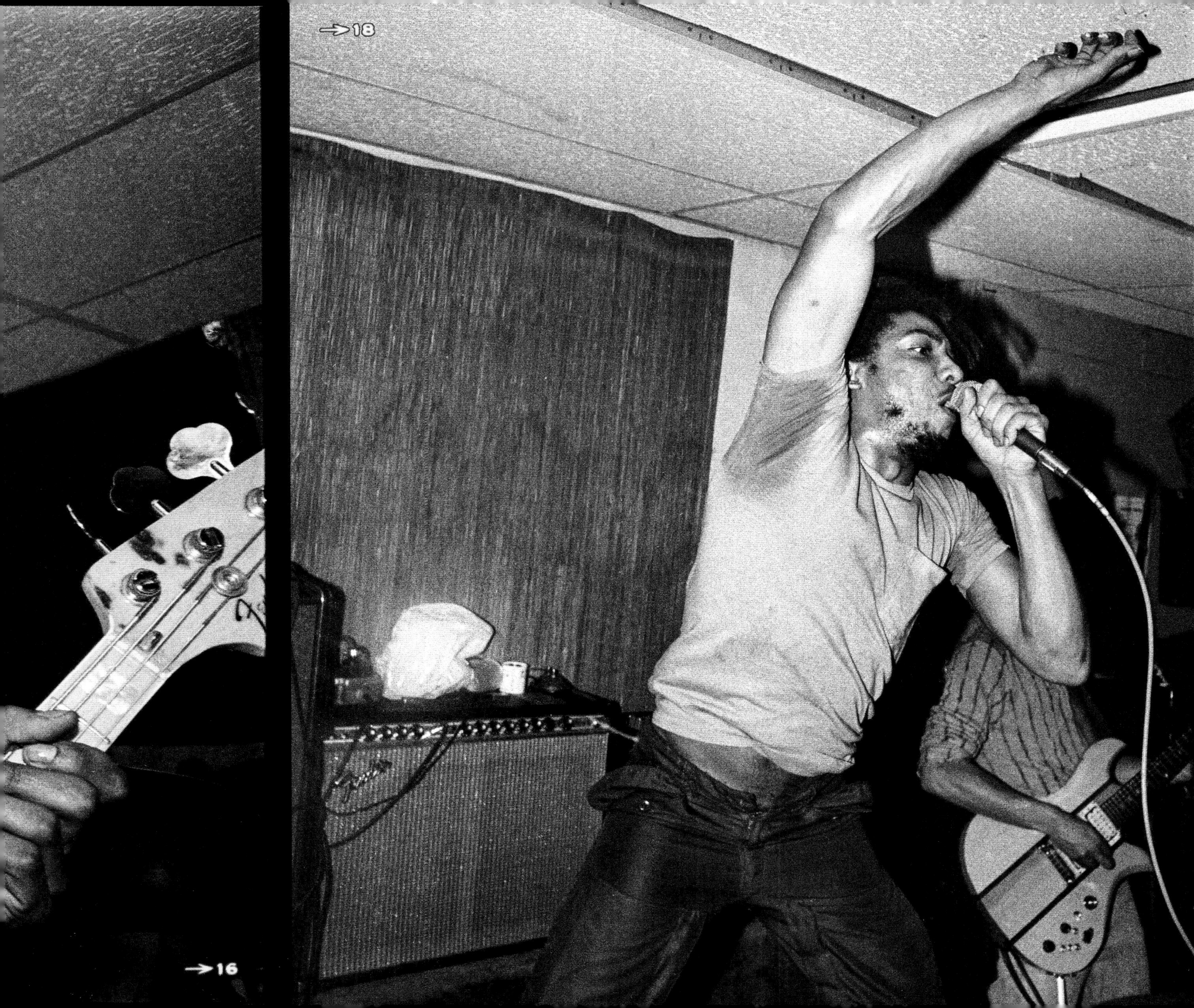
→ 18
→ 16

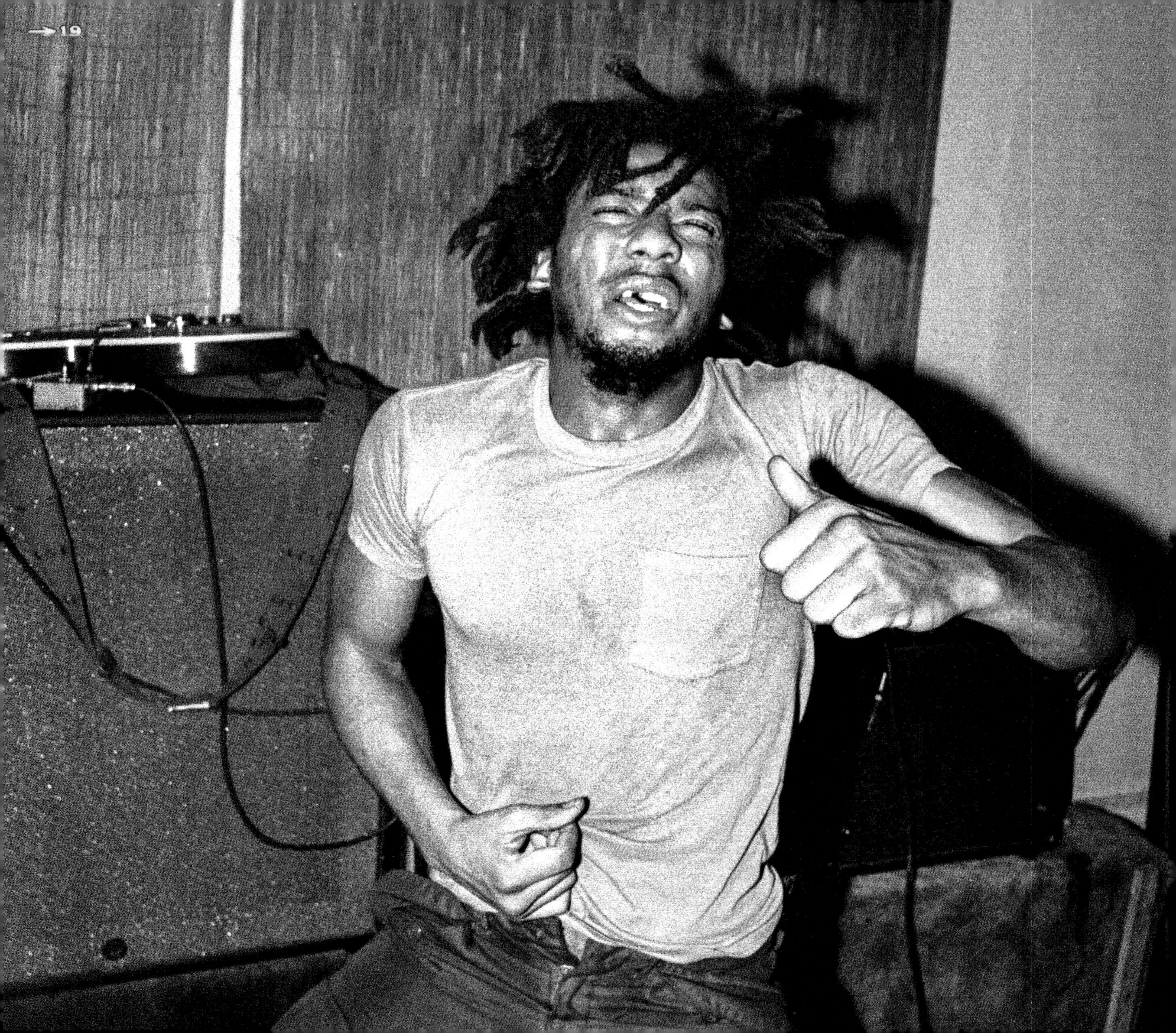
19

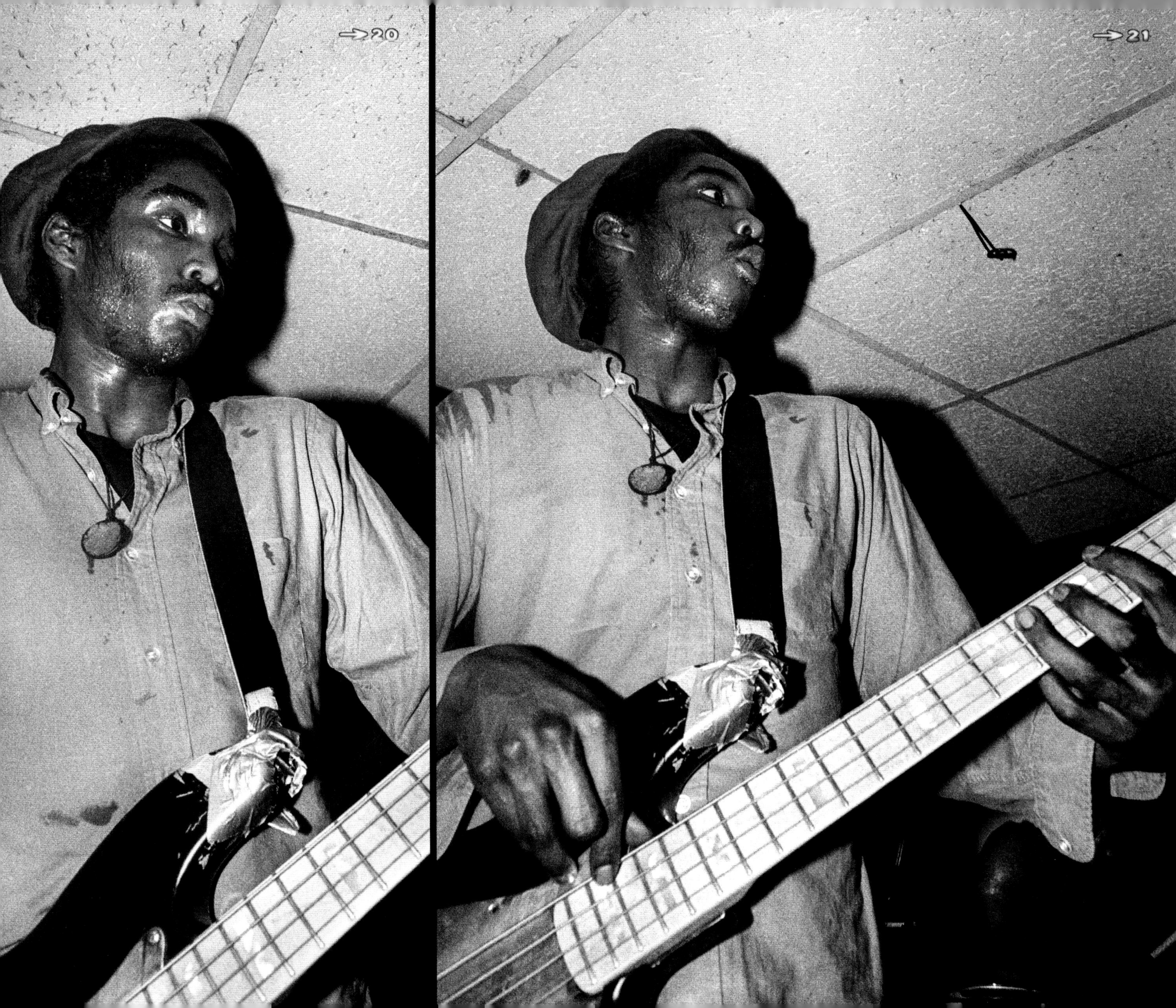

20
21

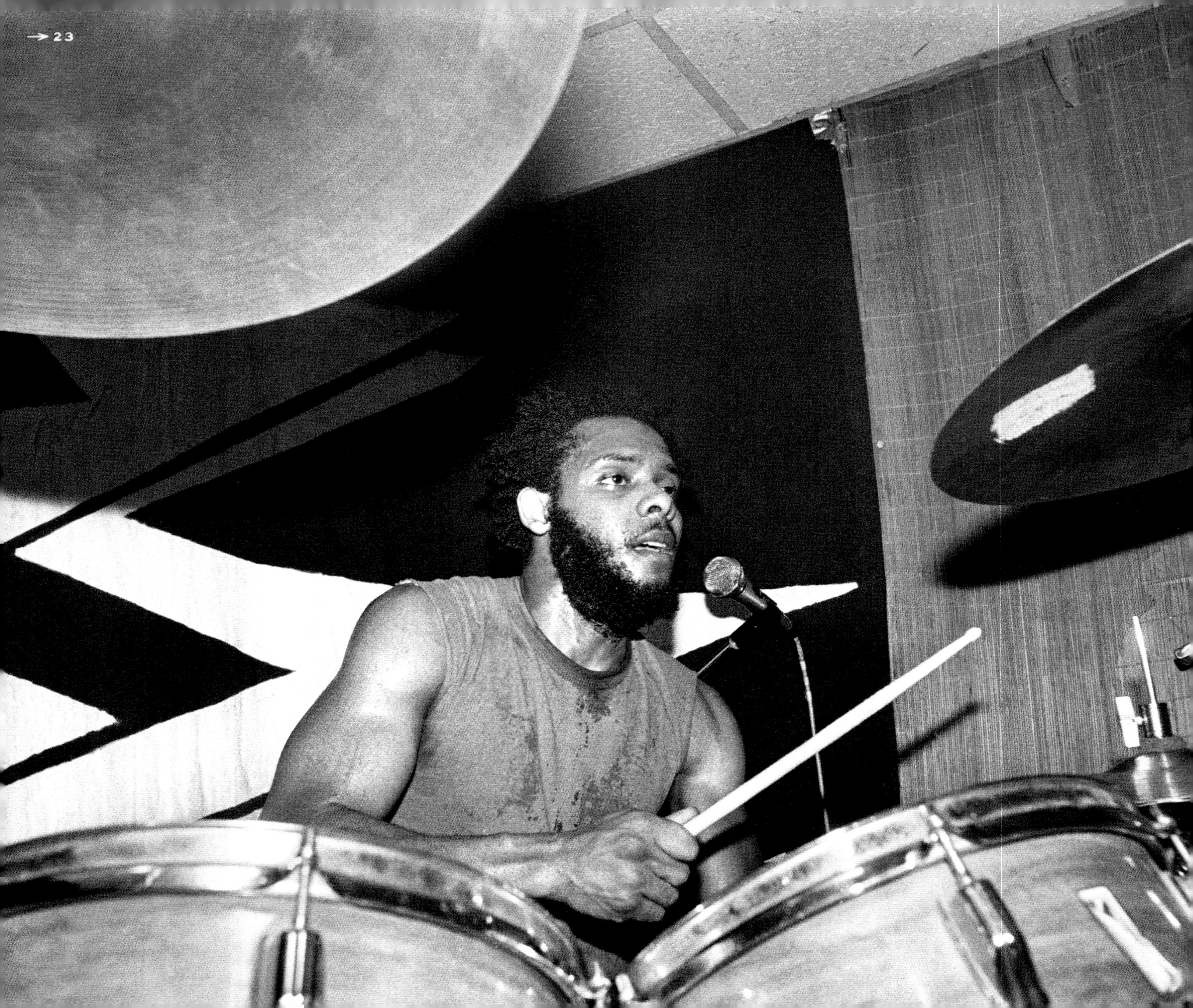

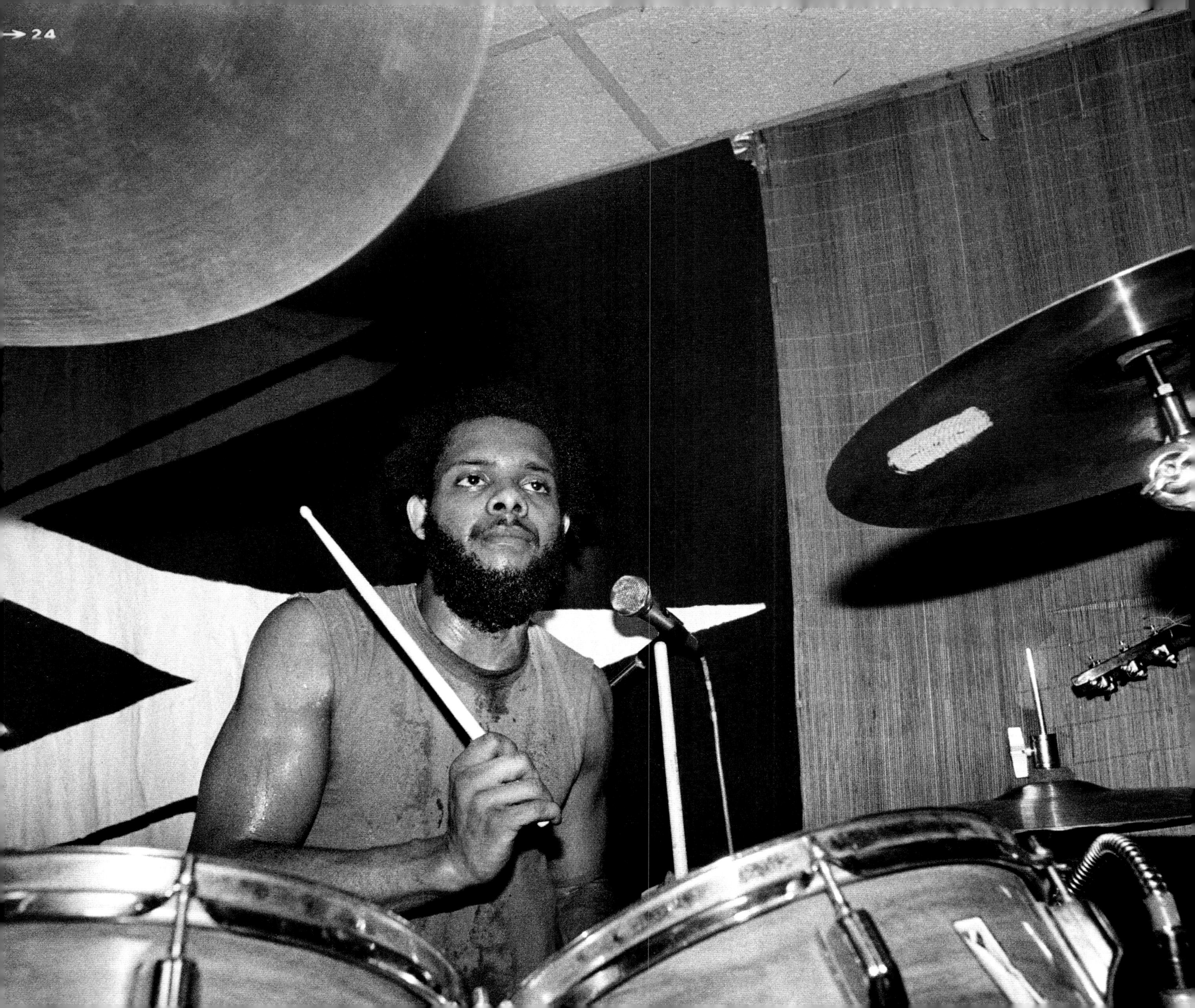

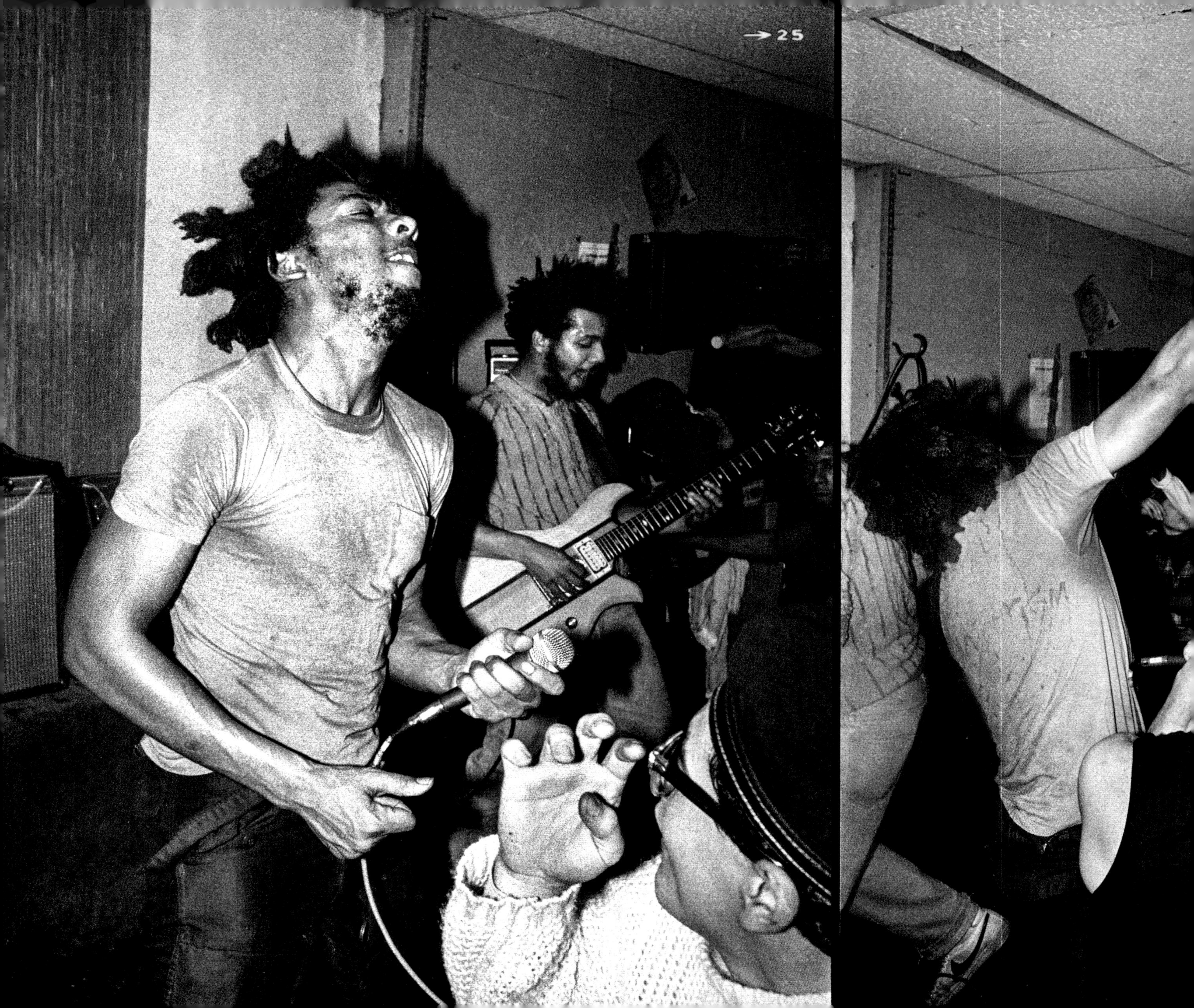
→ 25

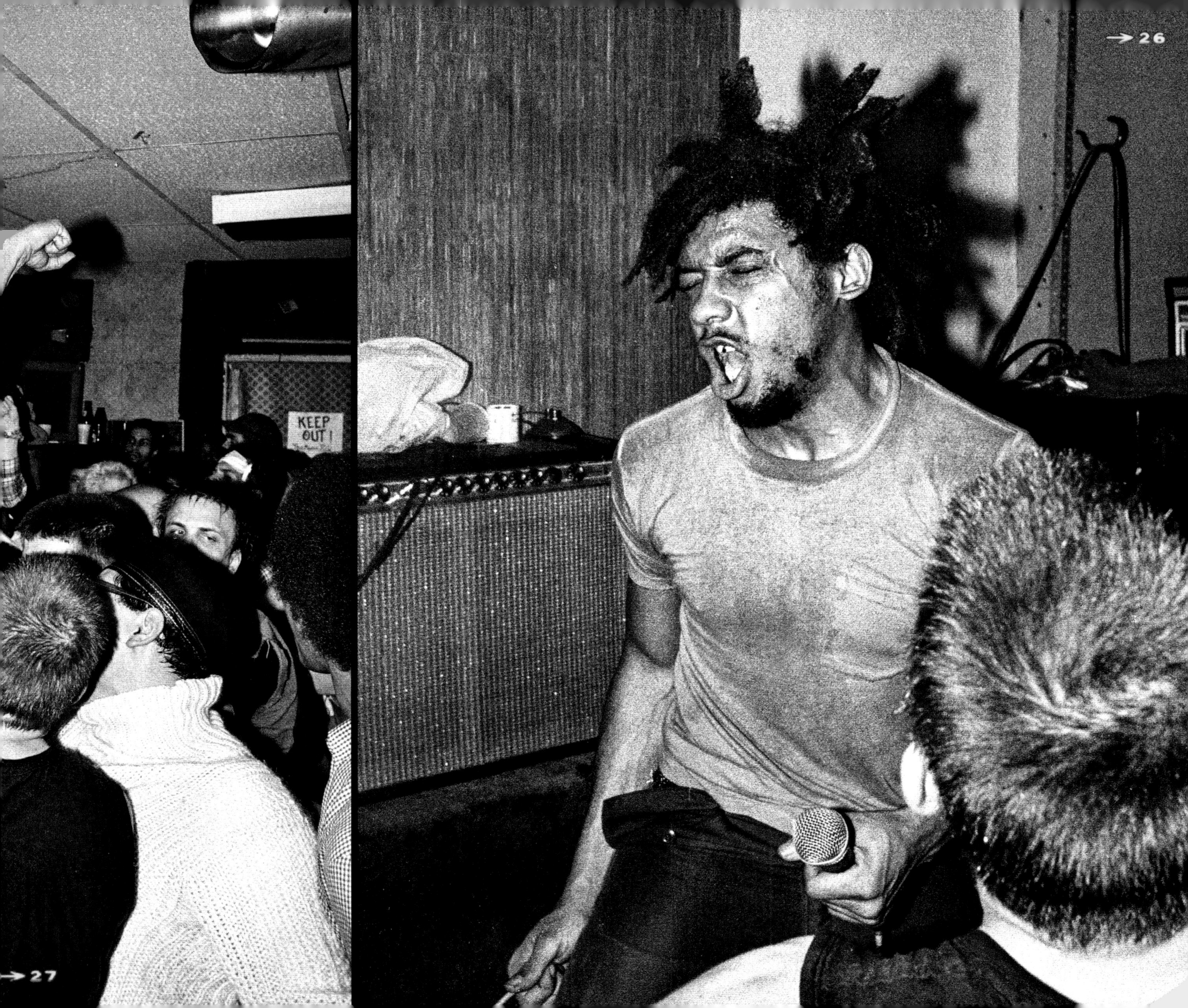
KEEP
OUT !

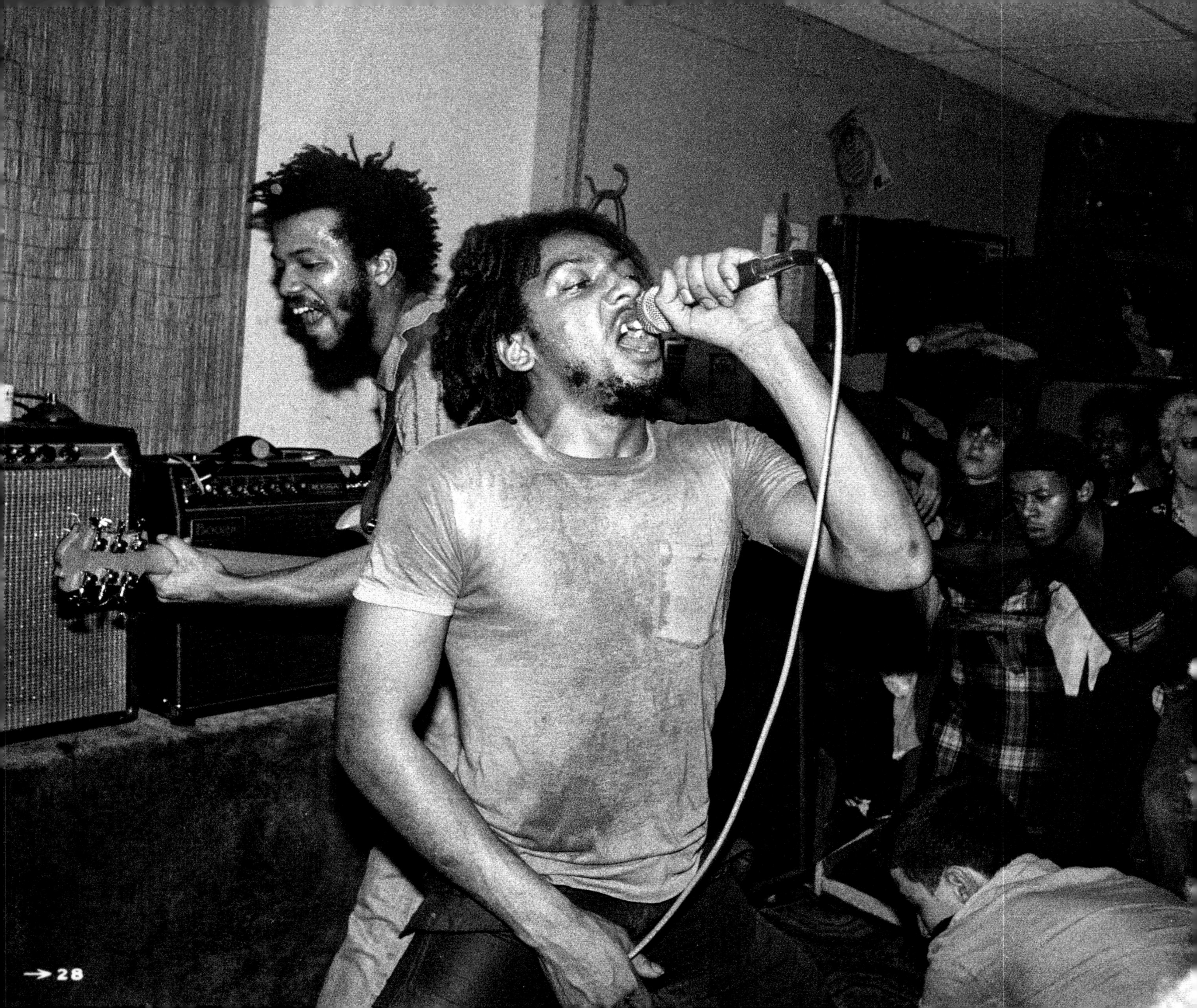
→ 28

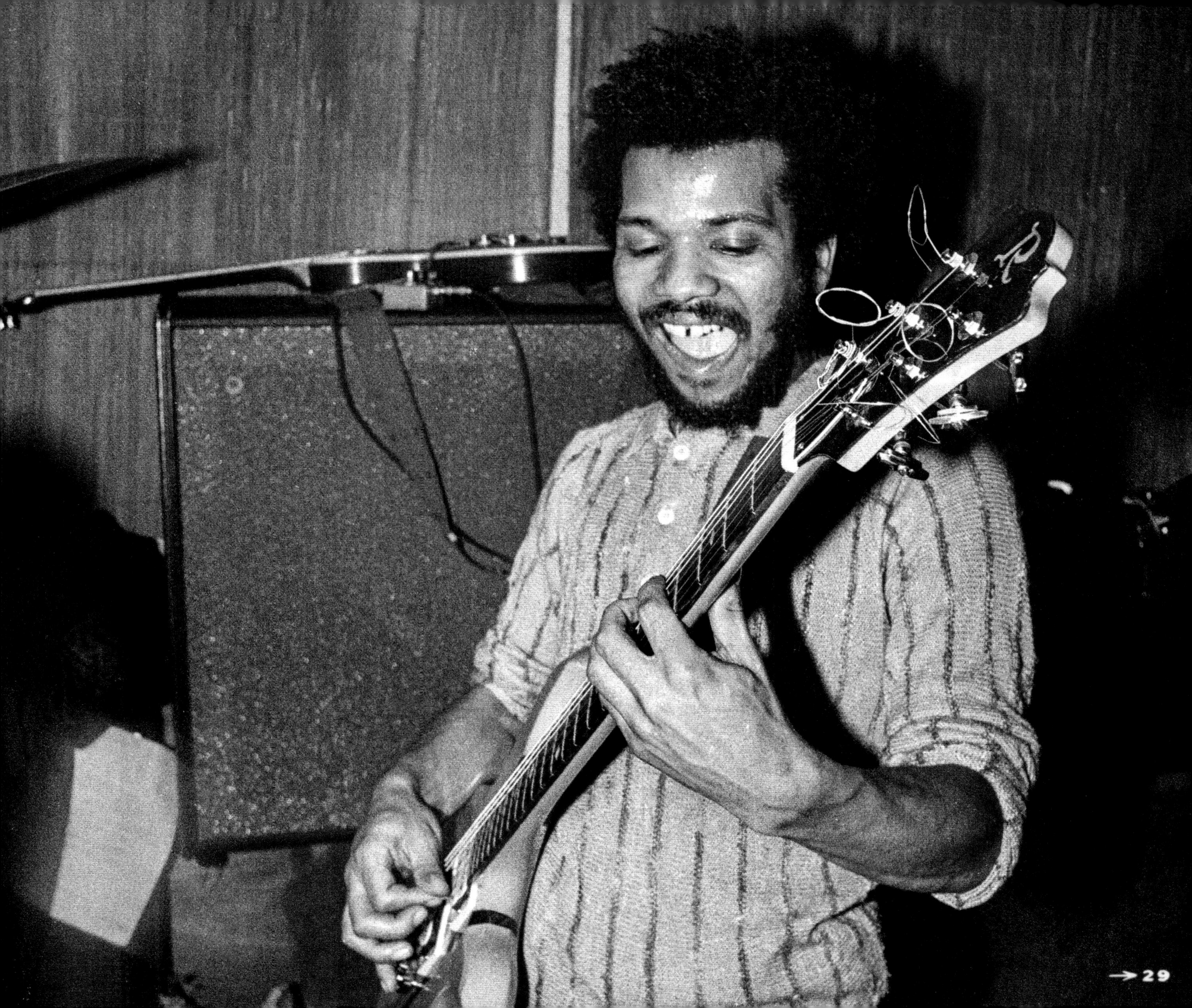
→ 29

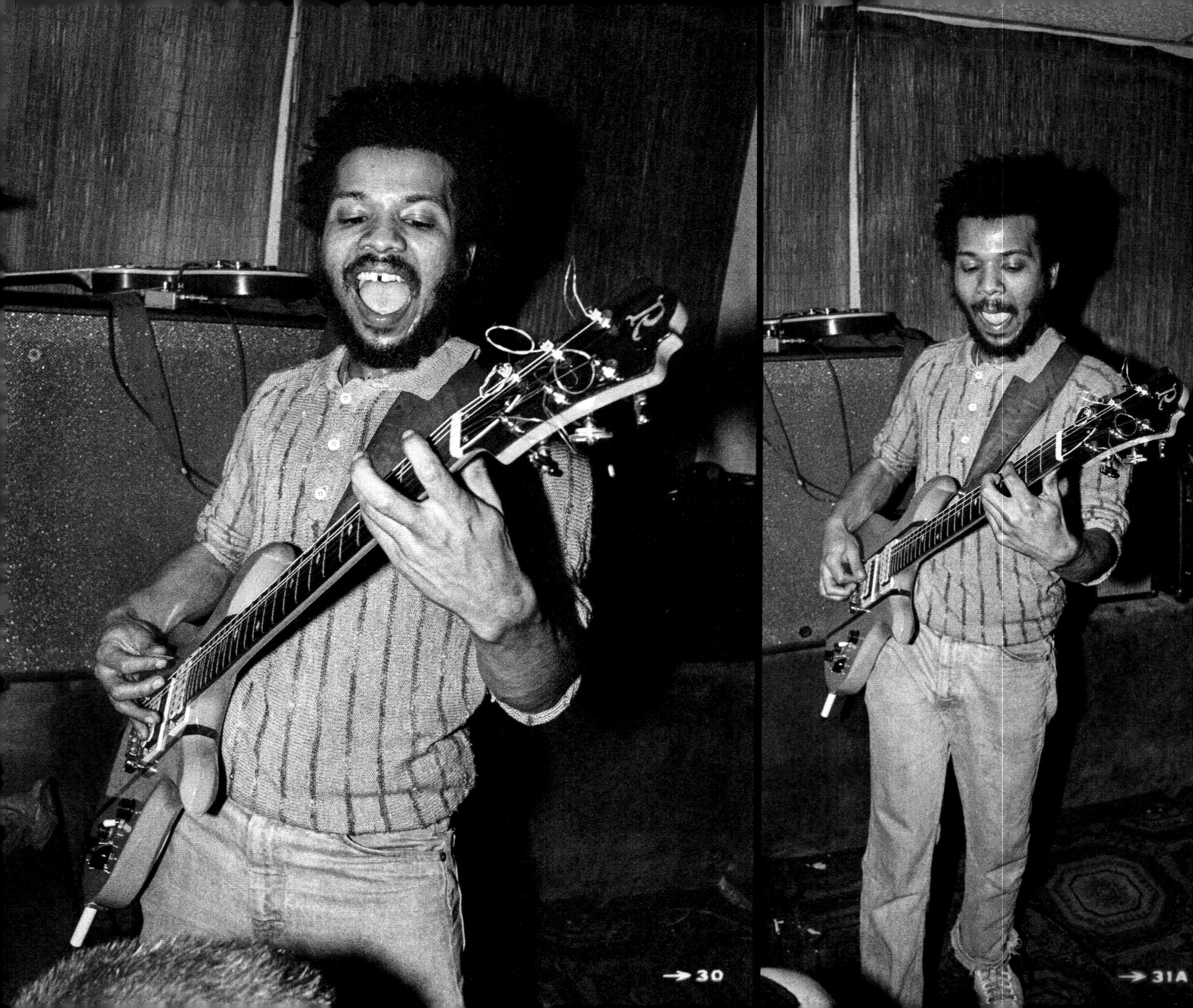

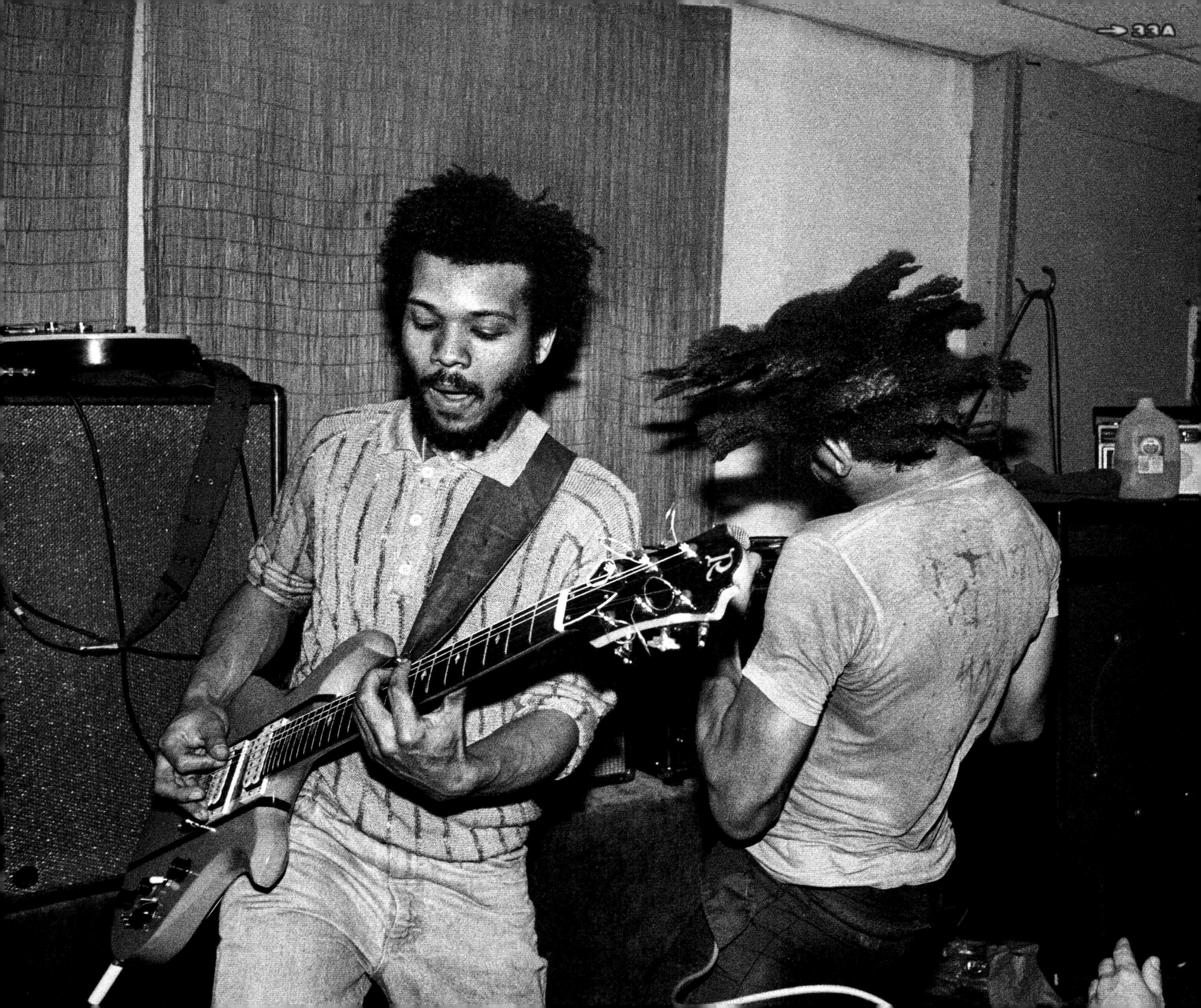

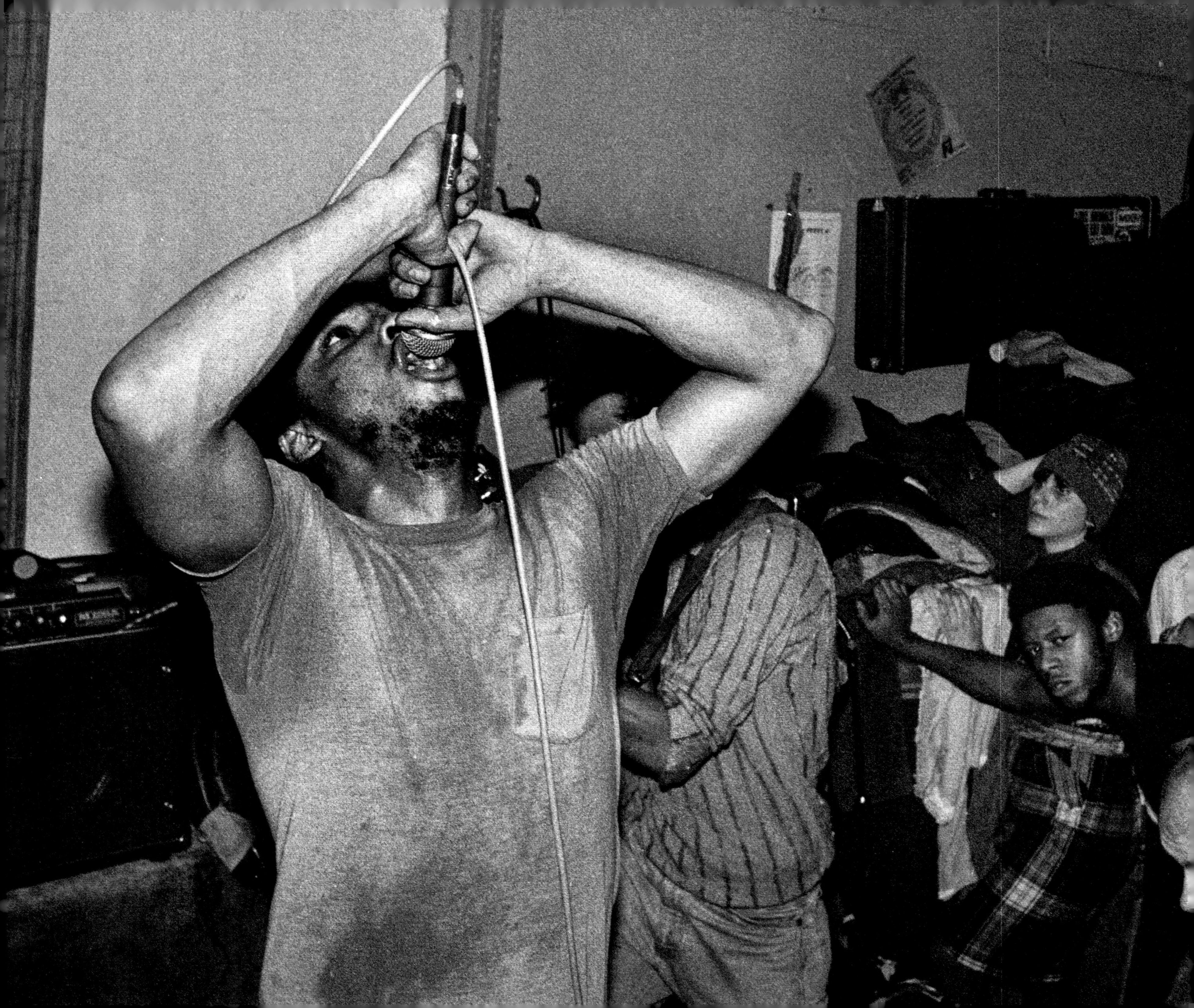

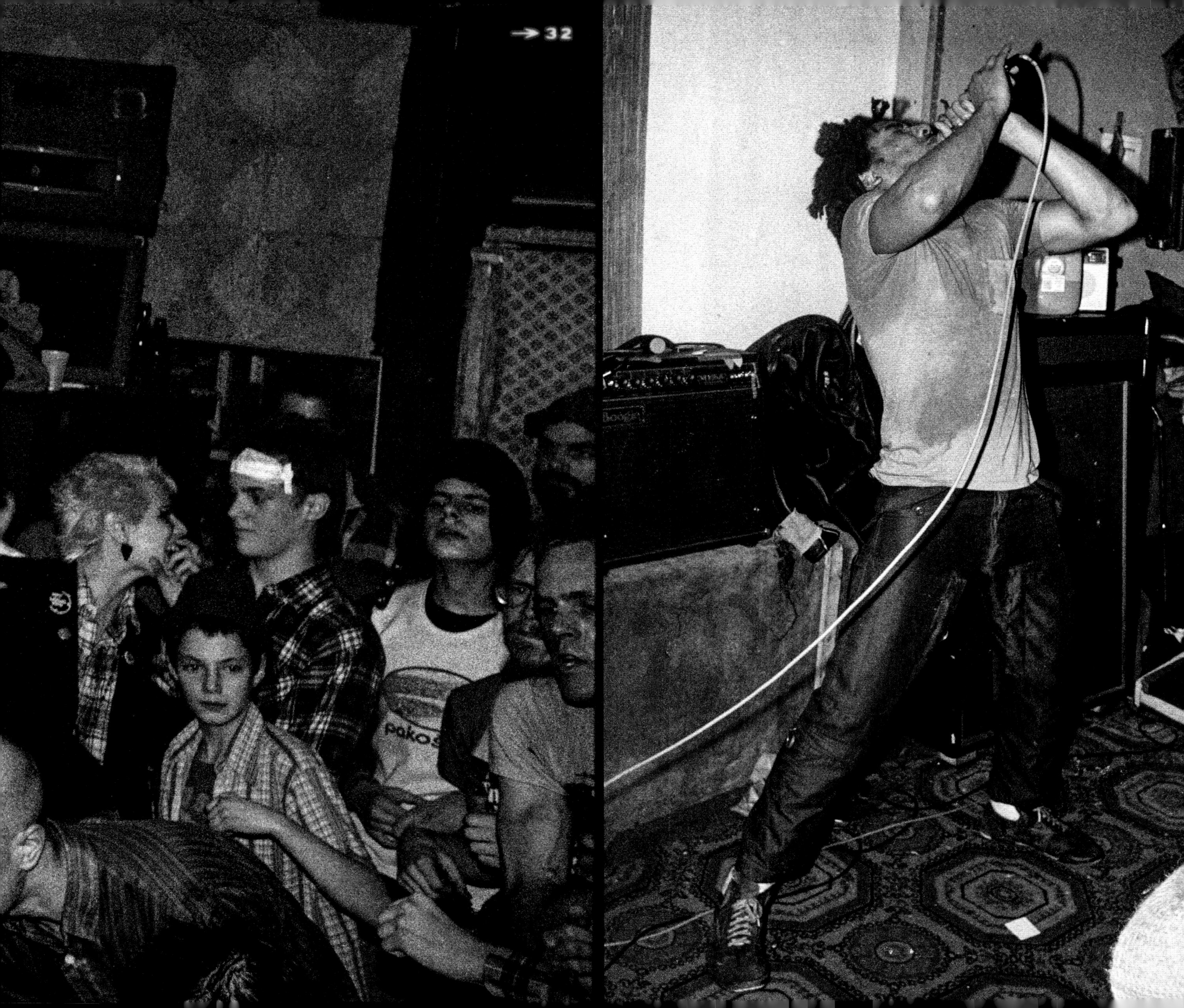

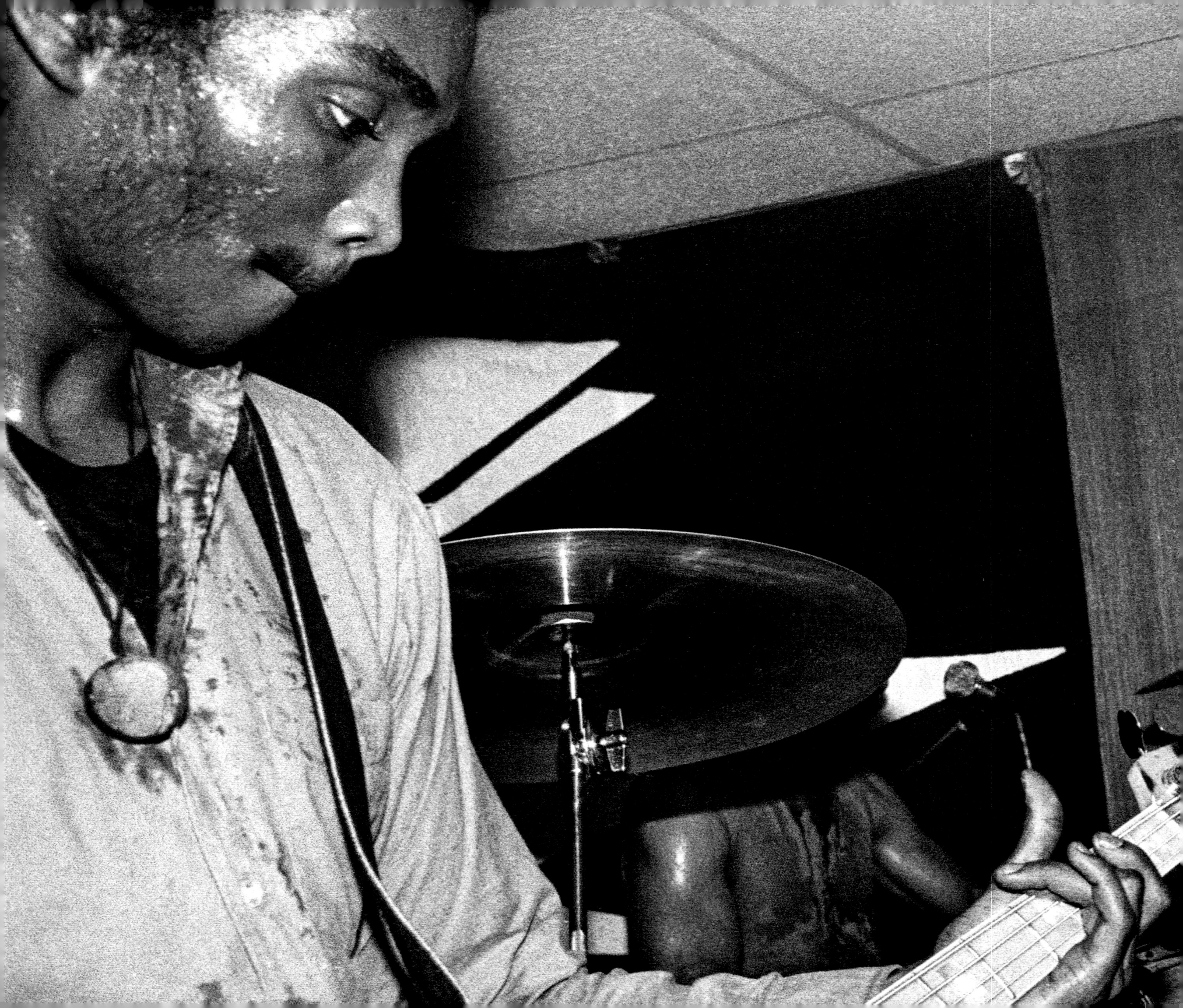

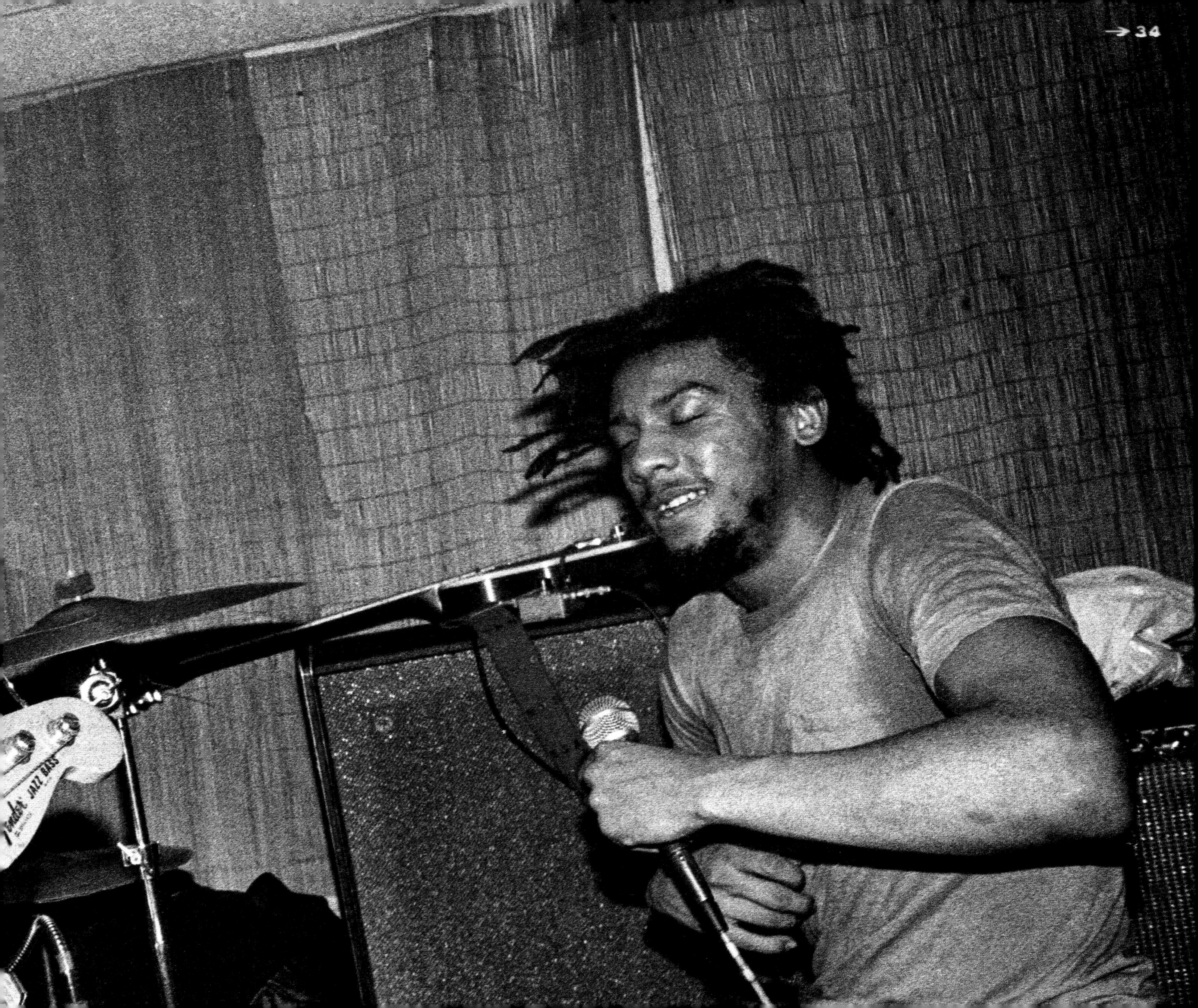

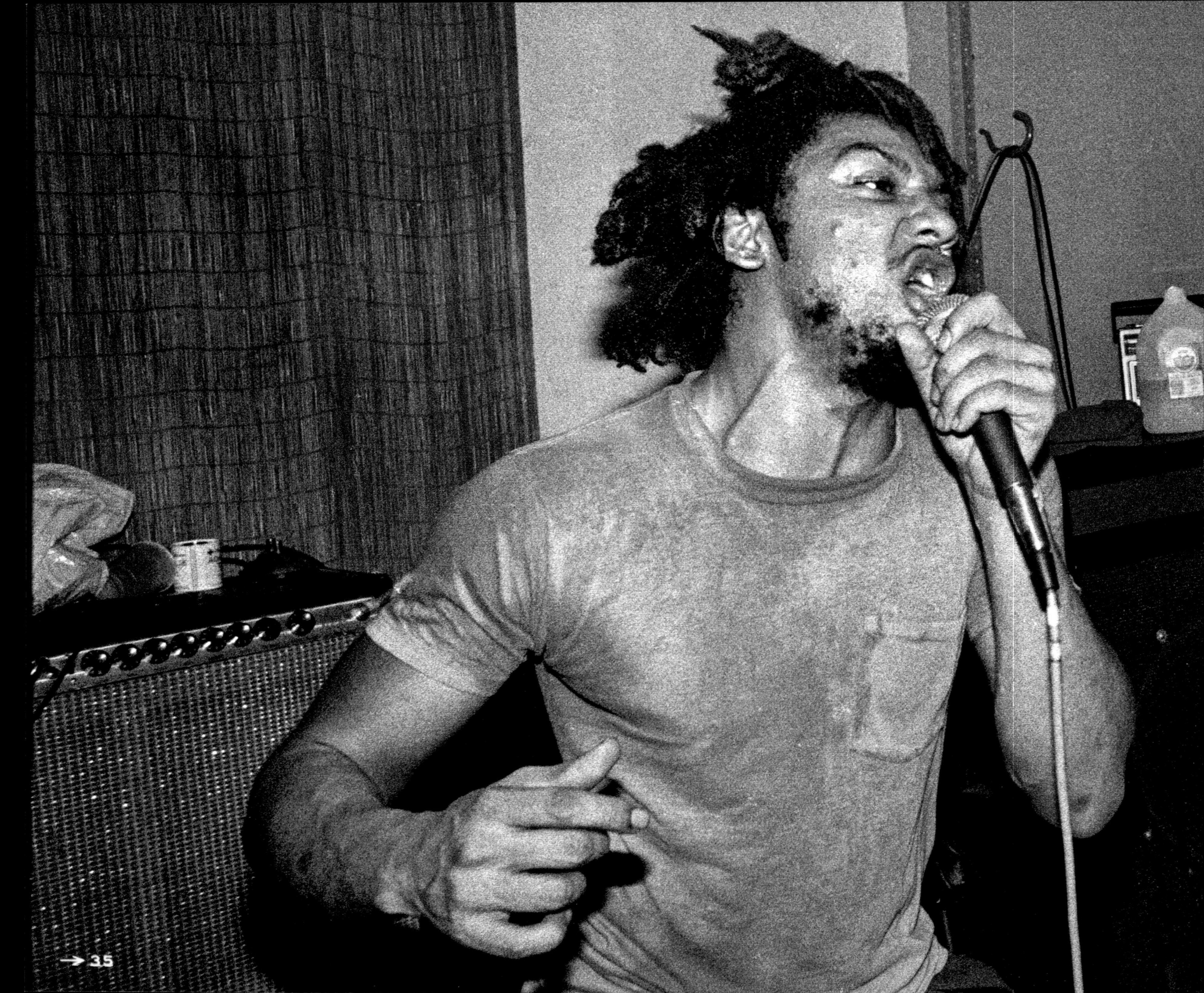
35

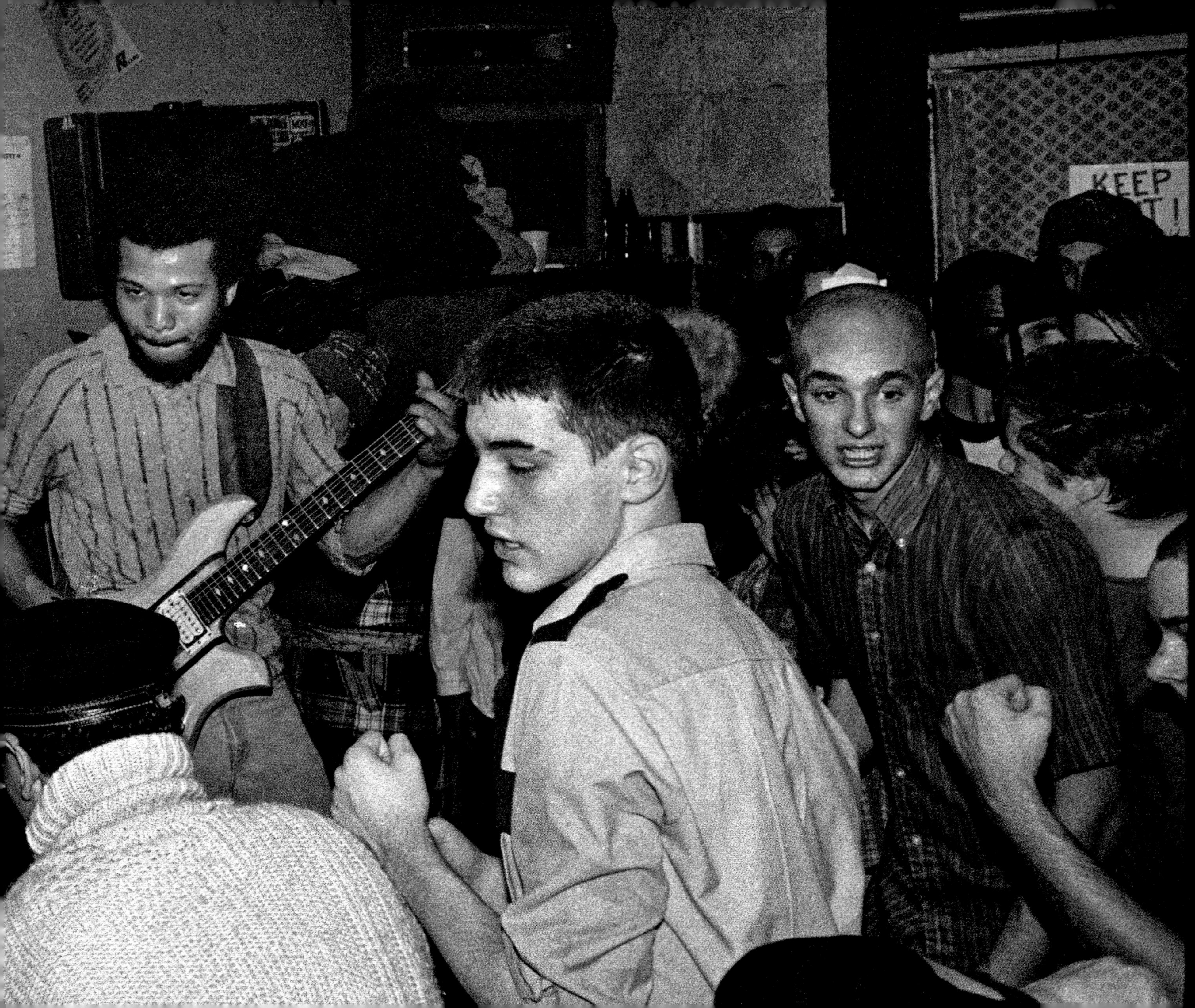
KEEP

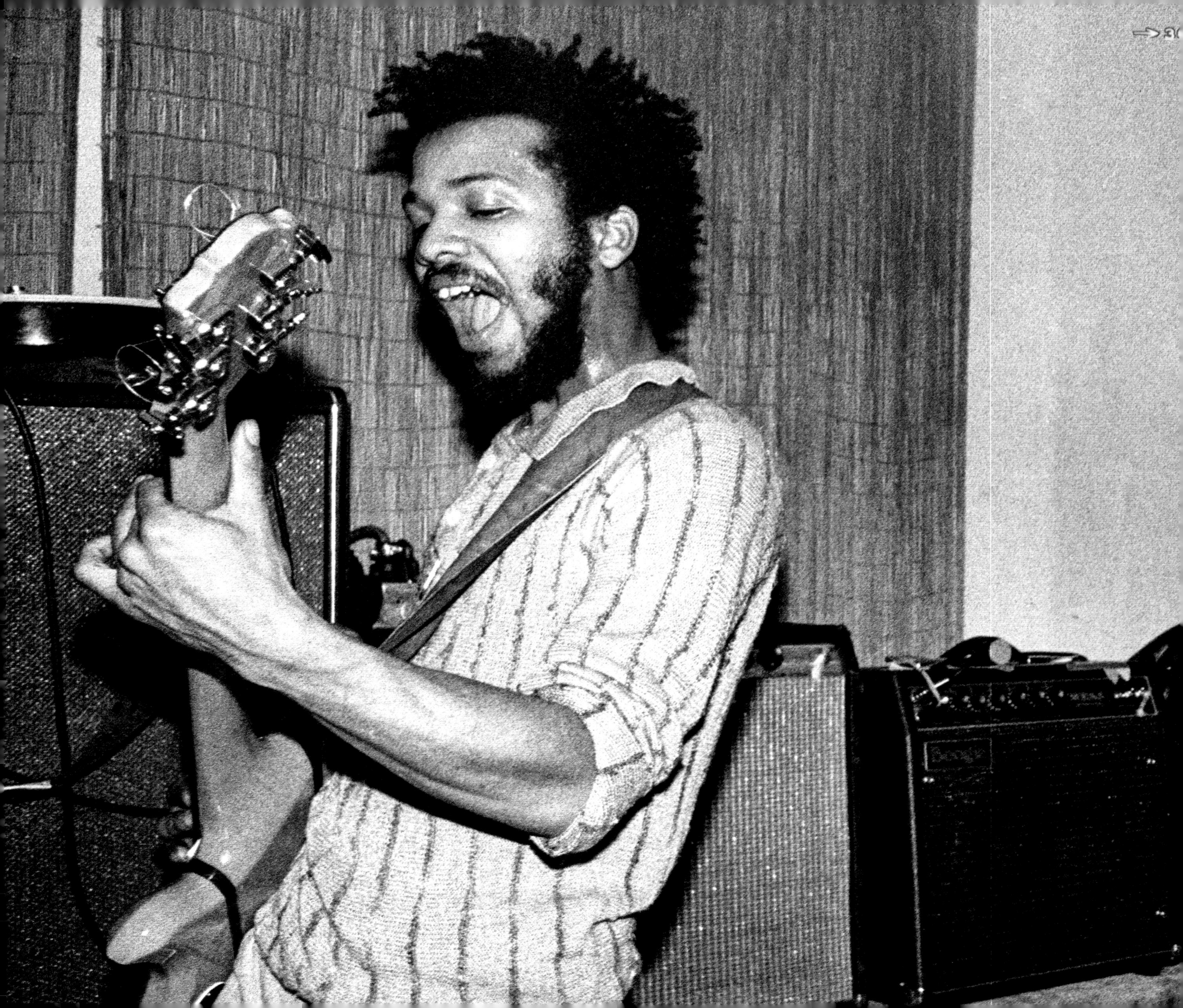

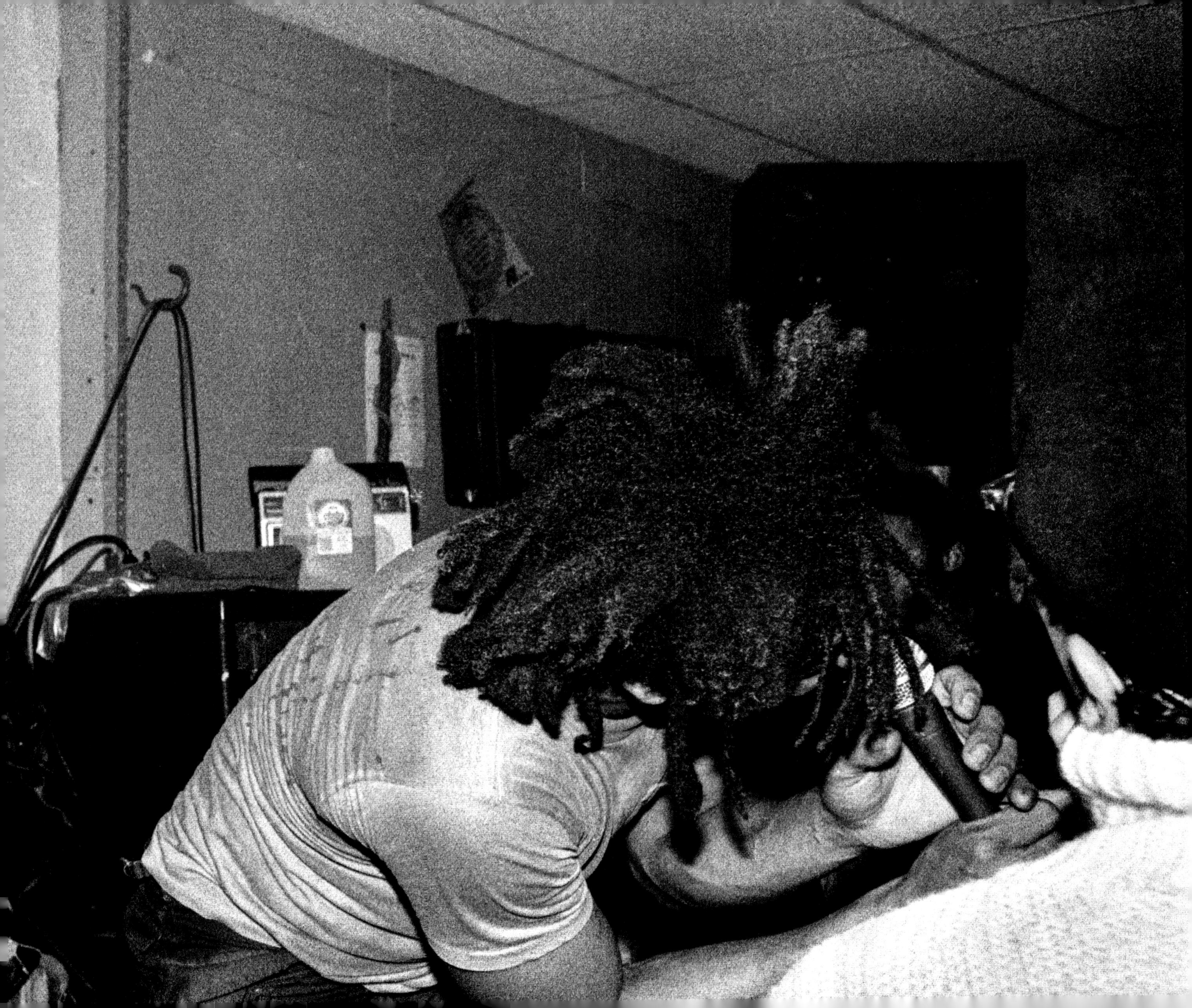

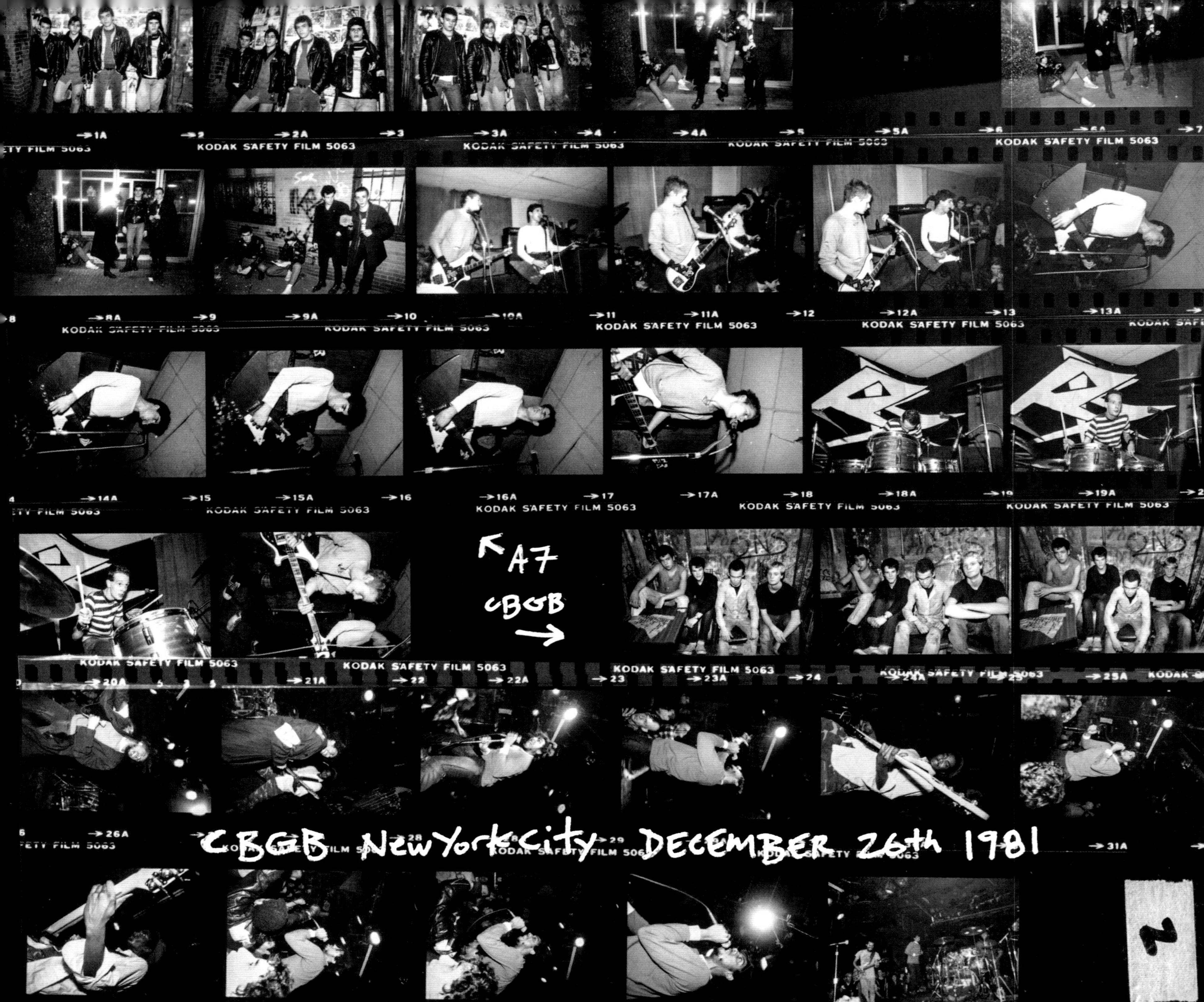

A7
CBGB →
CBGB New York City DECEMBER 26th 1981
KODAK SAFETY FILM 5063

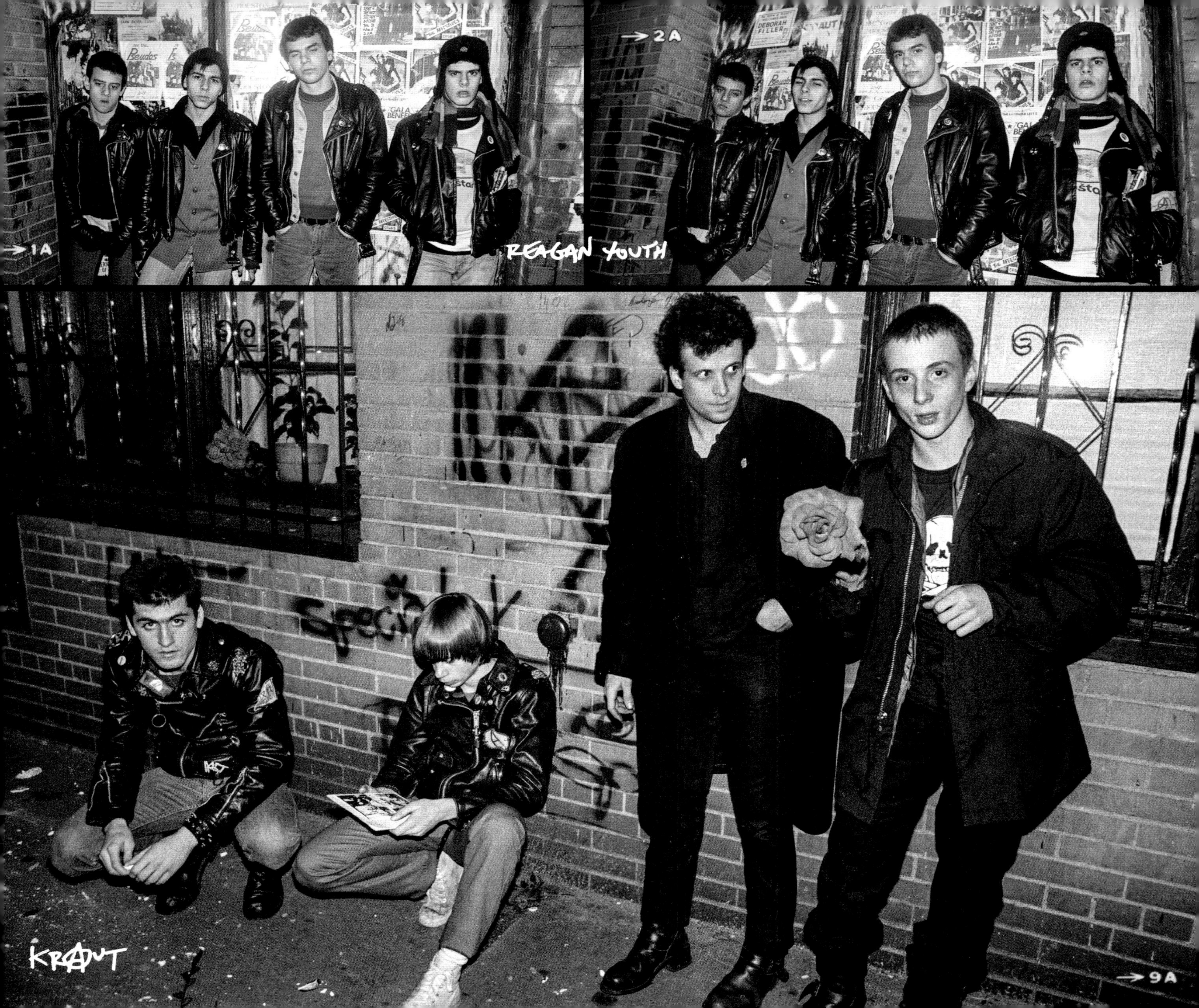

→1A
→2A
REAGAN YOUTH
KRAUT
→9A

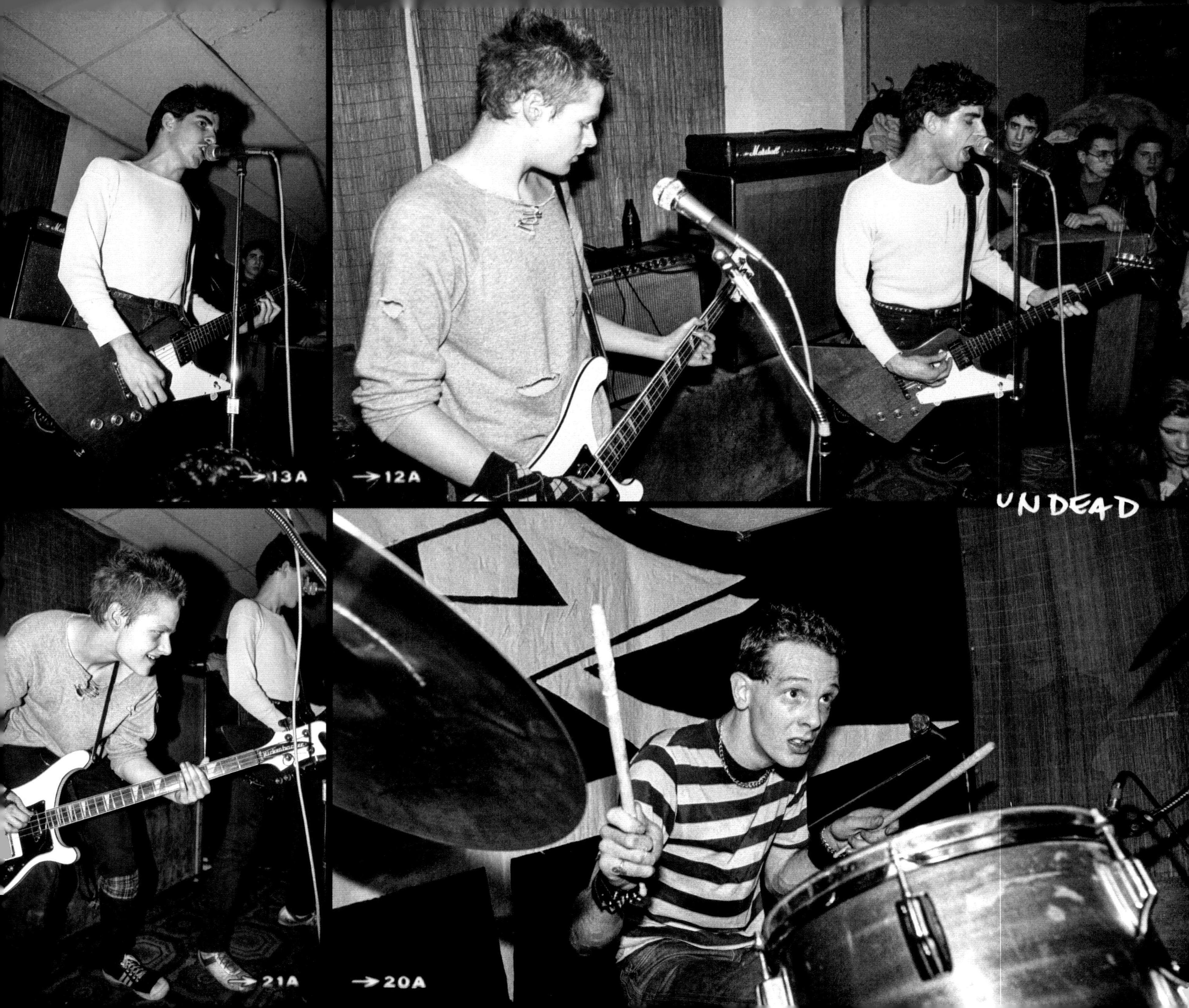

→13A
→12A
UNDEAD
→21A
→20A

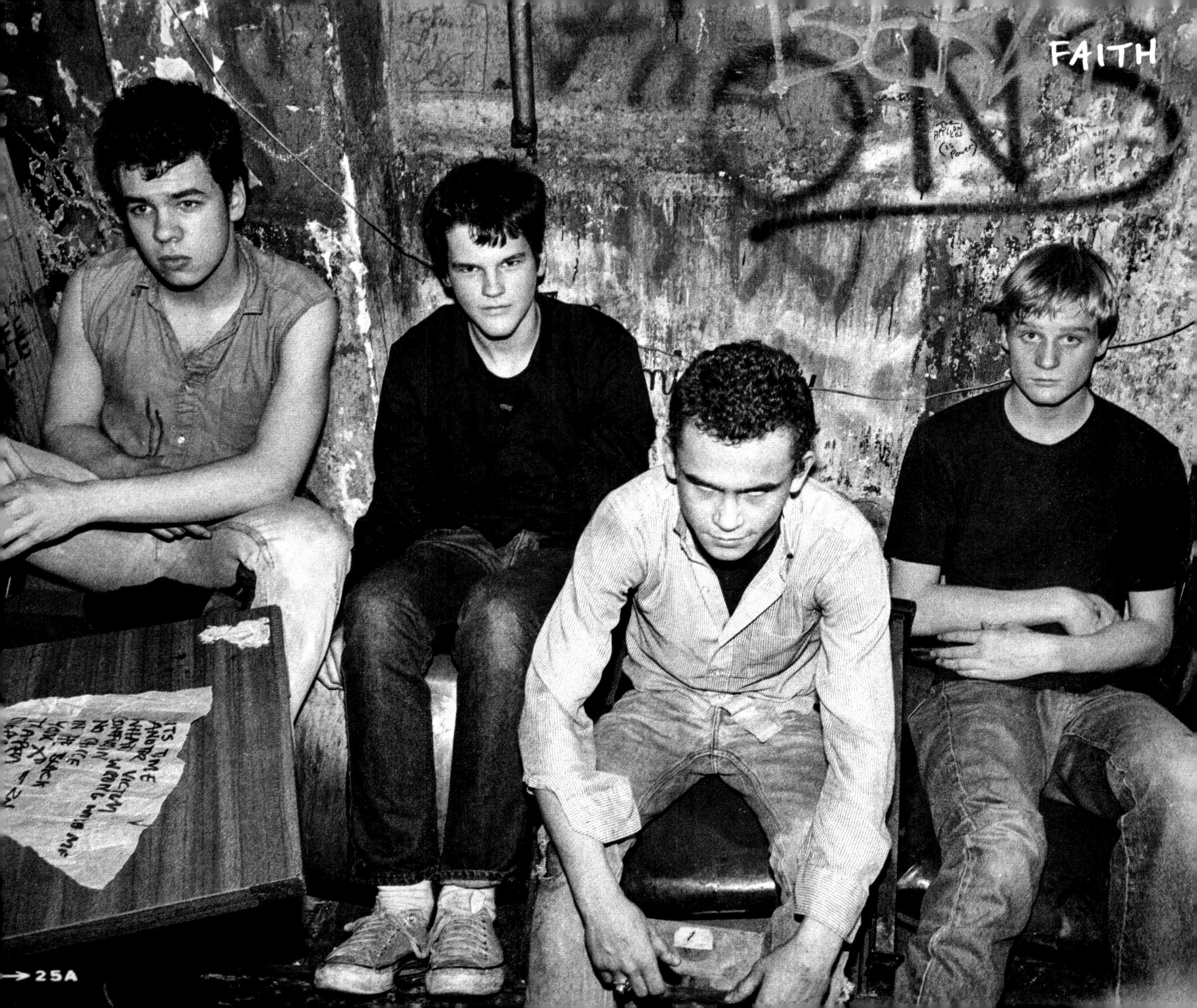

FAITH
25A

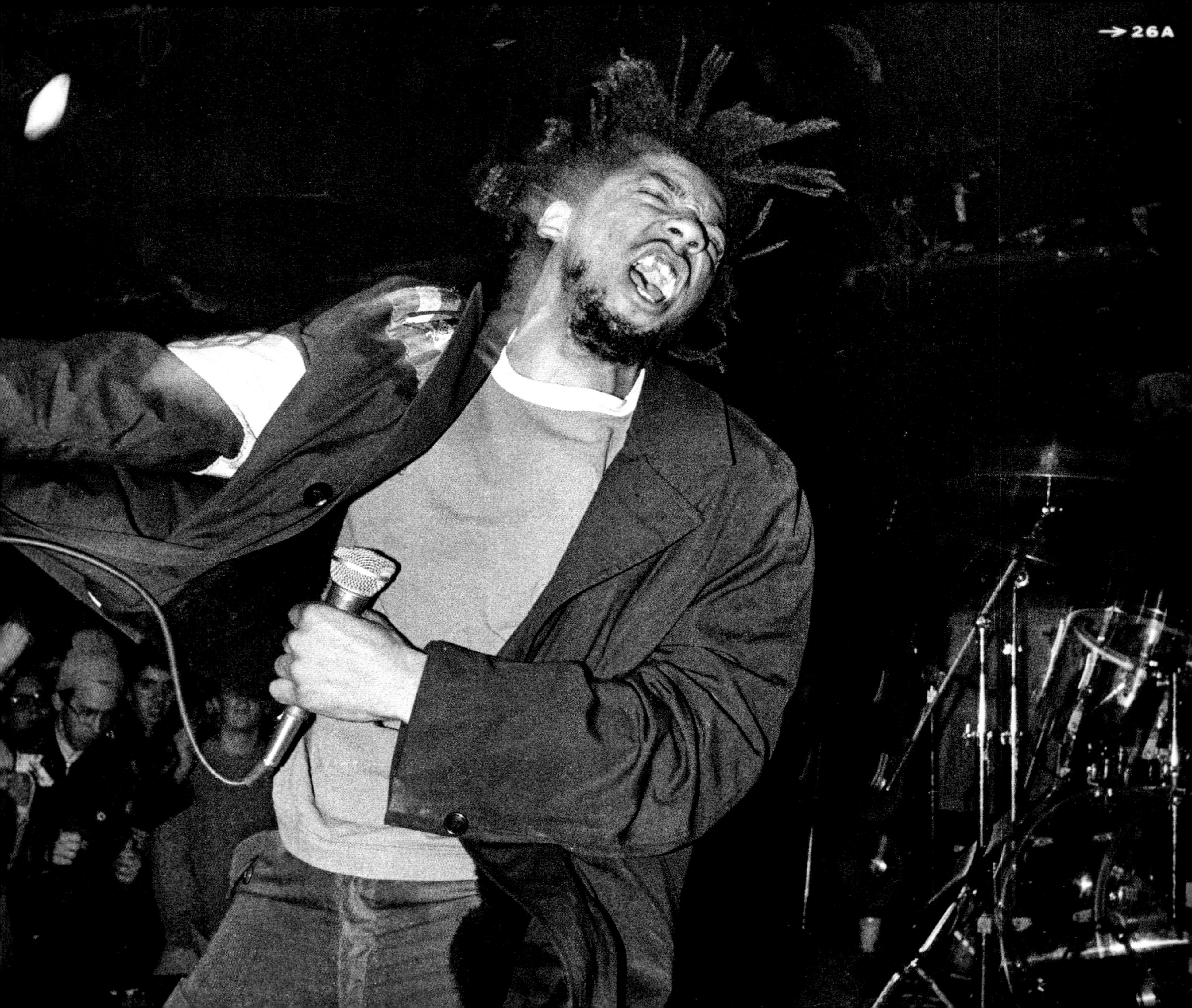
26A

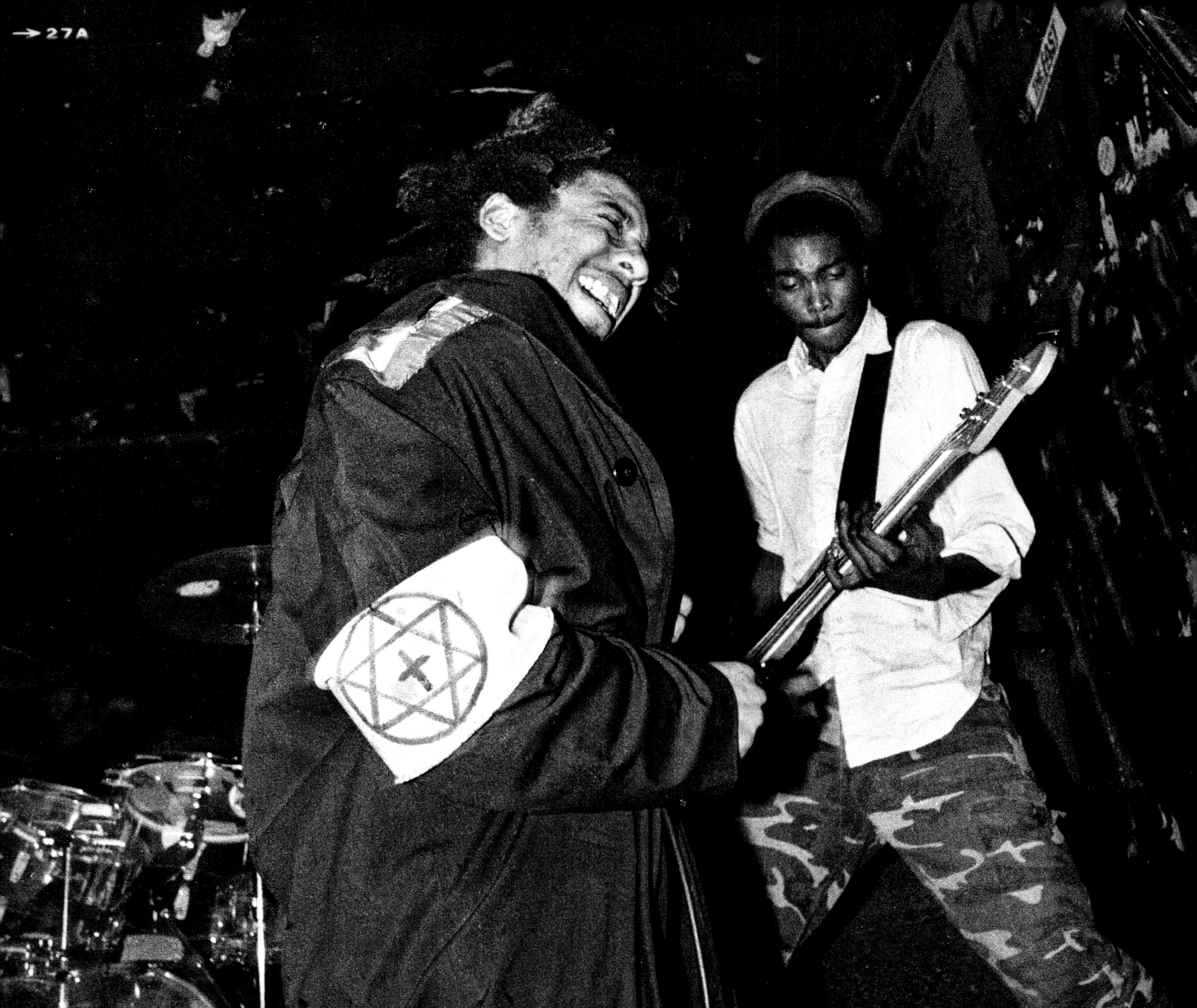

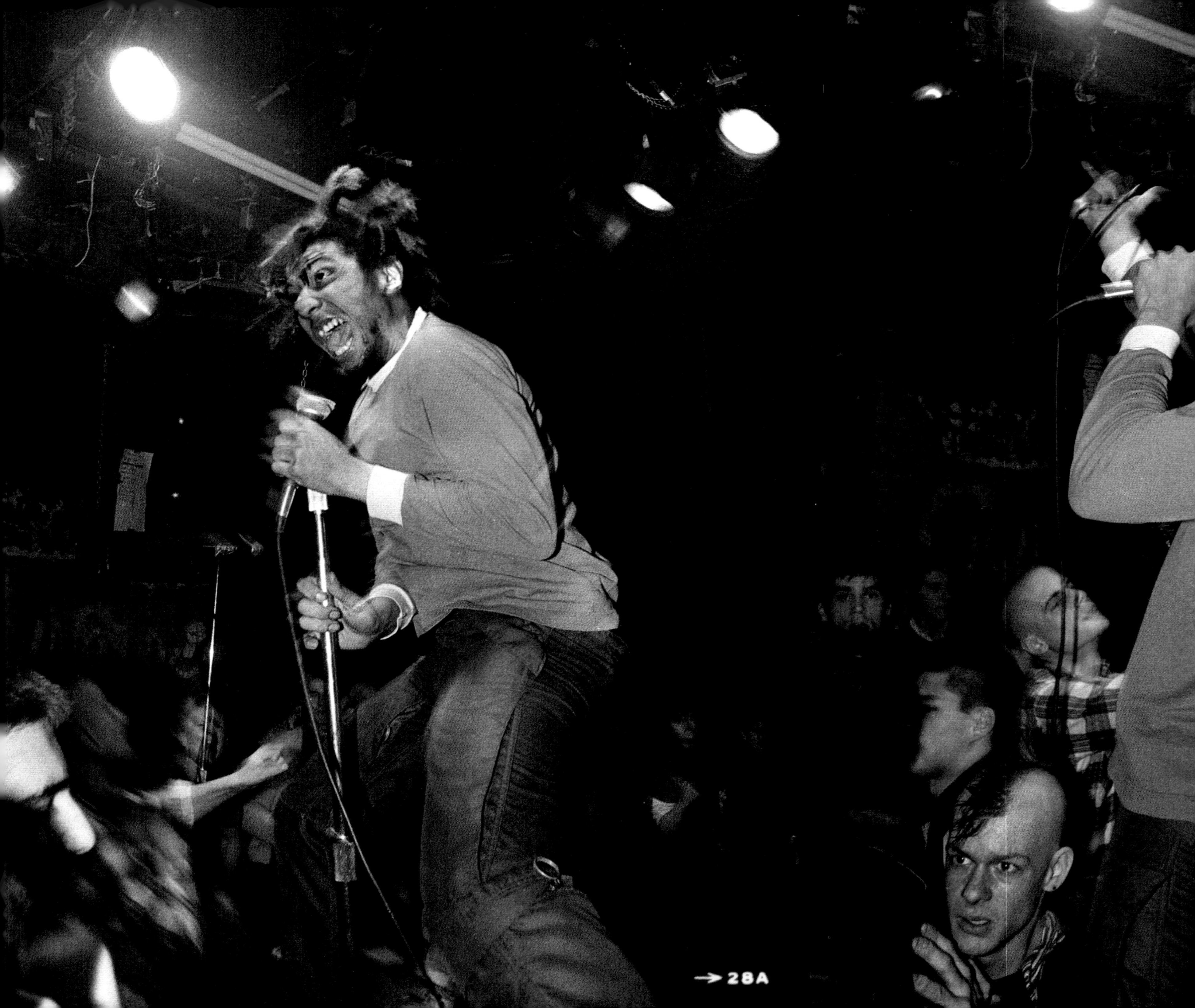
→ 28A

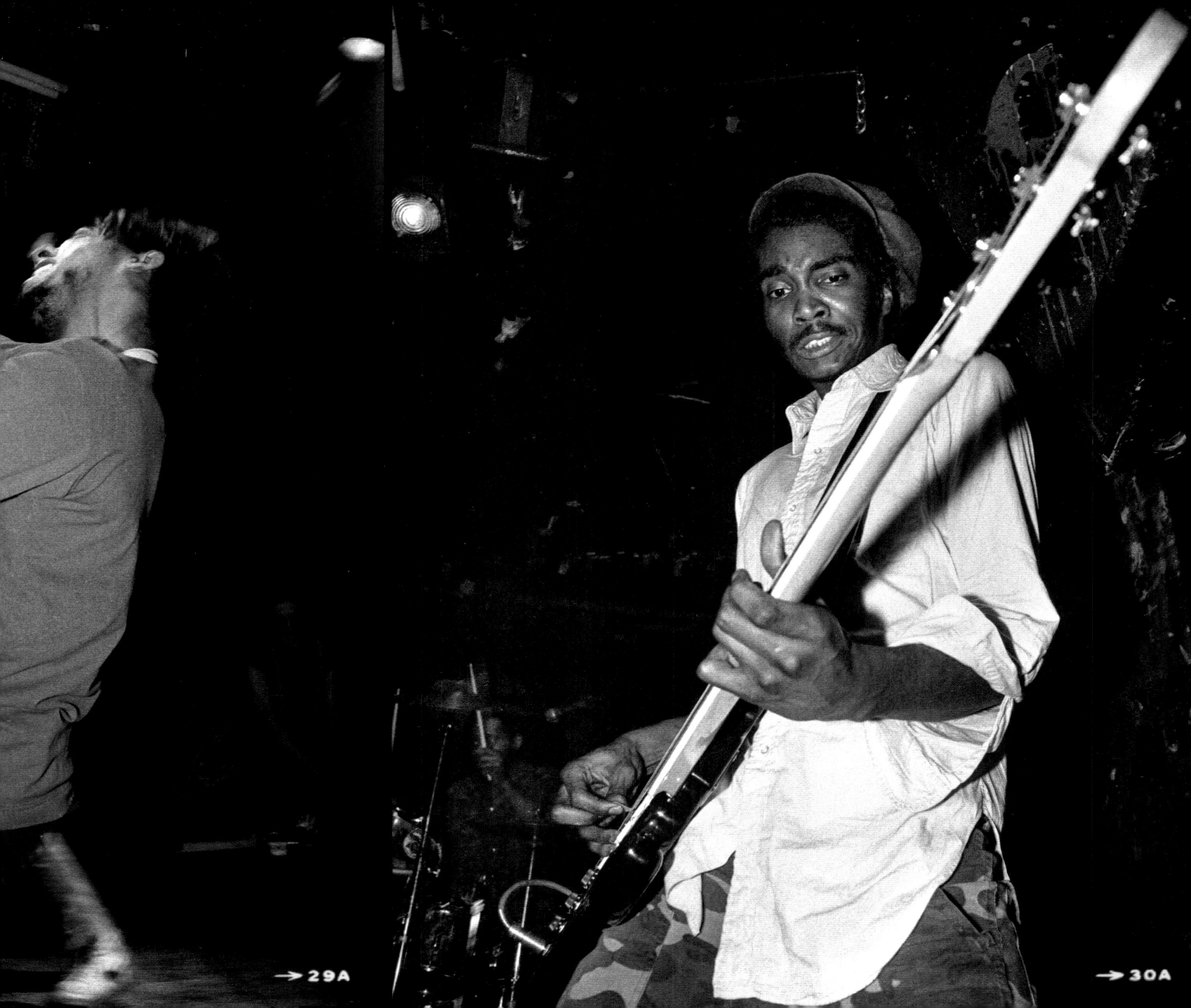
29A
30A

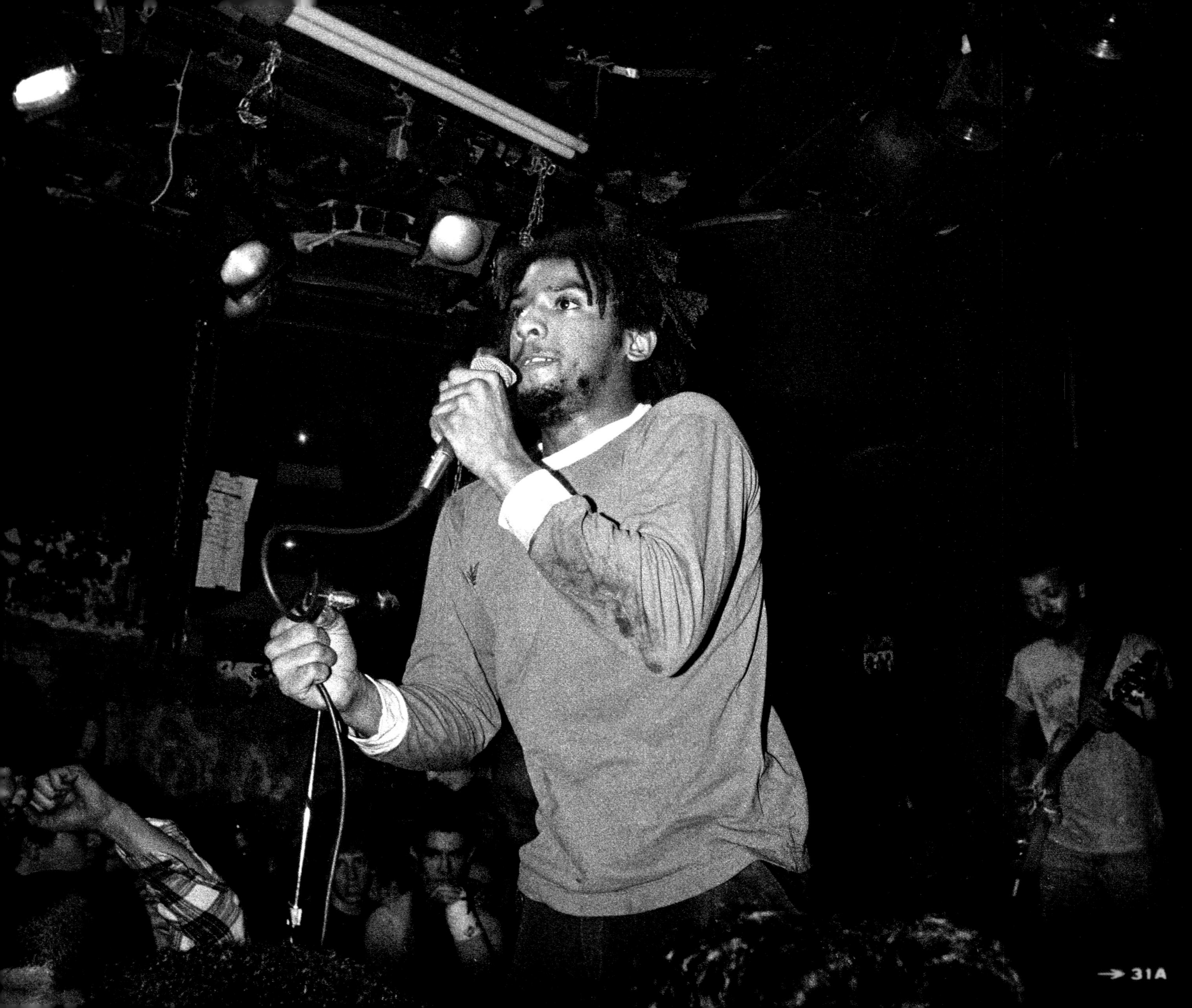
31A

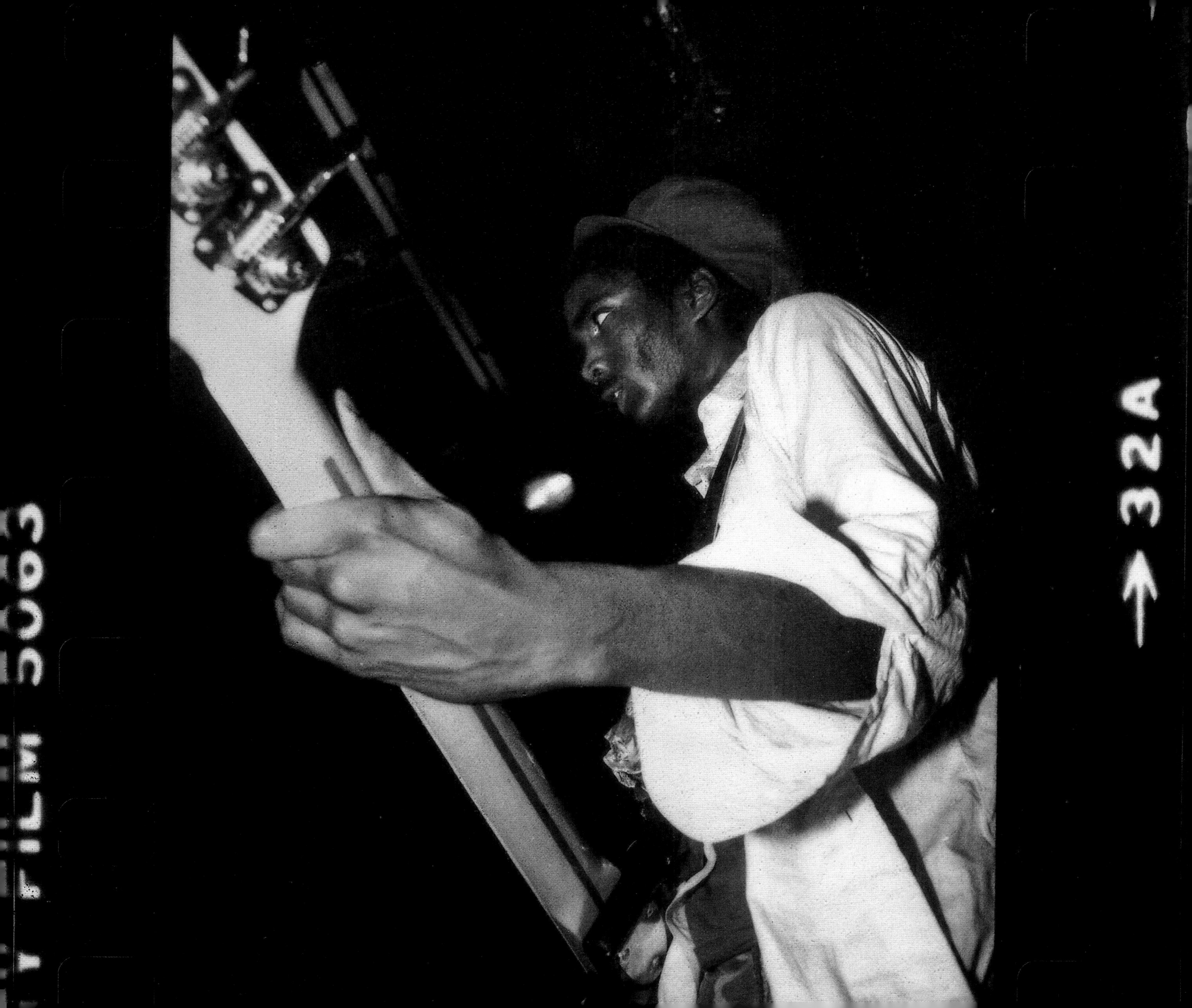

FILM 5063
32A

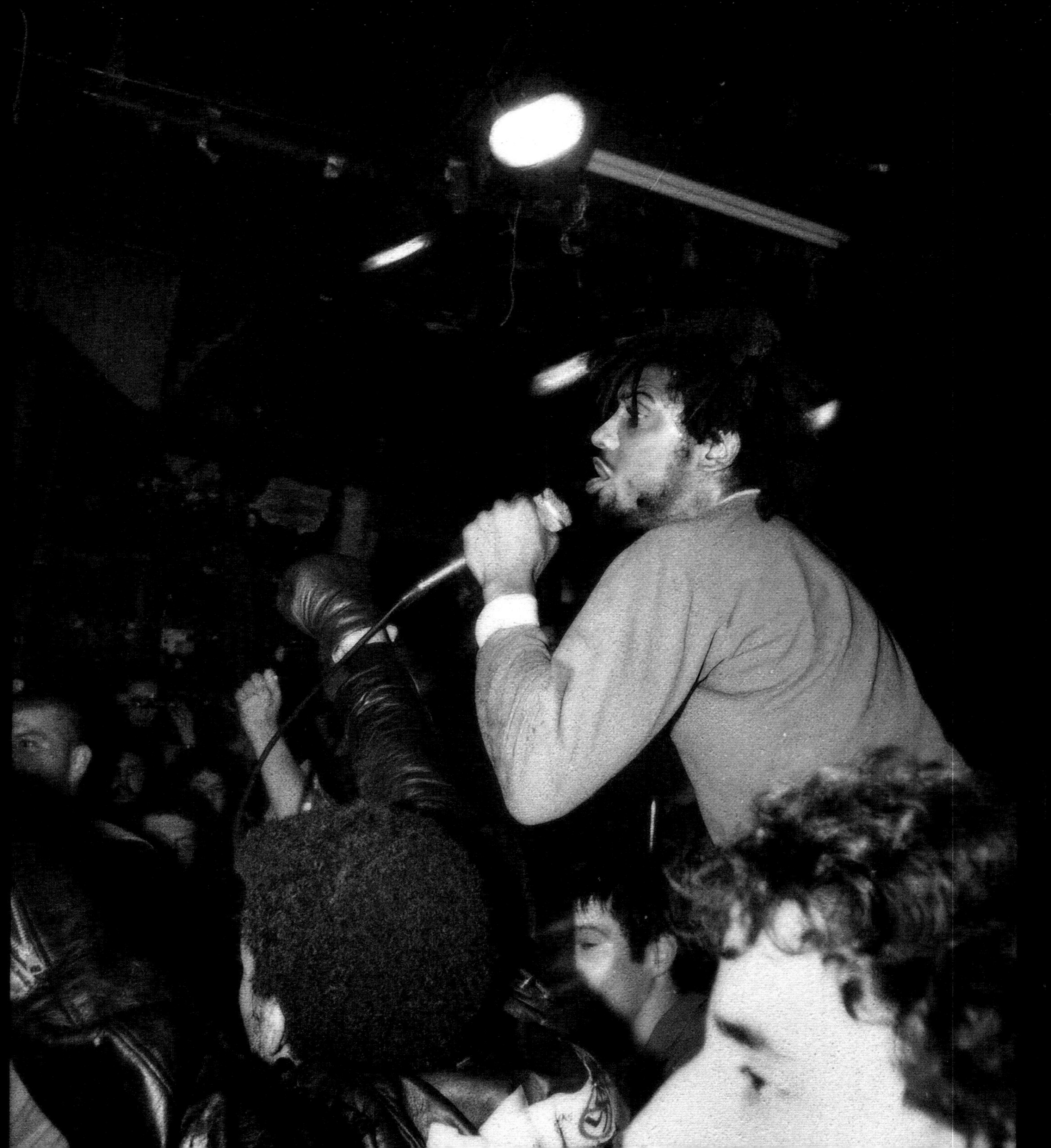

KODAK S'AFETY FILM 5063

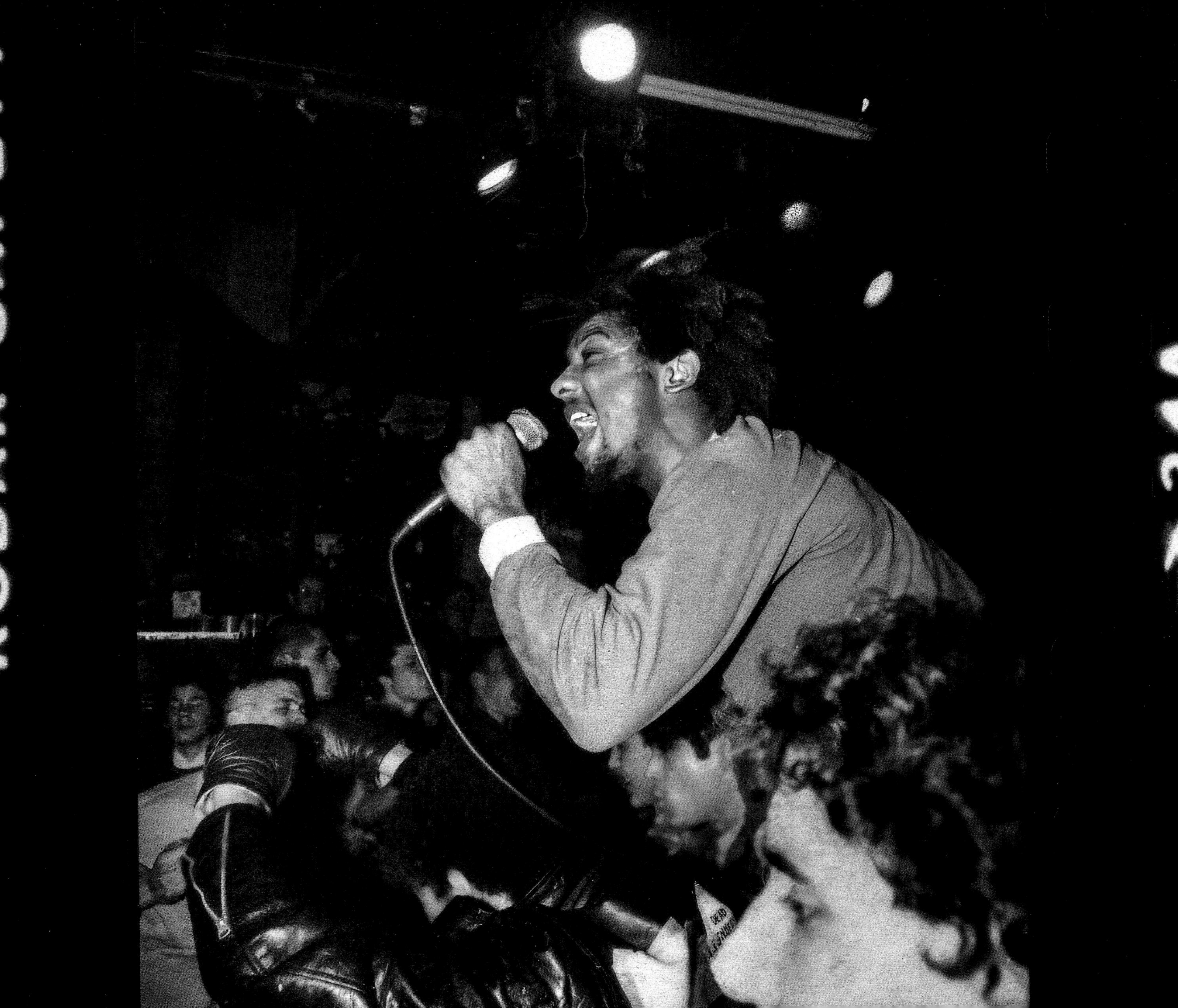
KODAK SAFETY

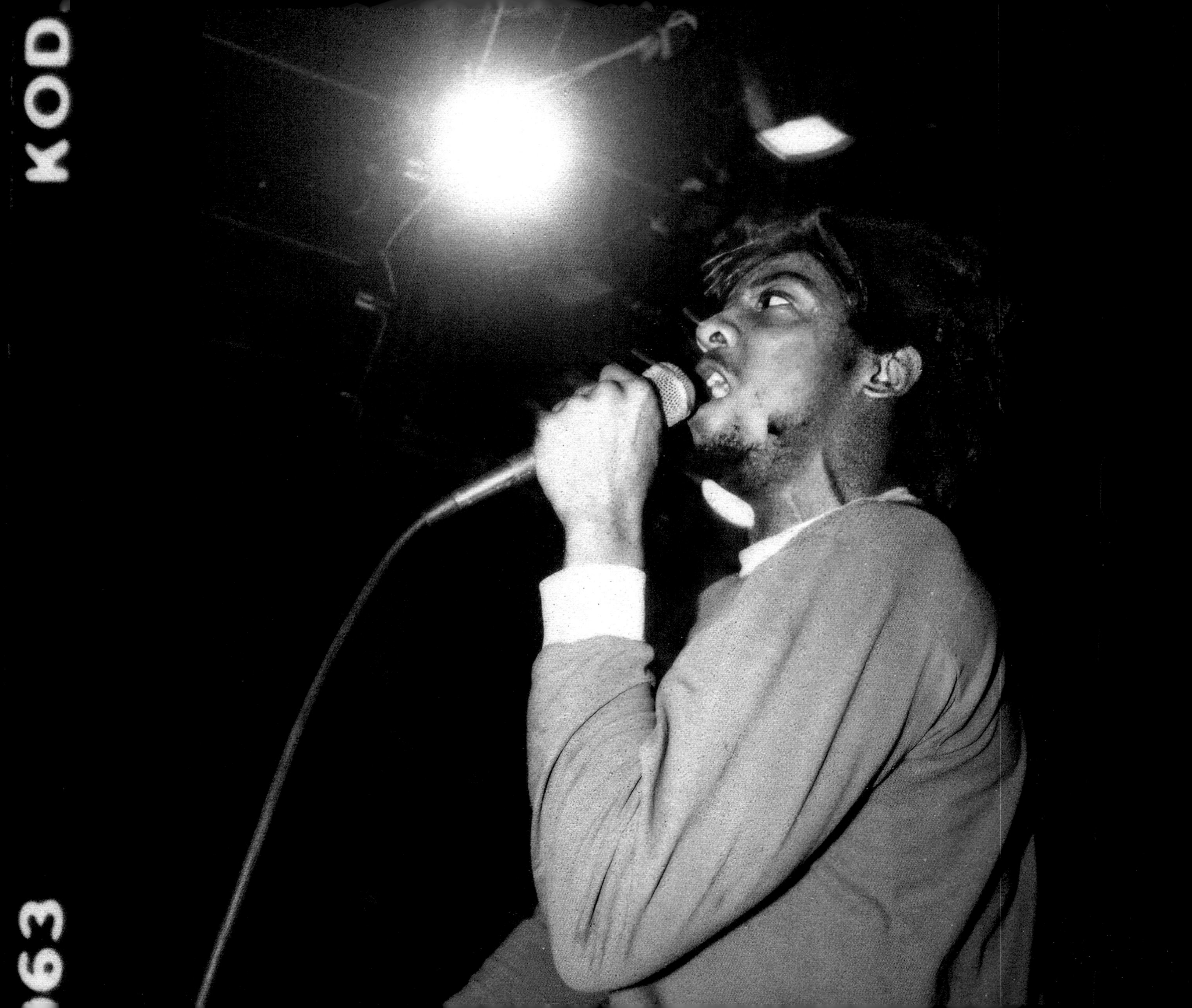

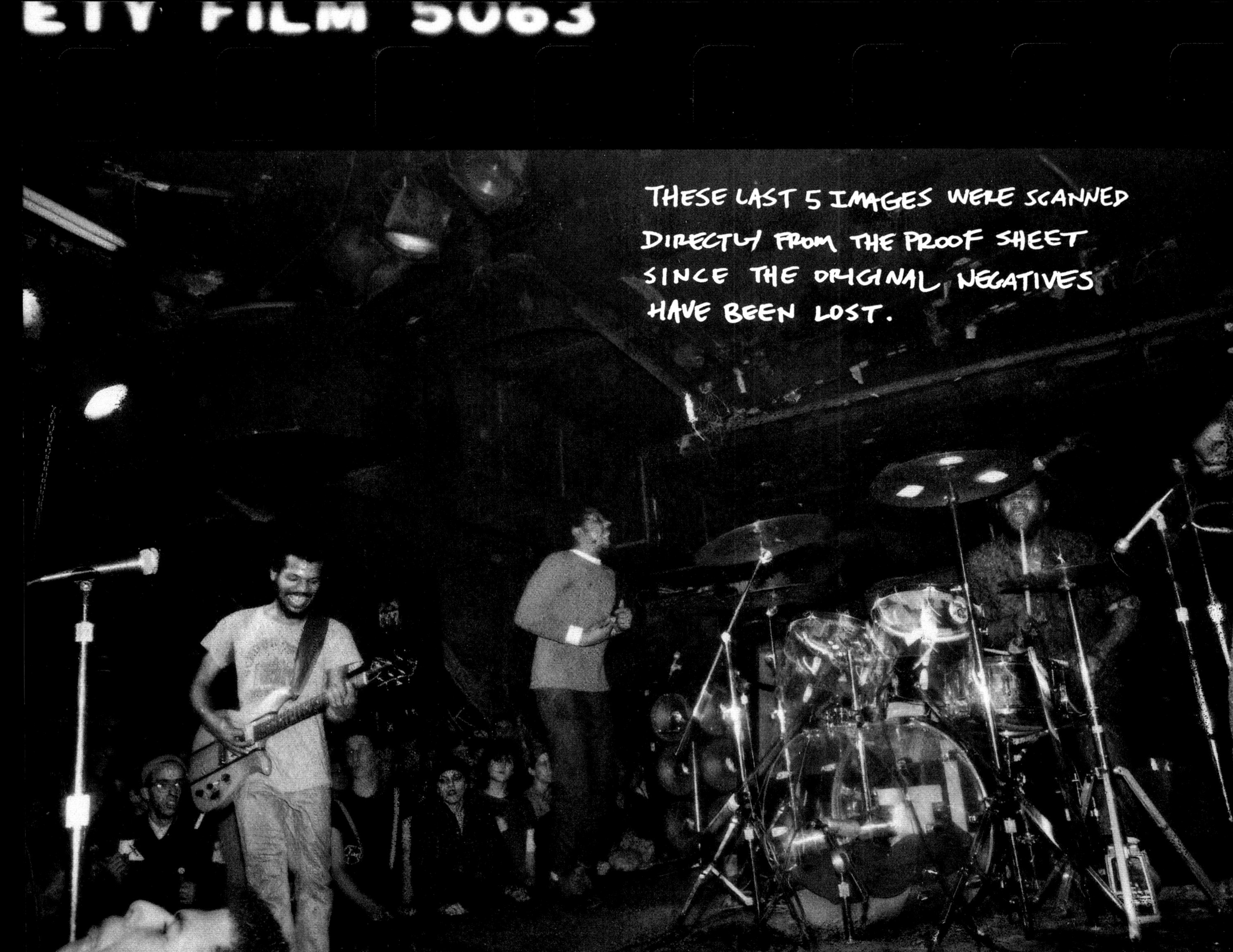


ETV FILM 5063
THESE LAST 5 IMAGES WERE SCANNED
DIRECTLY FROM THE PROOF SHEET
SINCE THE ORIGINAL NEGATIVES
HAVE BEEN LOST.

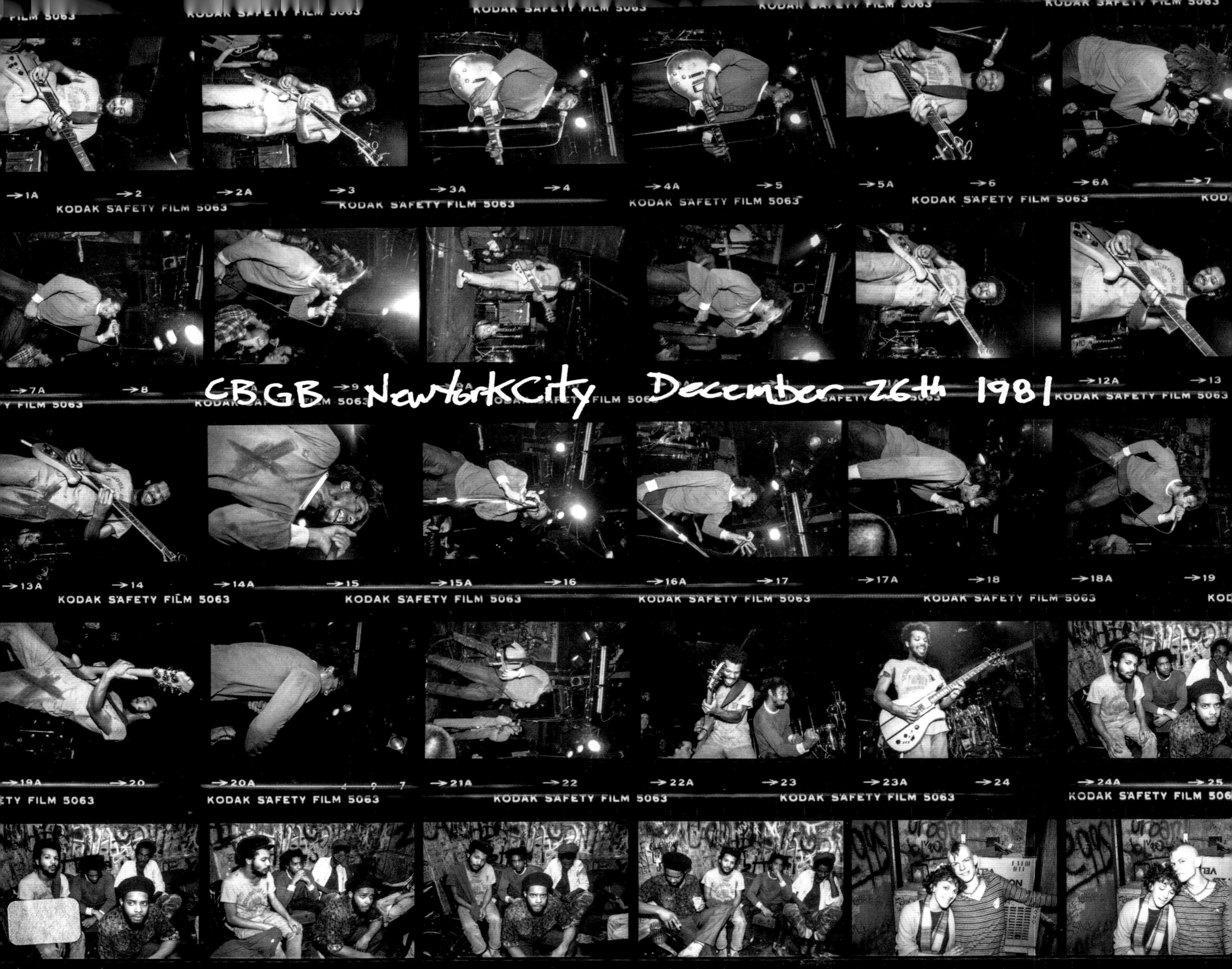

CBGB · NewYorkCity   December 26th 1981

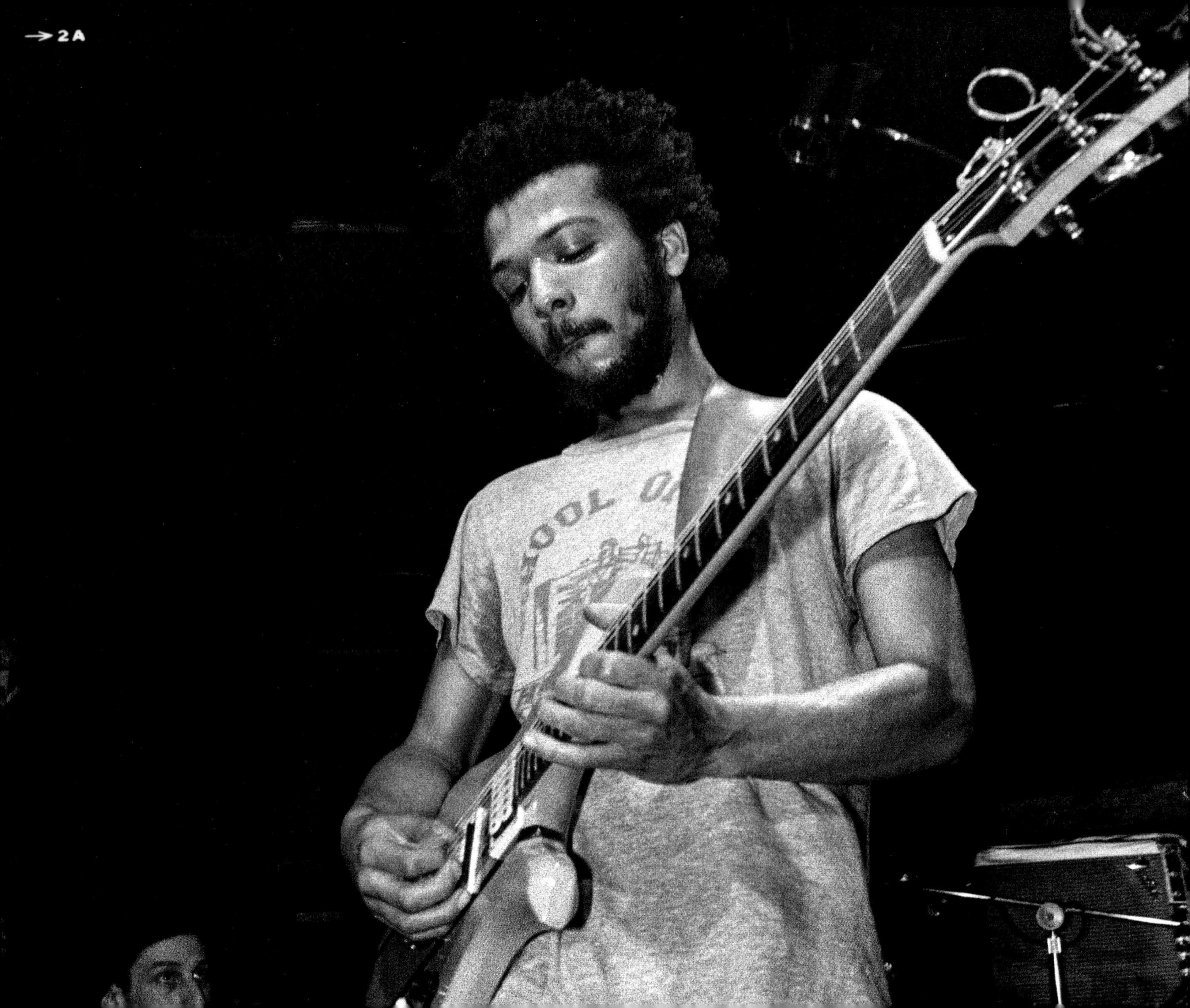
→2A

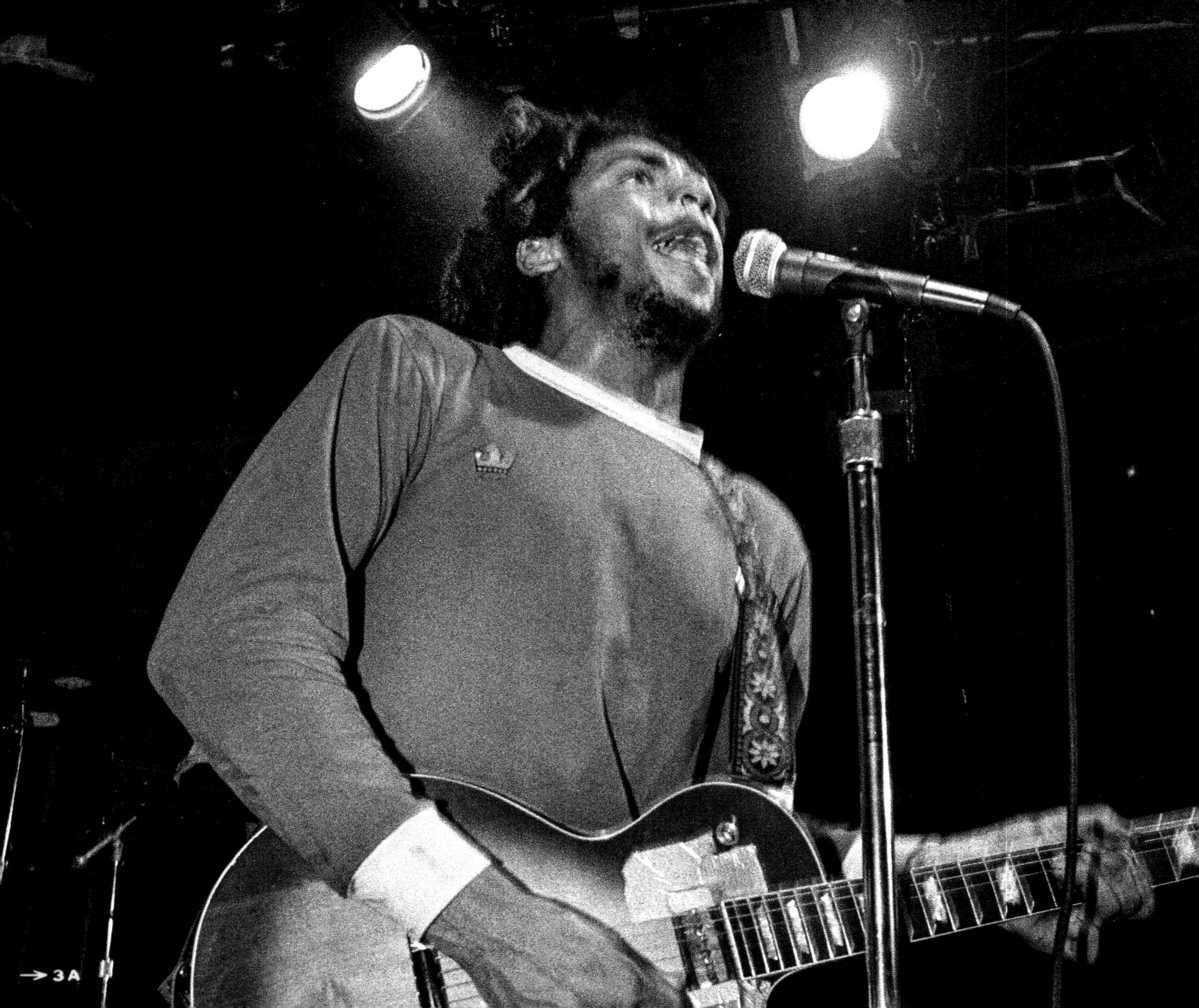
→ 3A

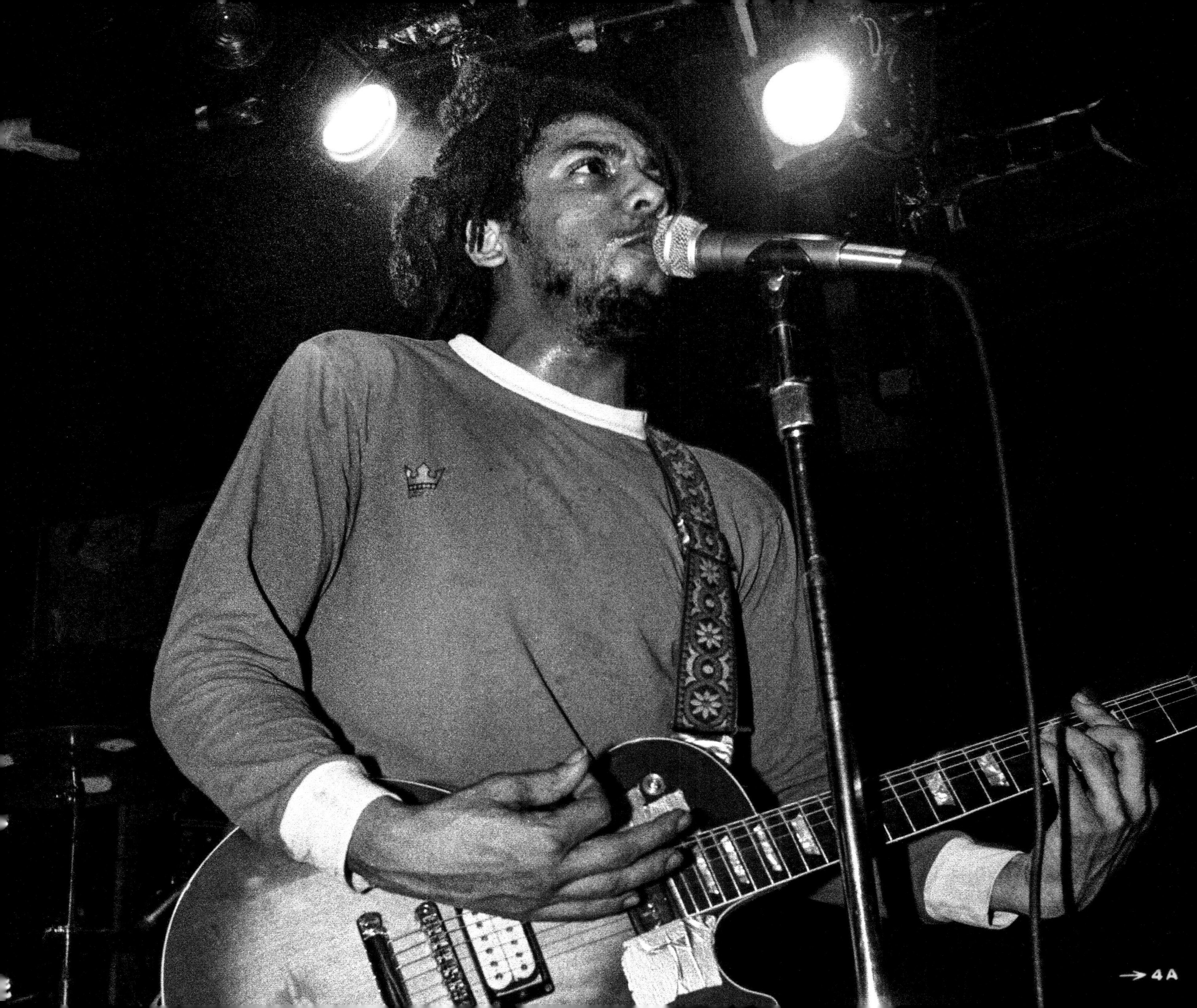

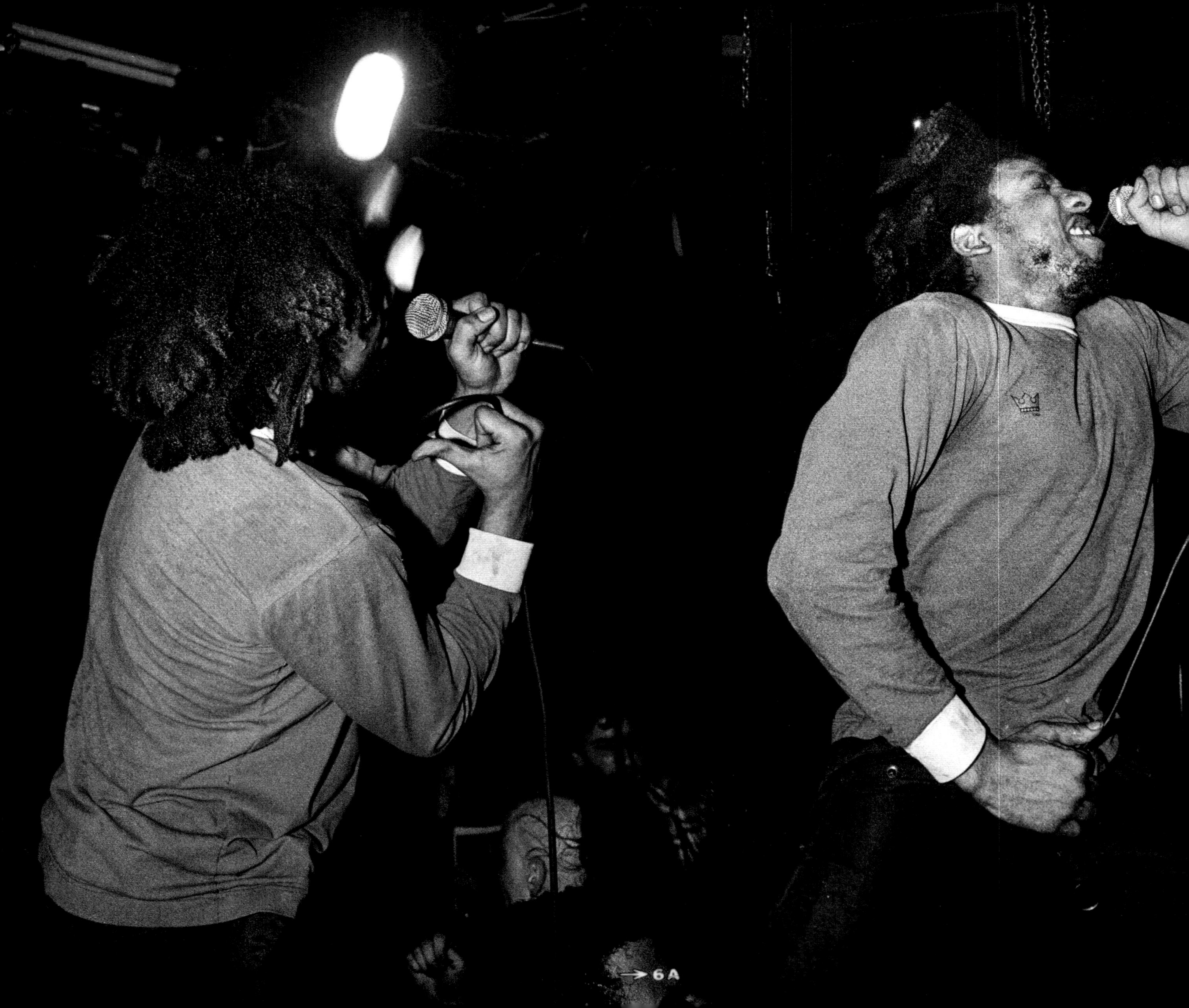
→ 6A

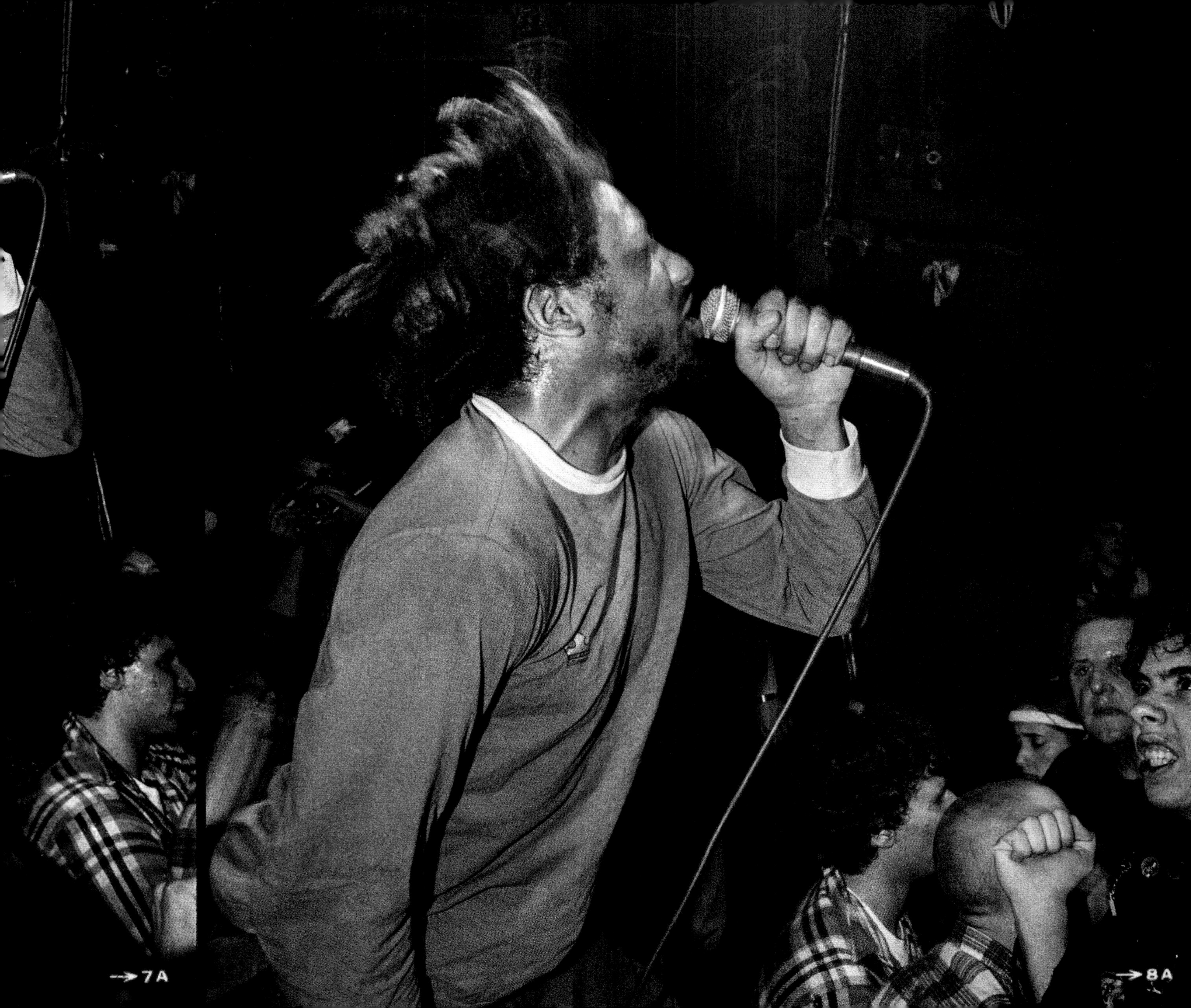
7A
8A

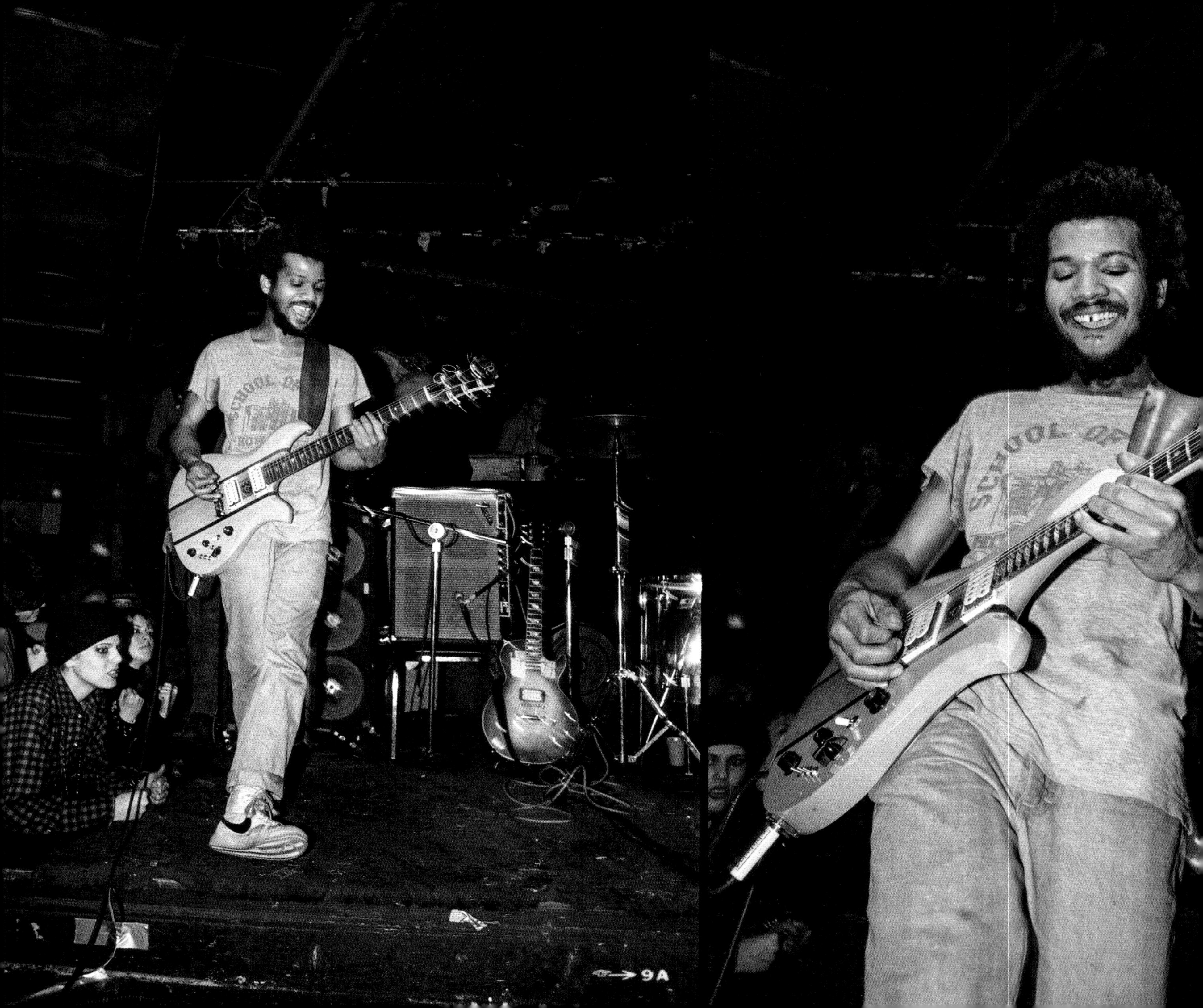
9A

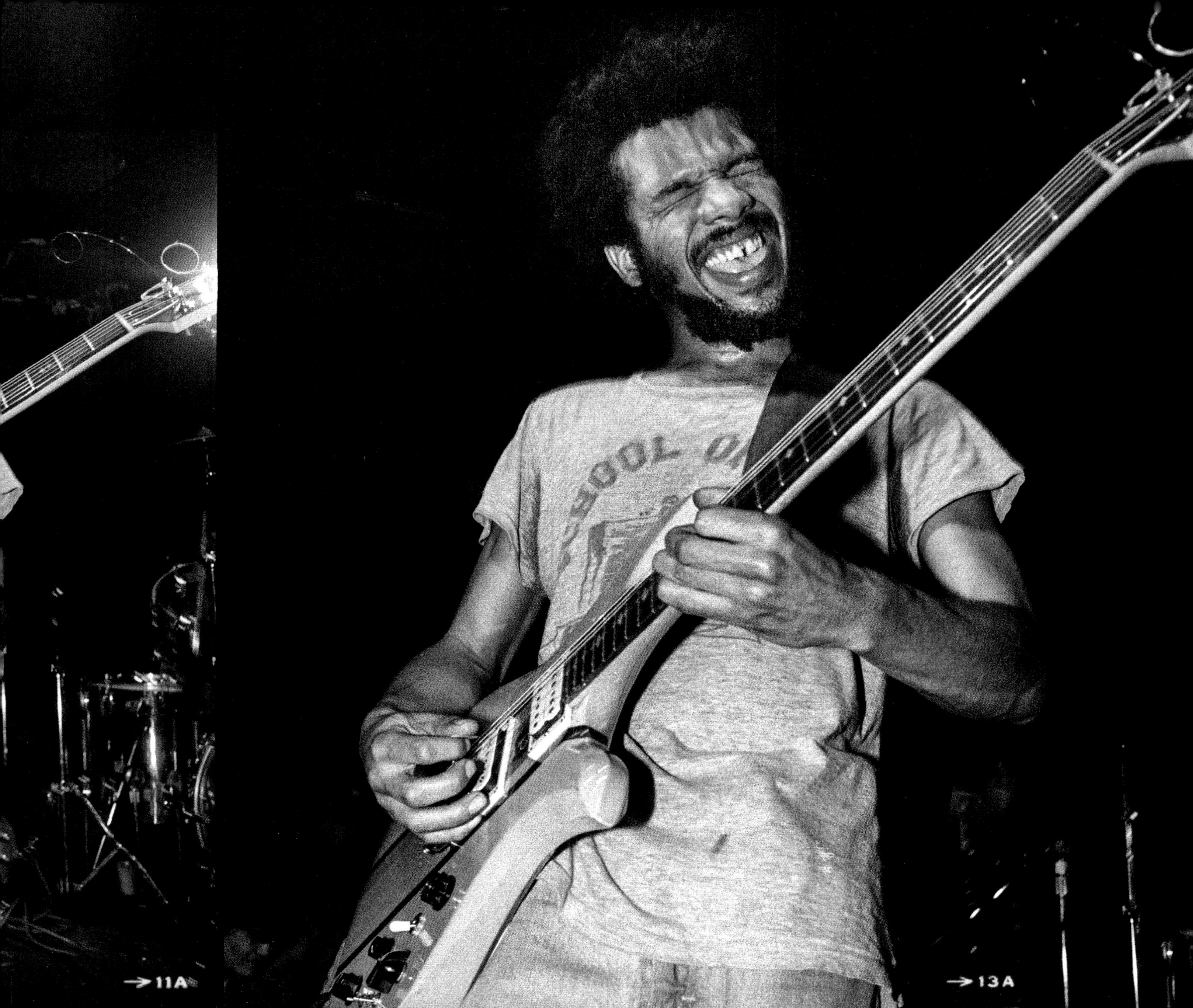
→11A
→13A

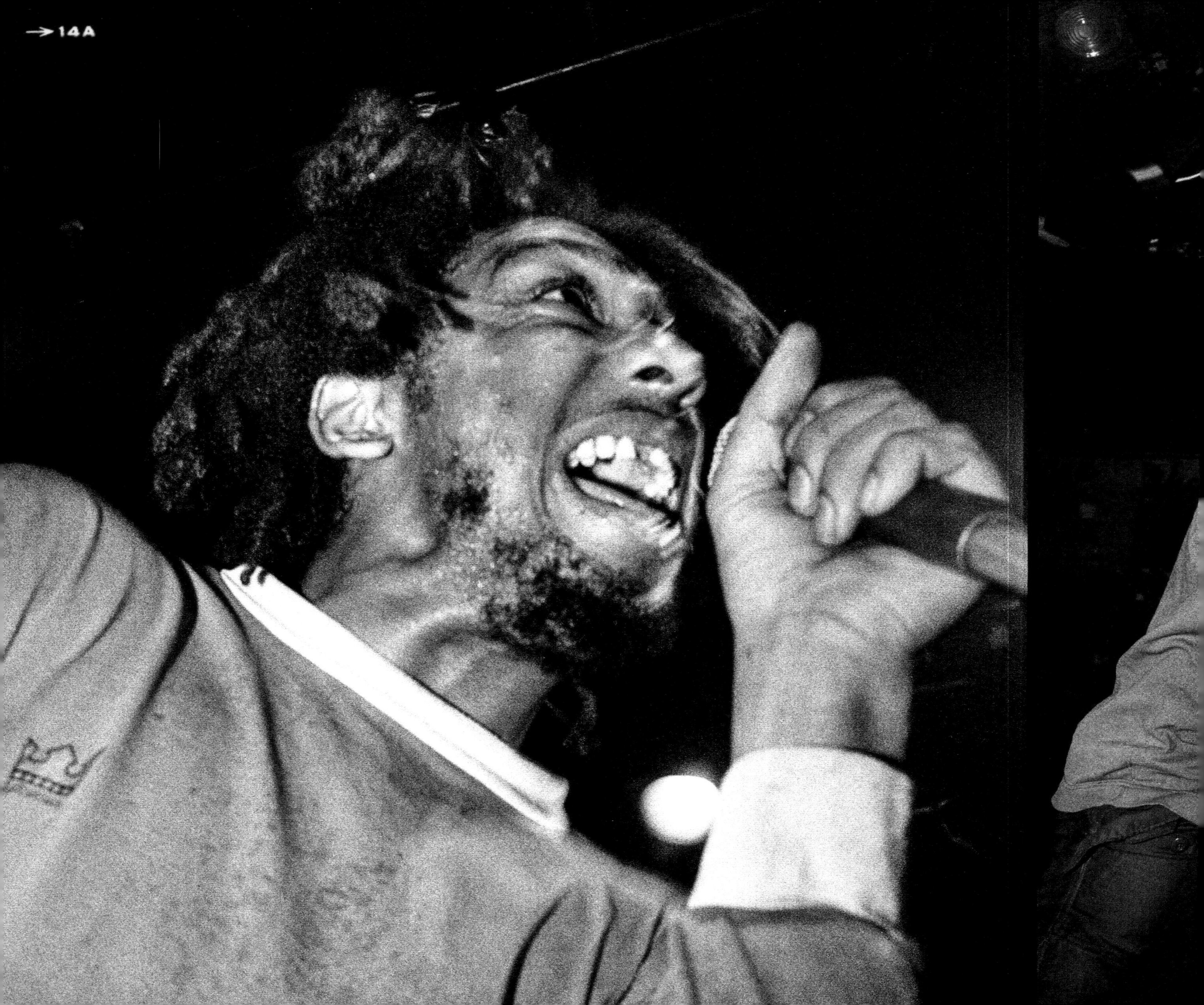
14A

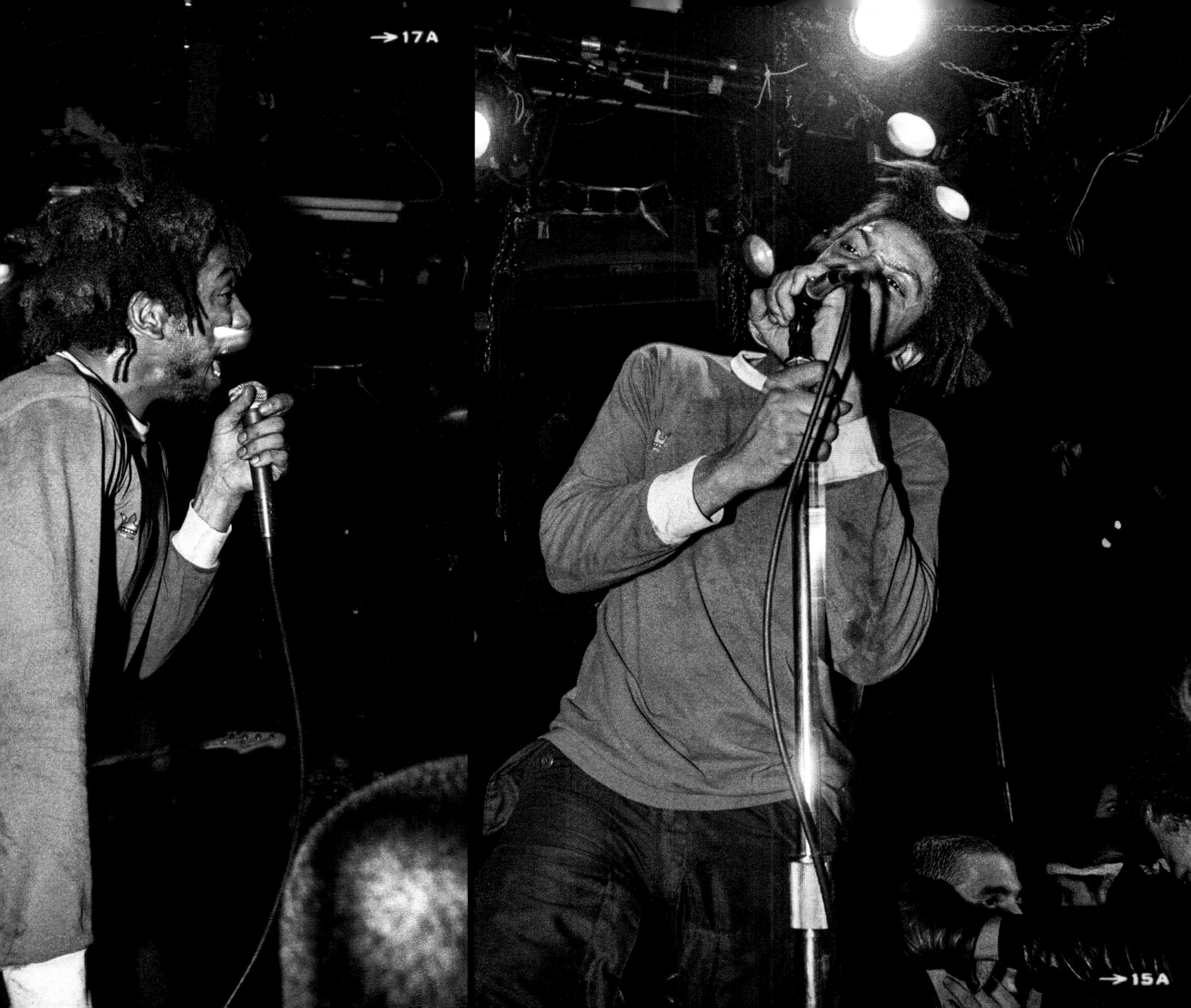

→17A
→15A

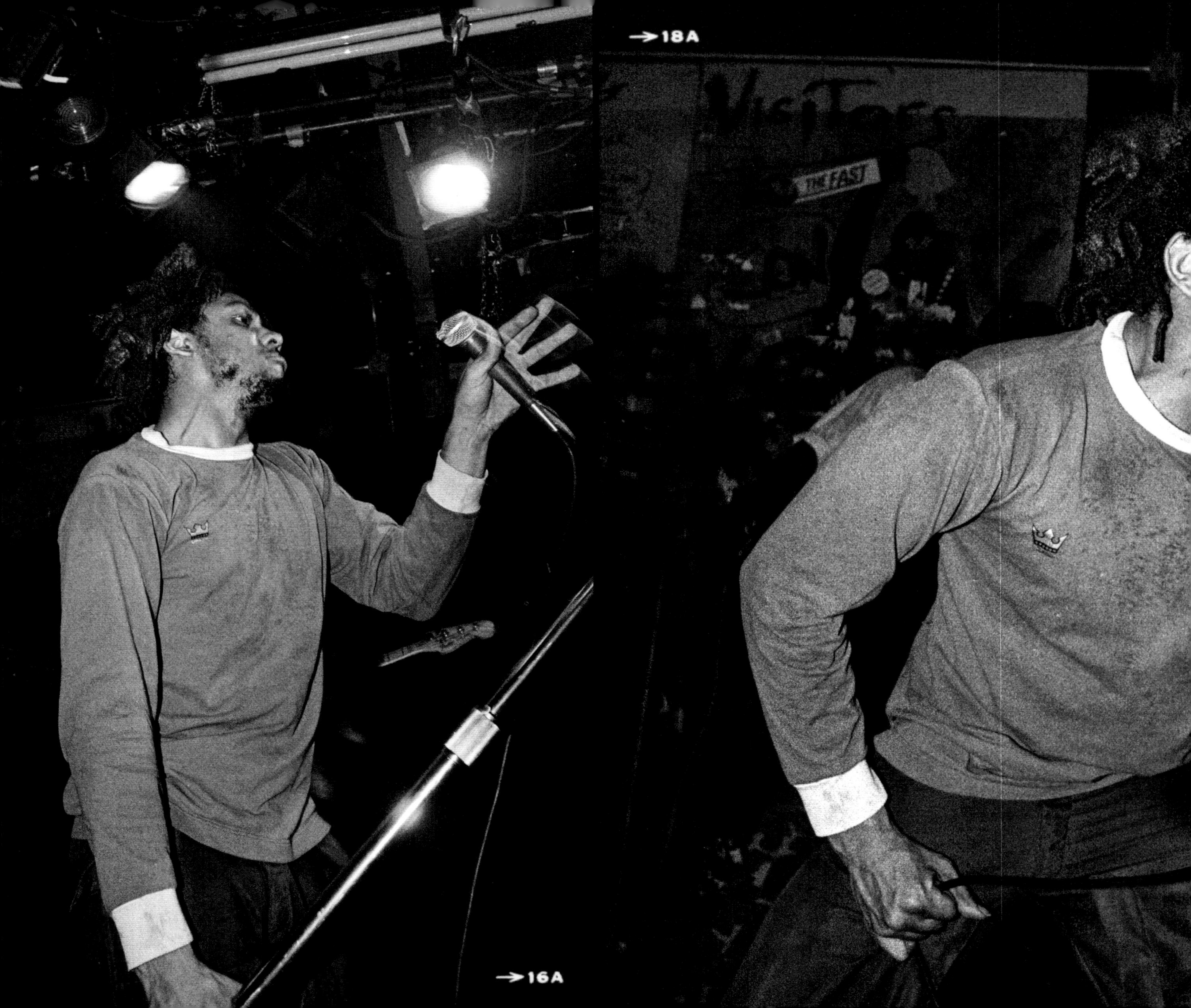
→18A
VisiTors
THE FAST
→16A

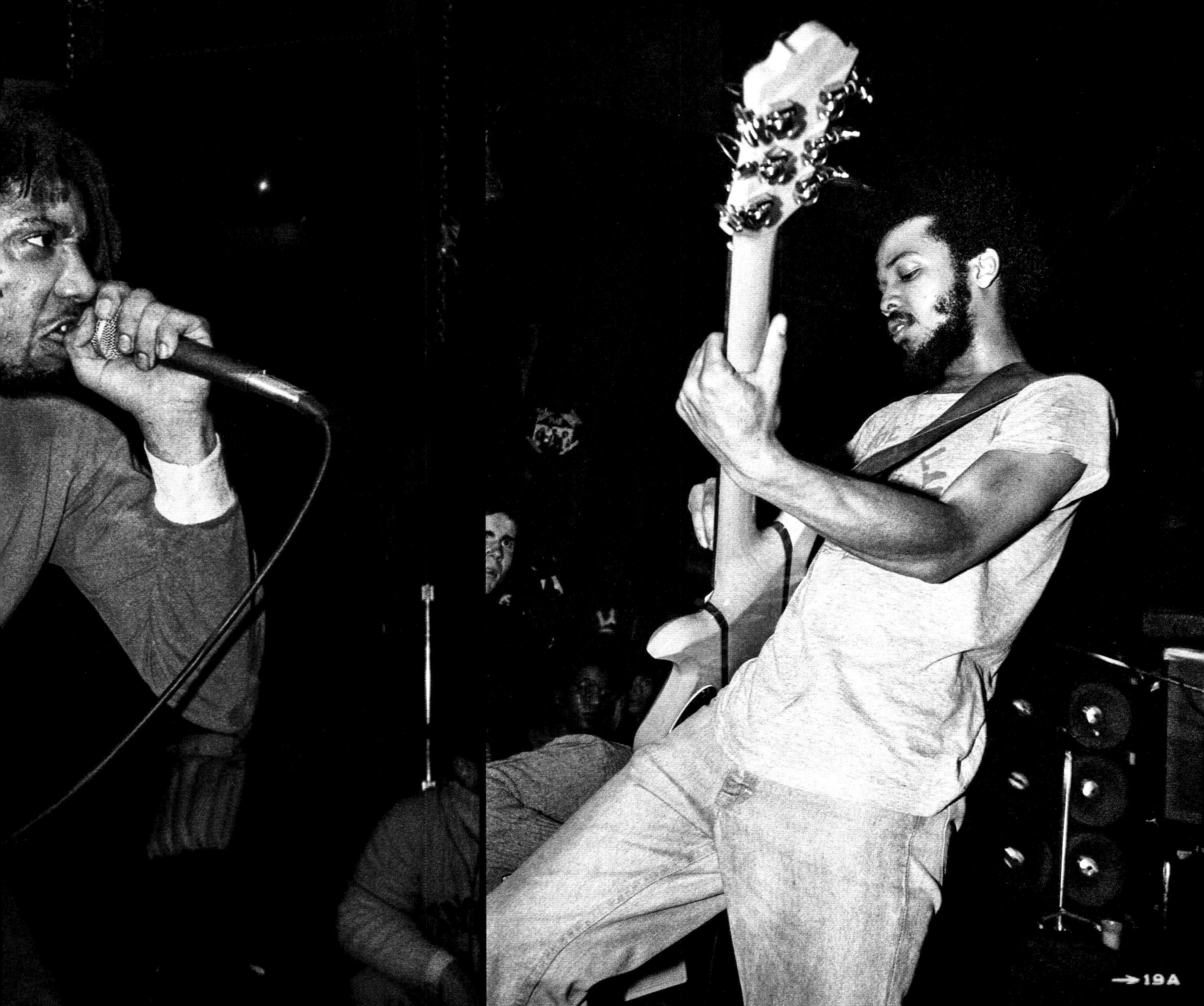

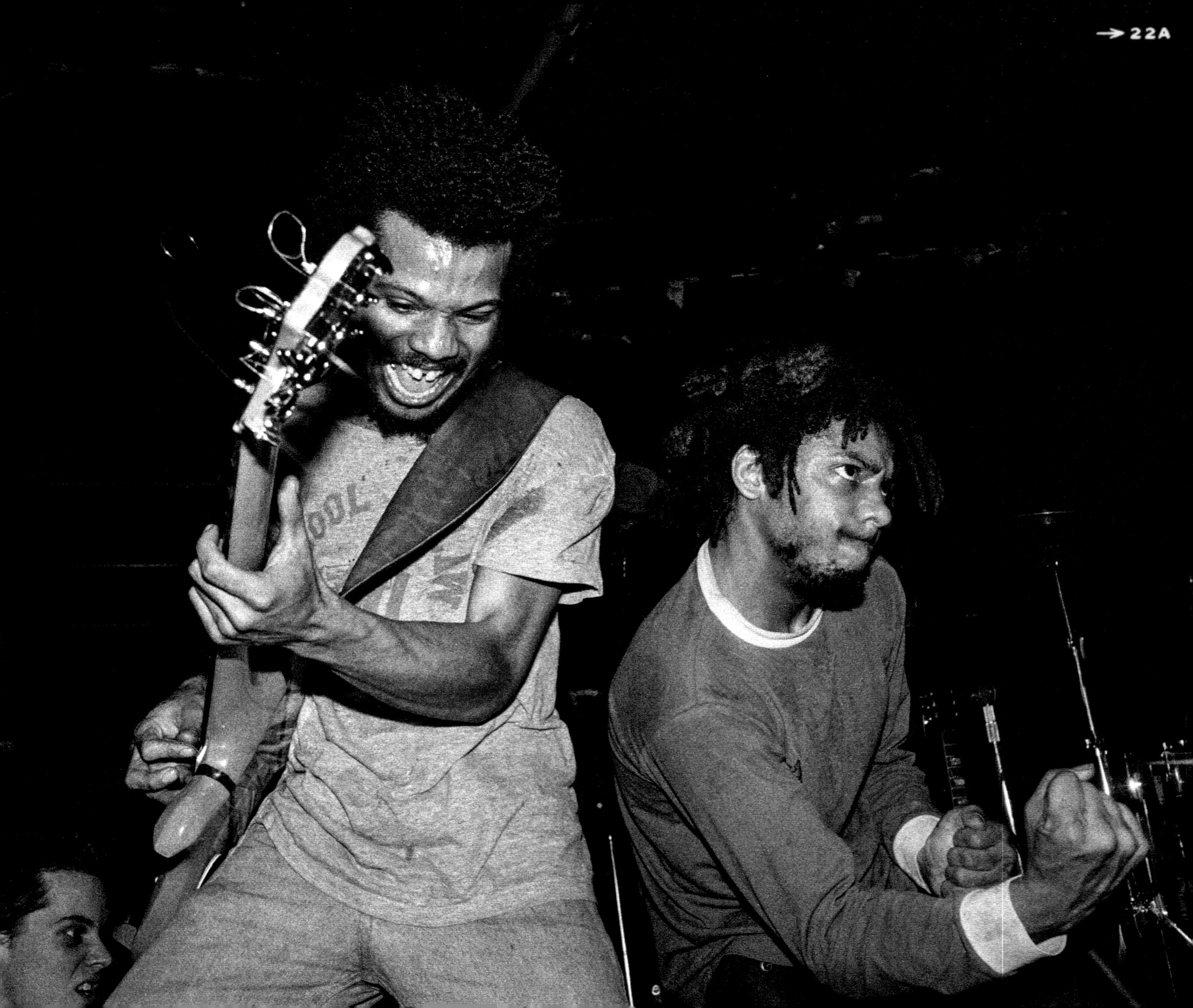
→ 22A

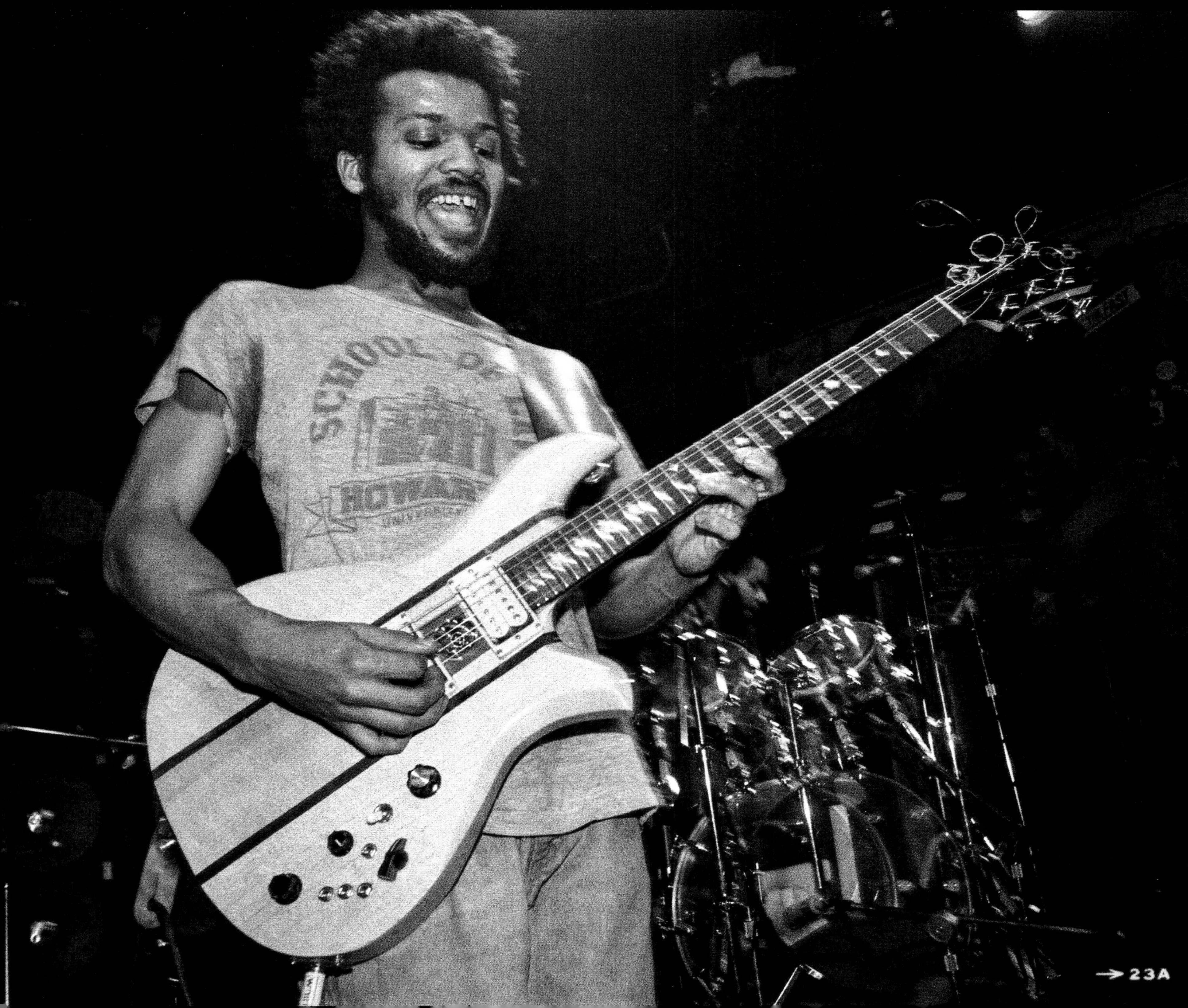
SCHOOL OF
HOWARD
UNIVERSITY
23A

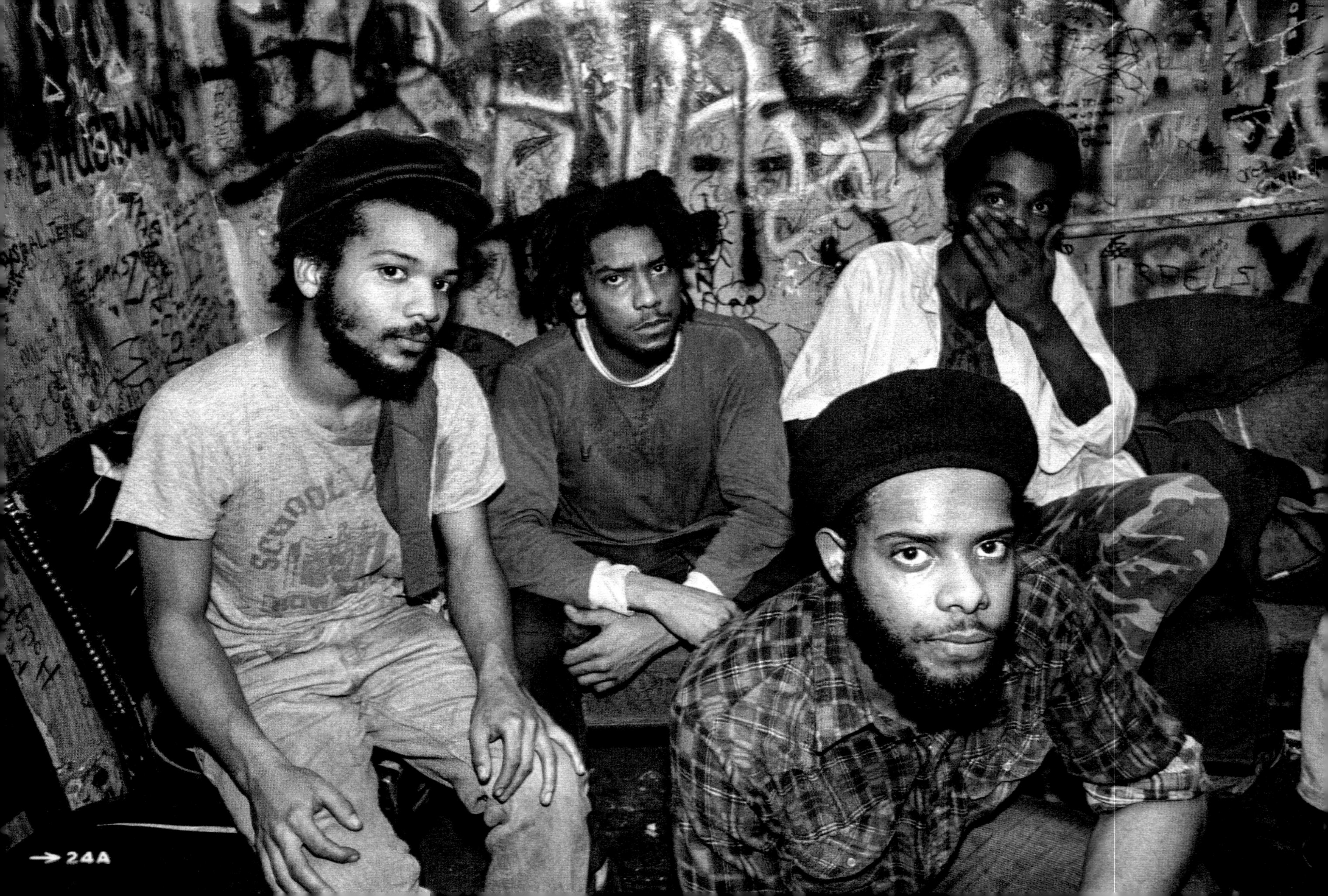

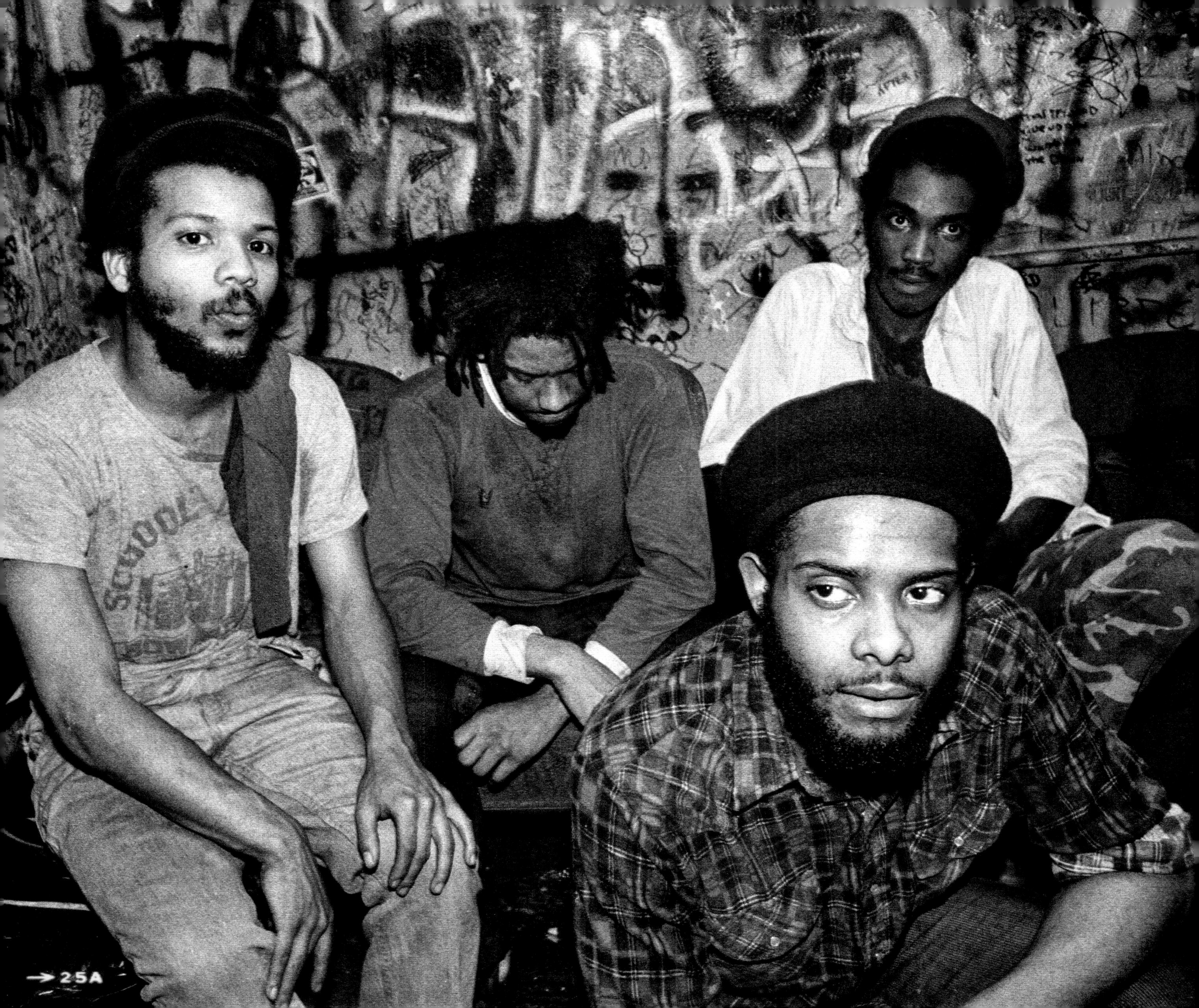

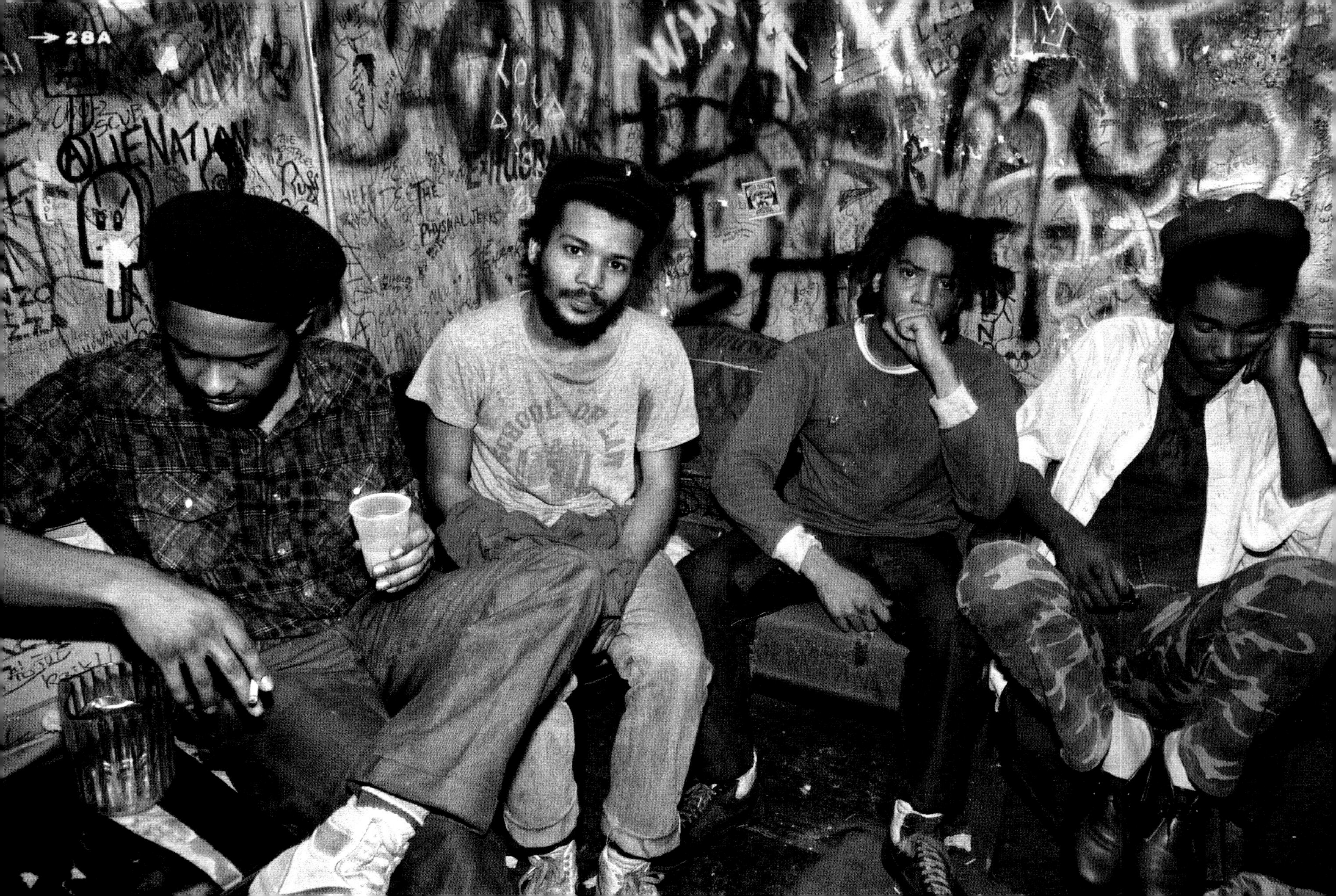
28A
ALIENATION

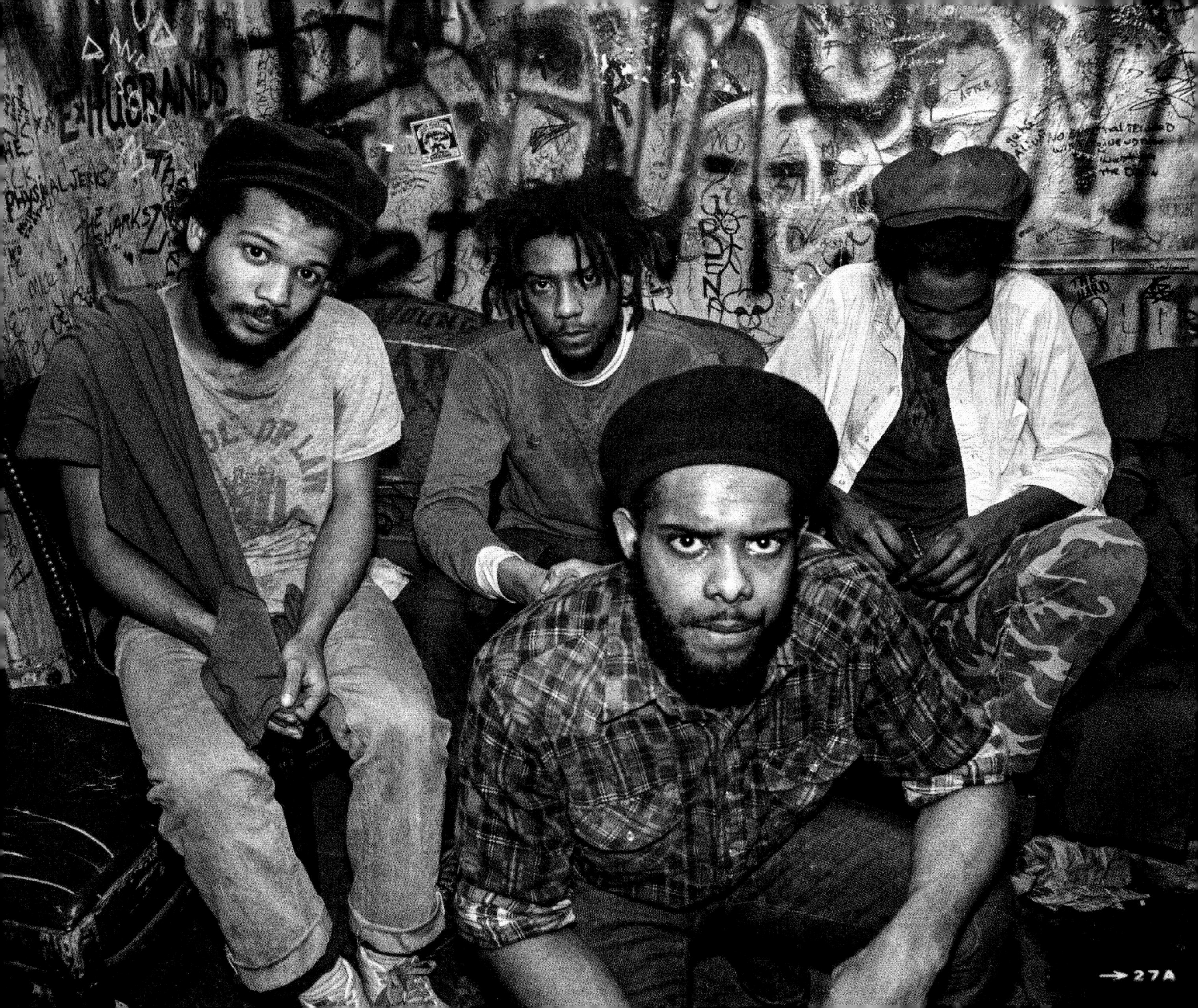
EX HUSBANDS
PHYSICAL JERKS
THE SHARKS
27A

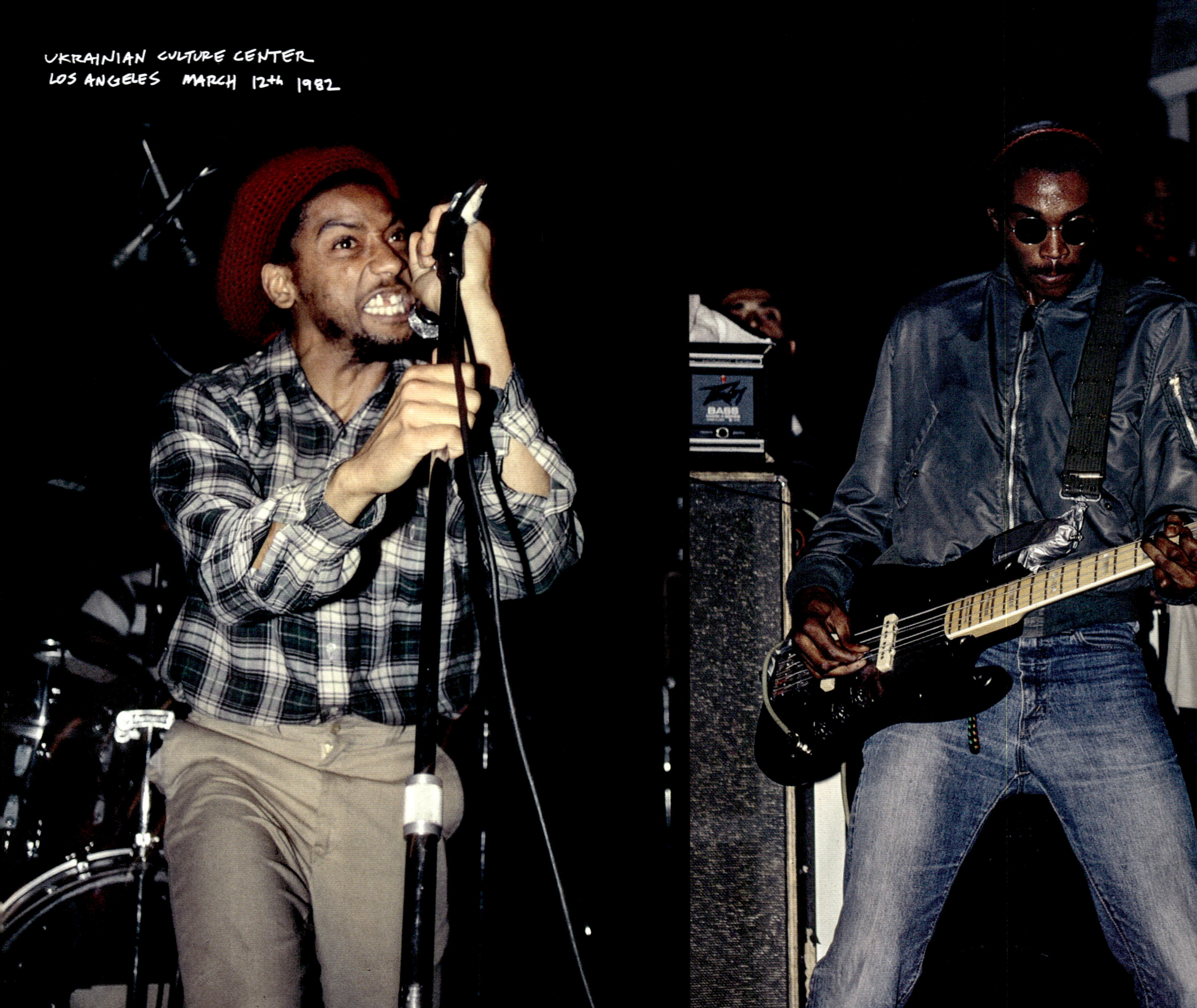

UKRAINIAN CULTURE CENTER
LOS ANGELES   MARCH 12th 1982

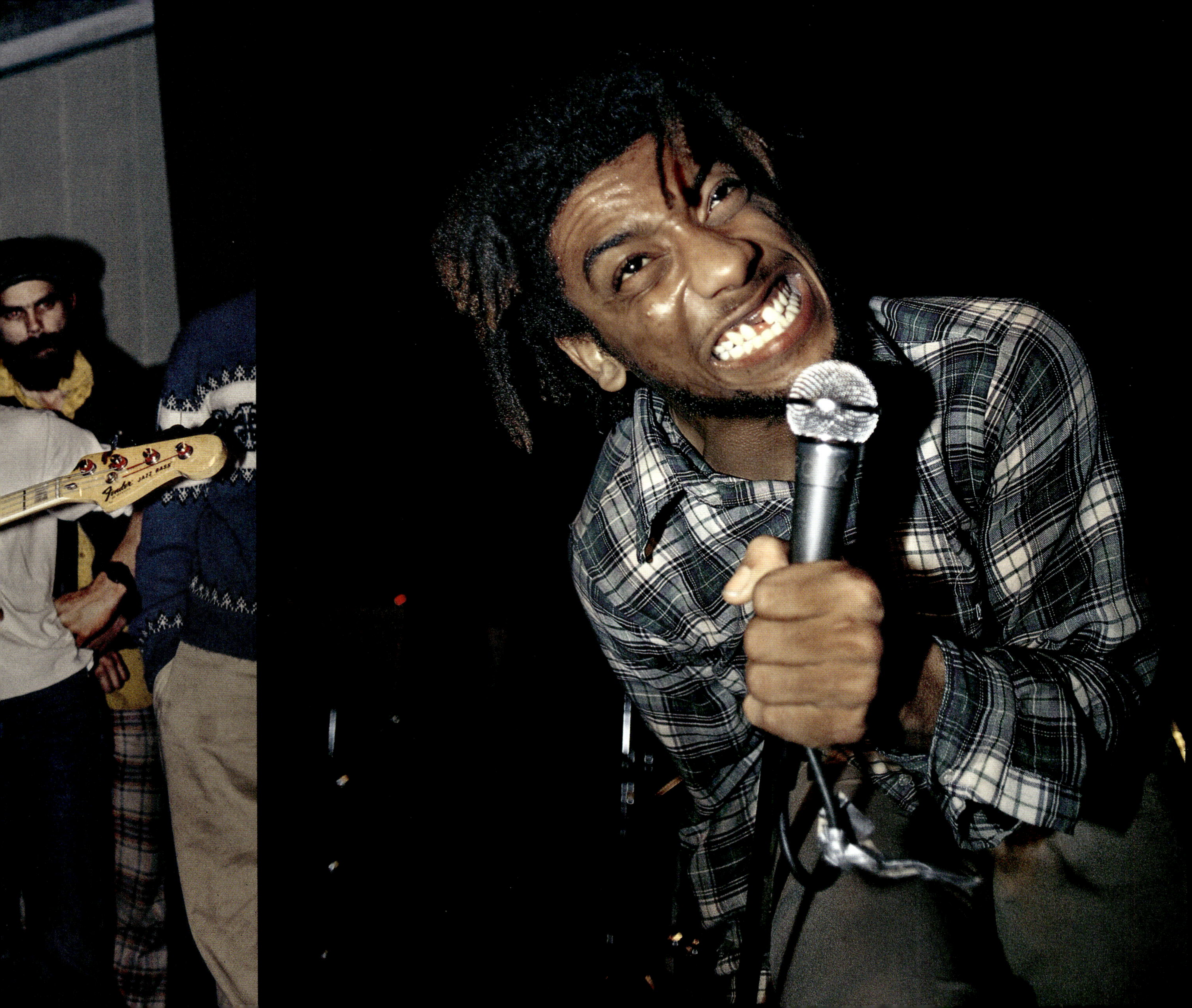

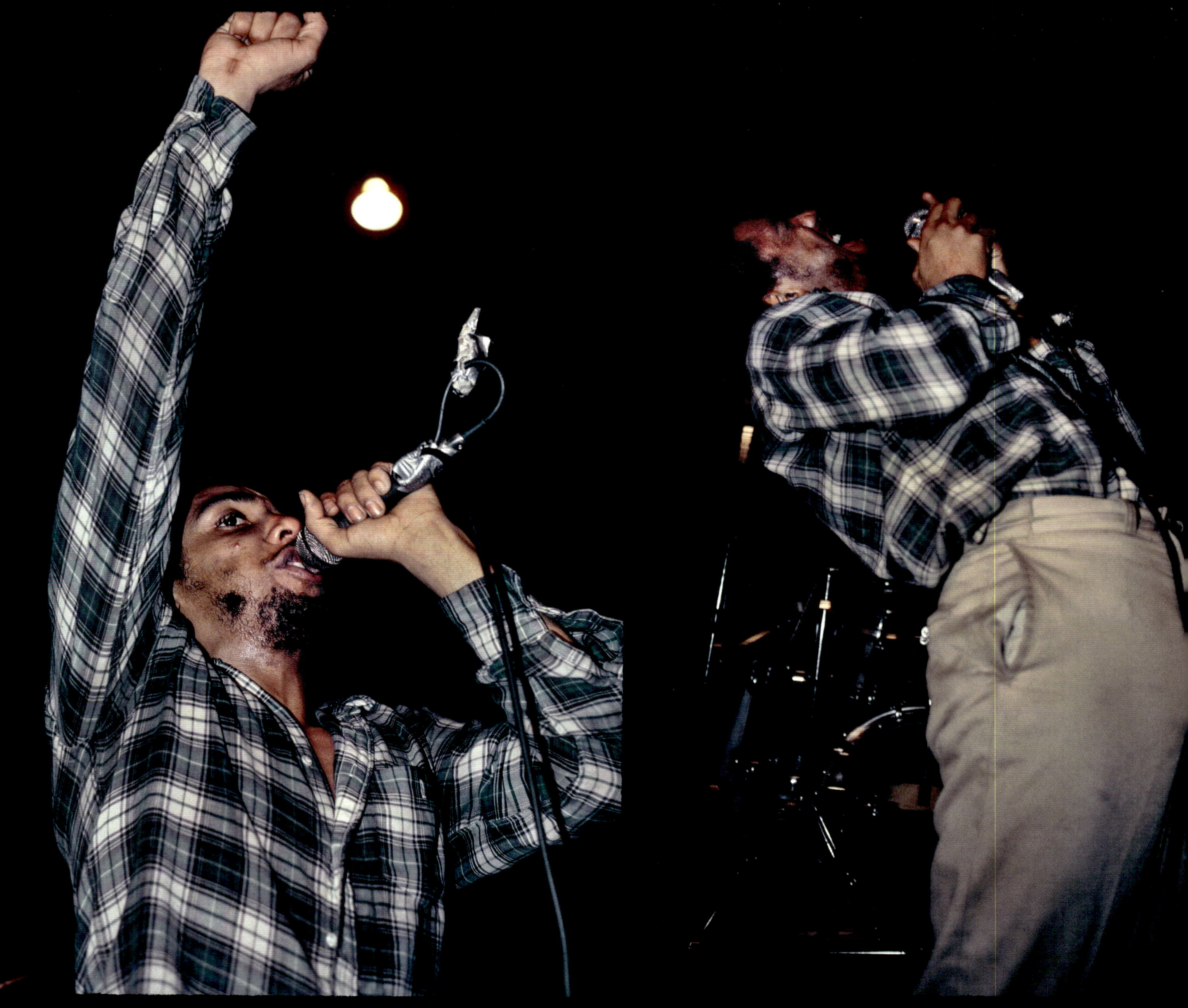

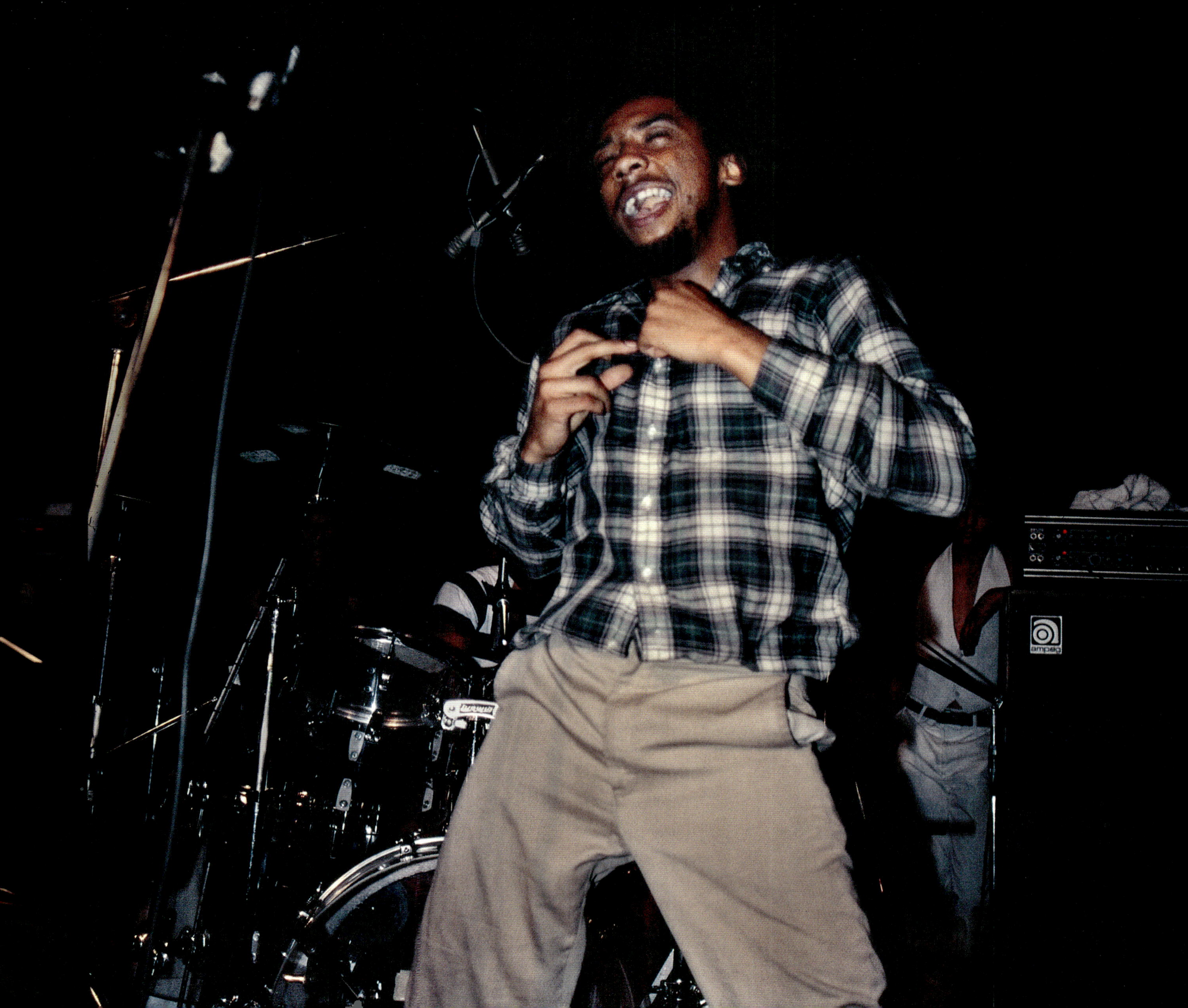

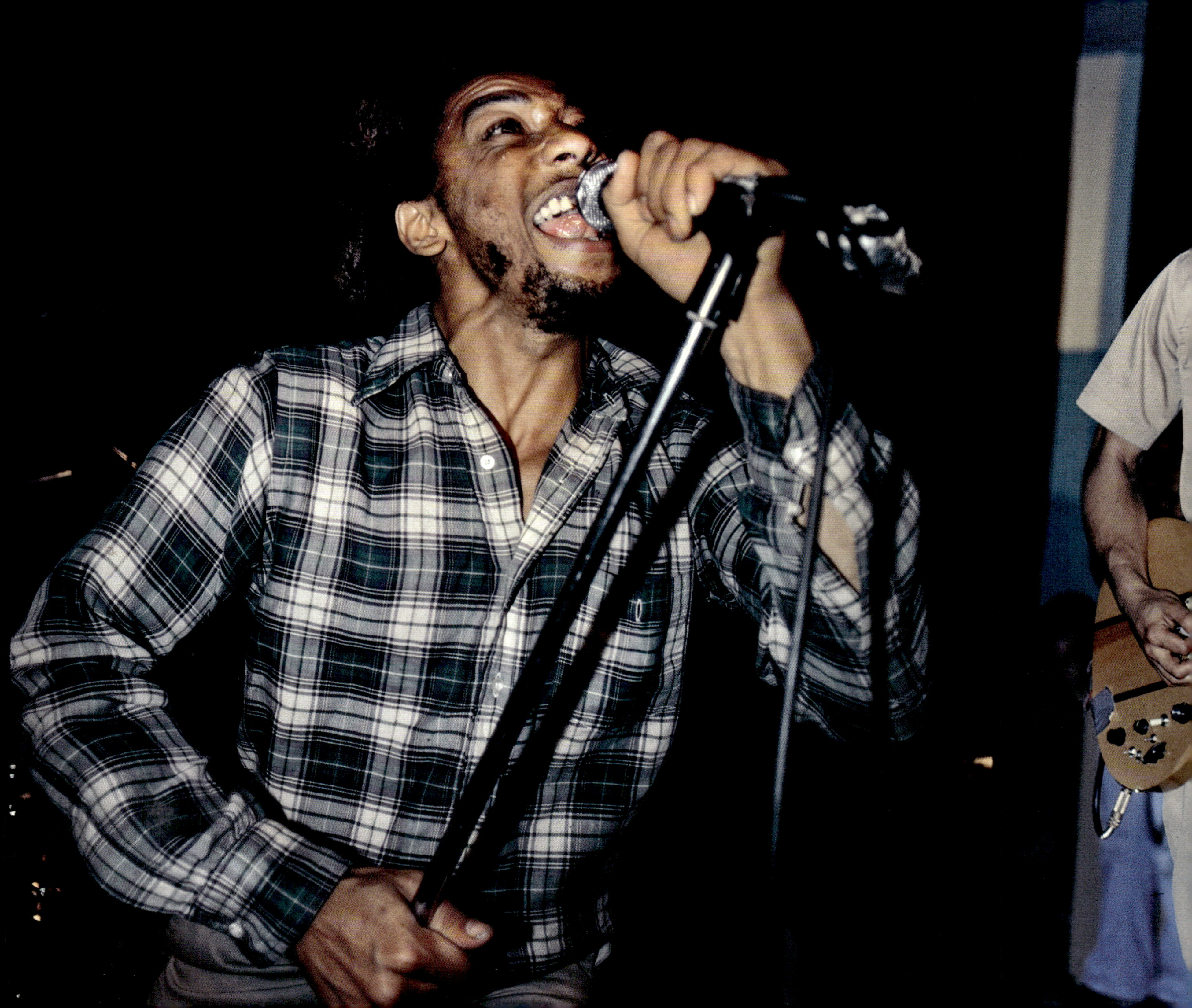

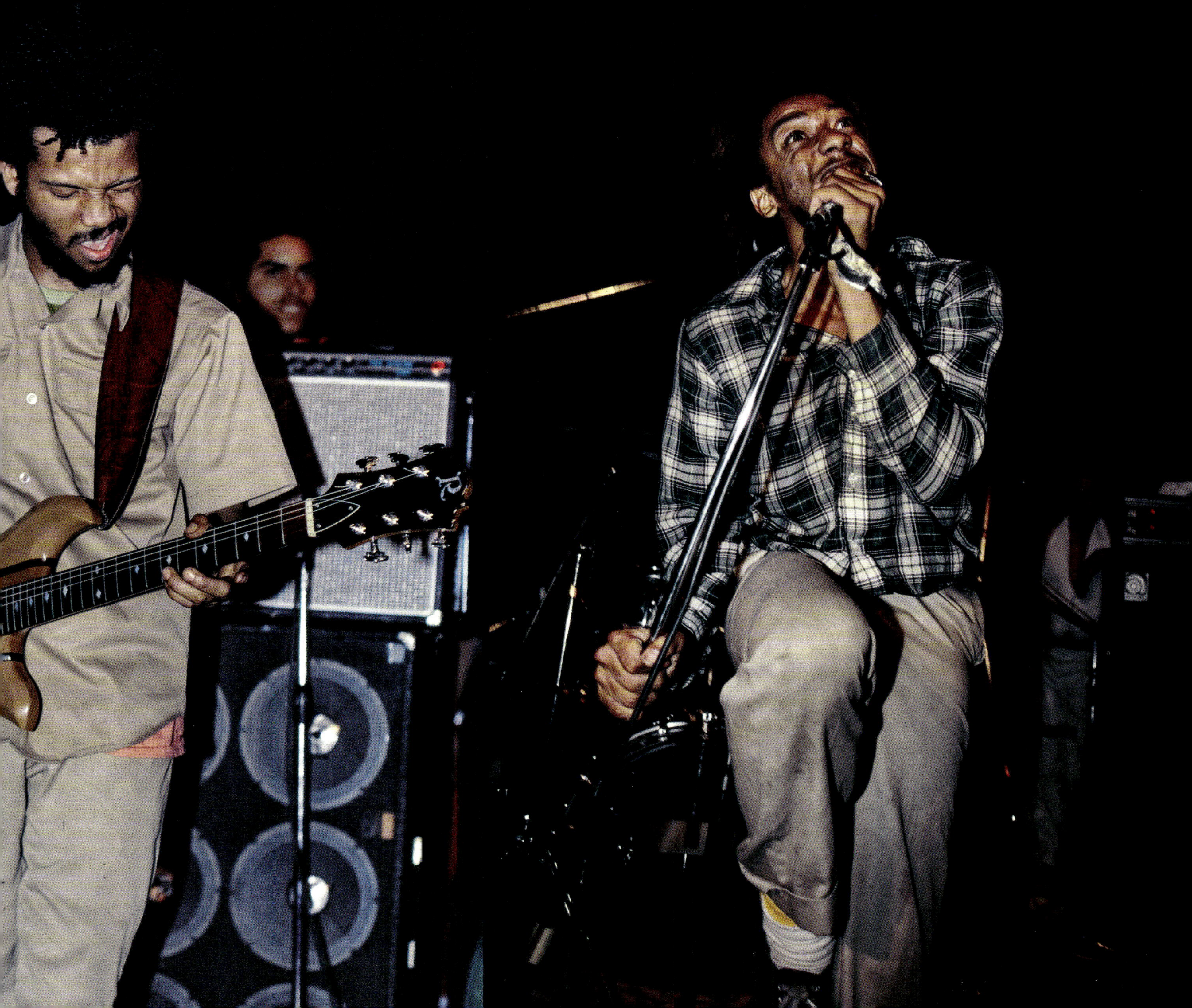

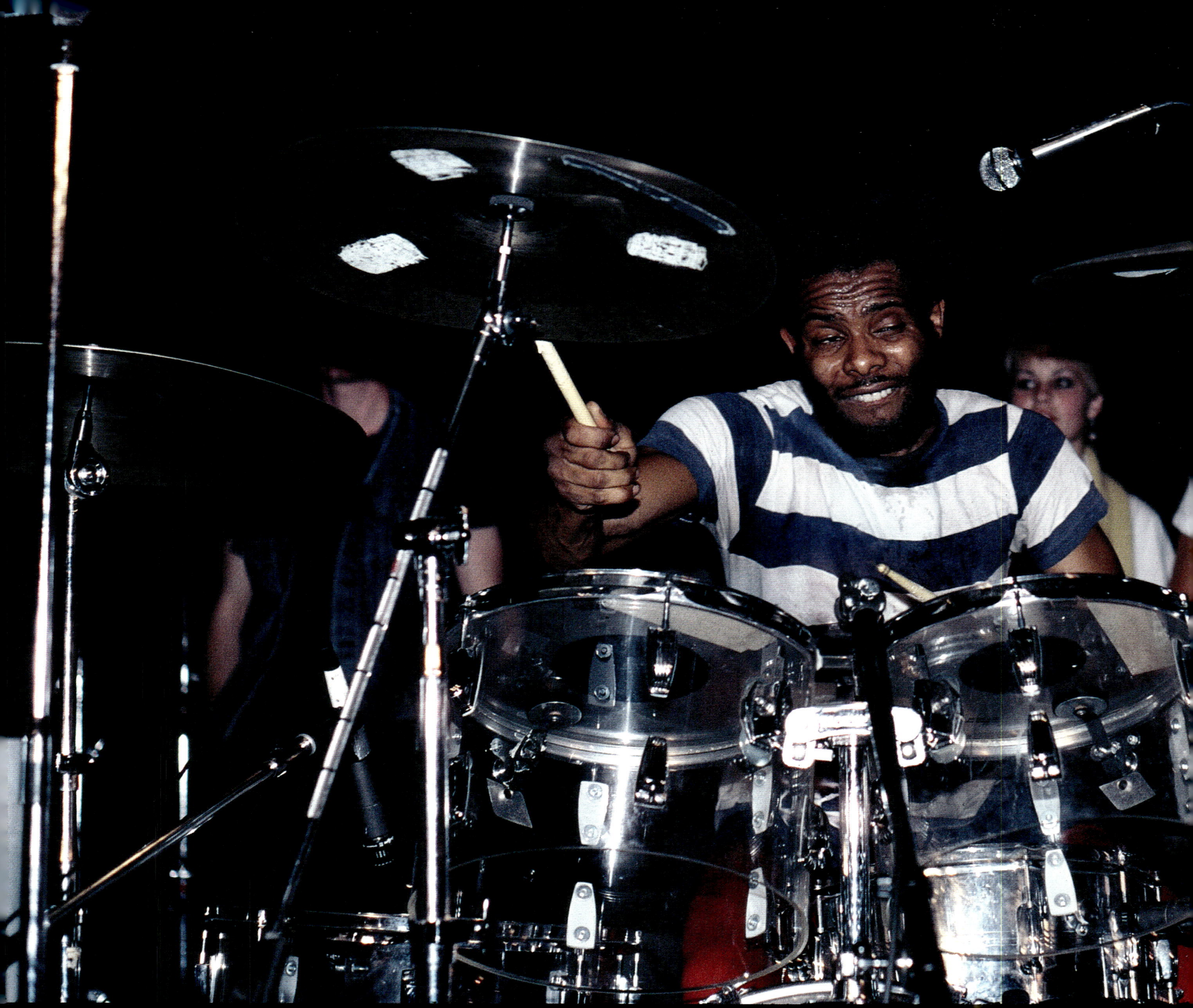

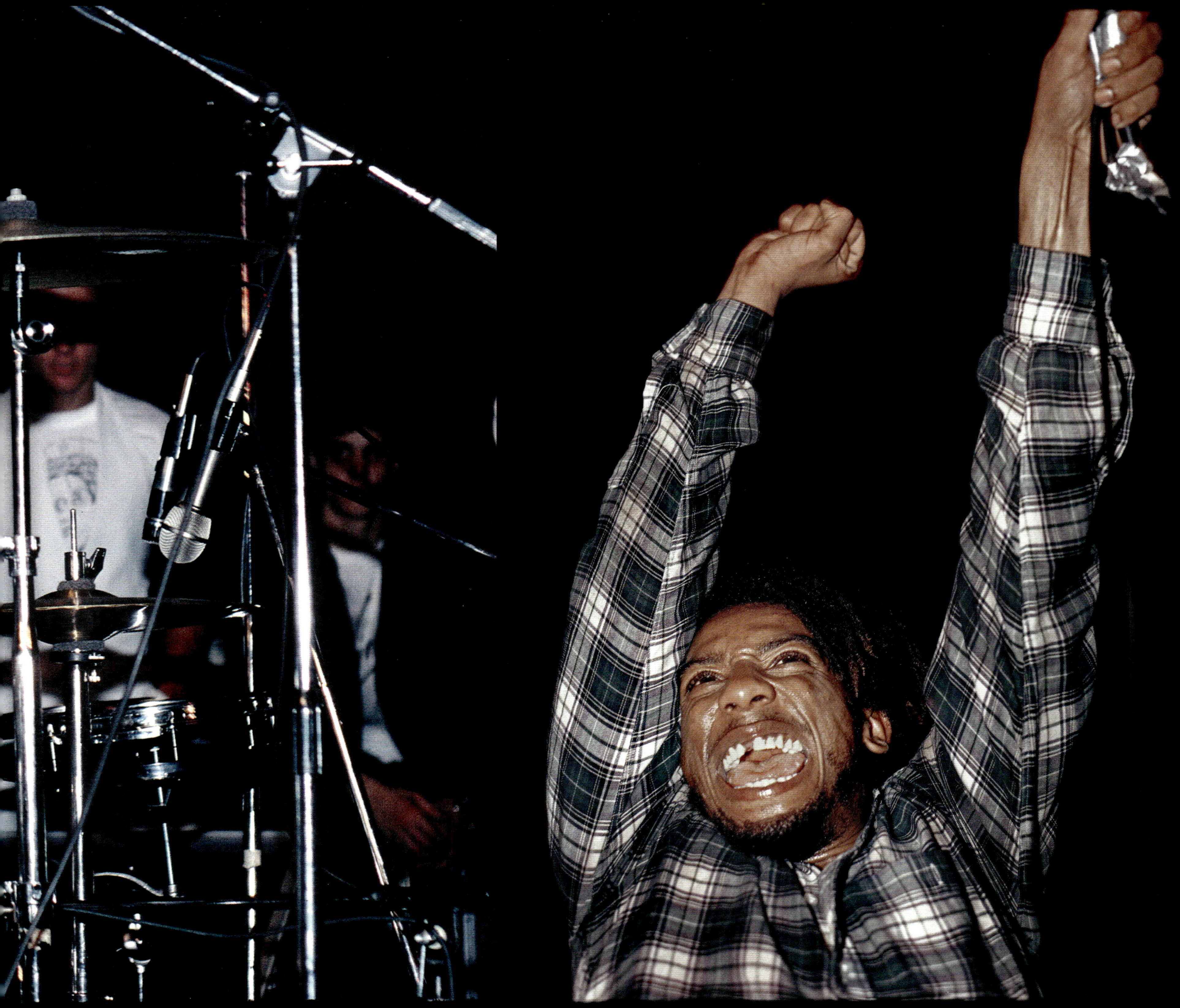

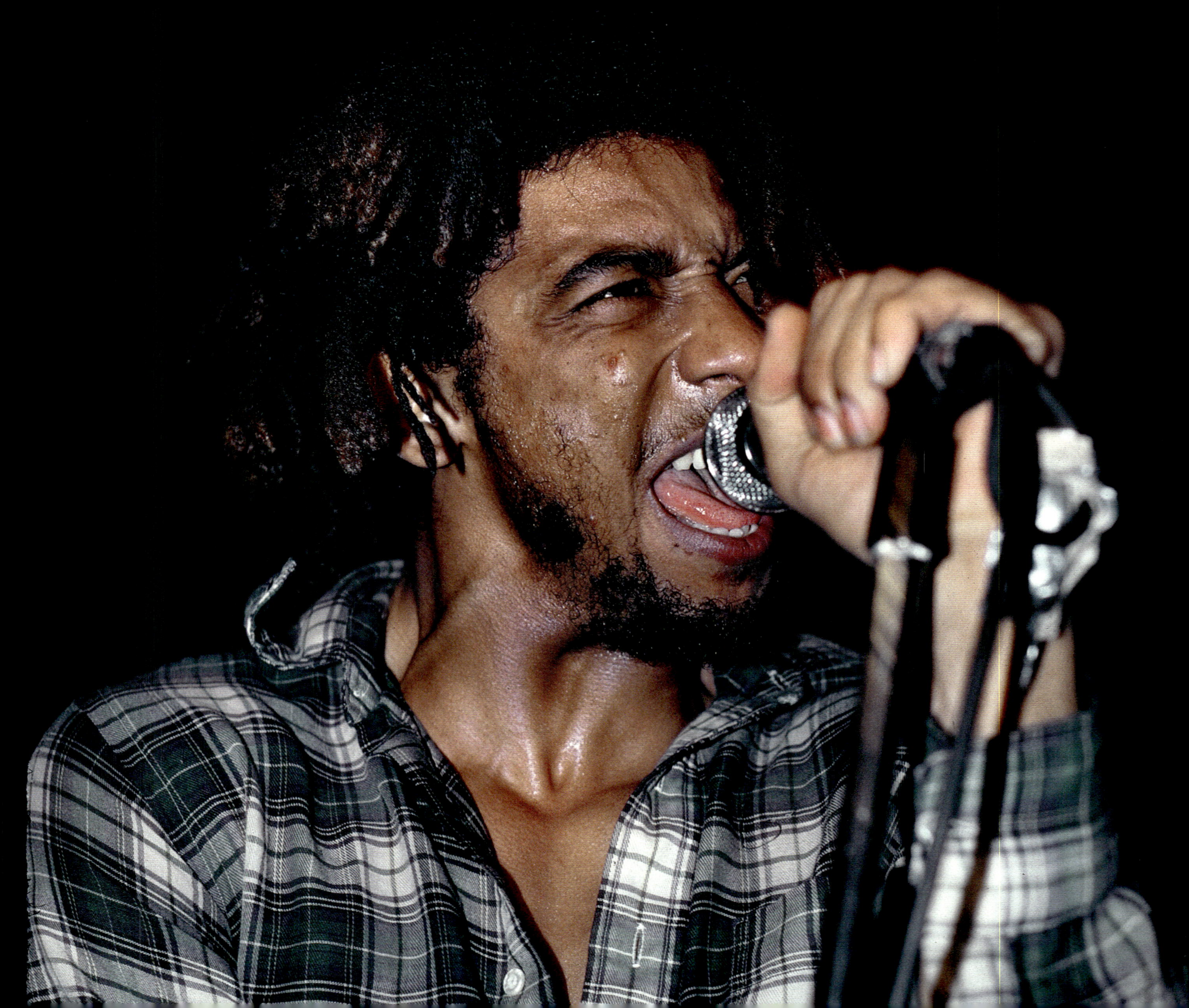

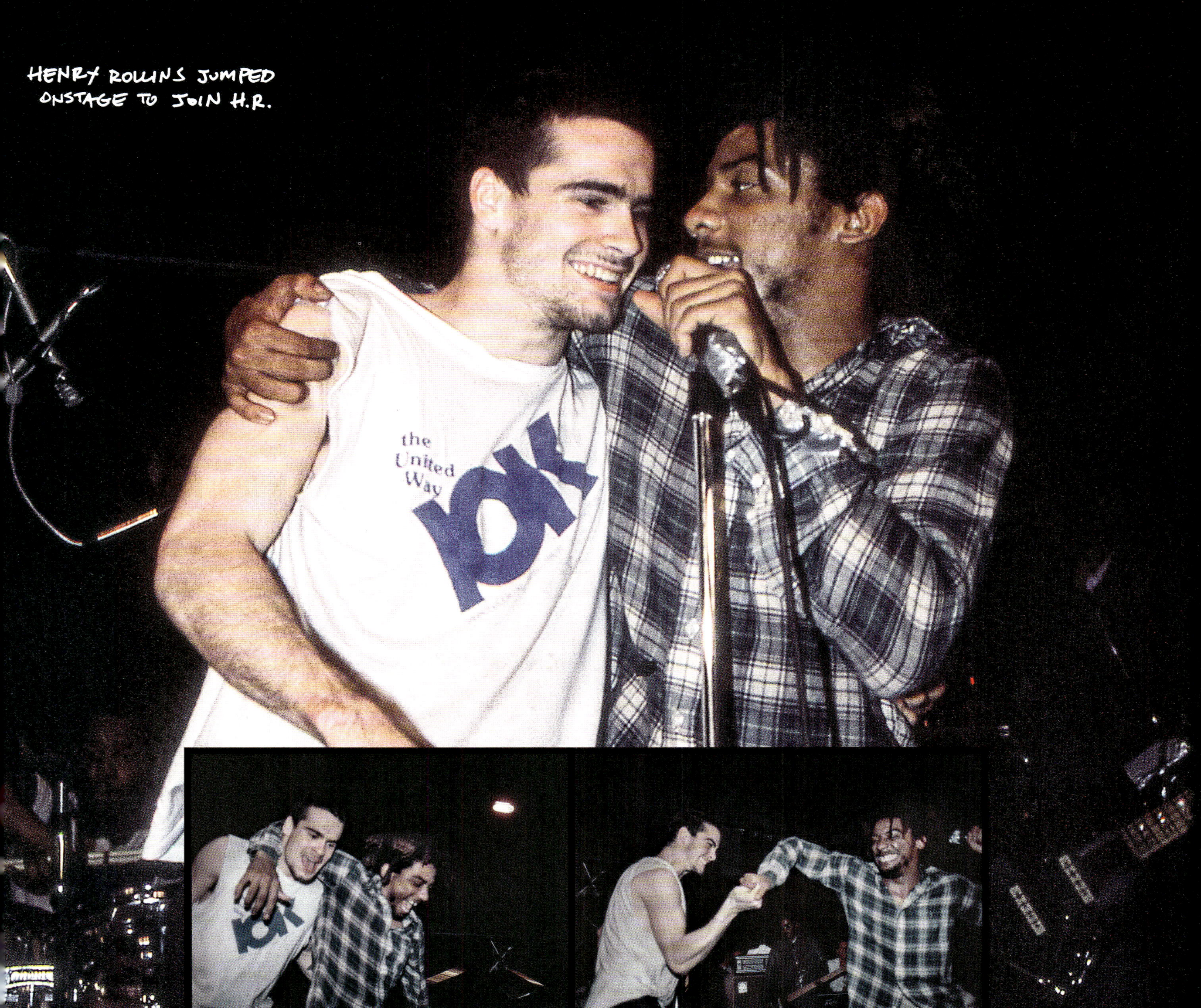
HENRY ROLLINS JUMPED
ONSTAGE TO JOIN H.R.

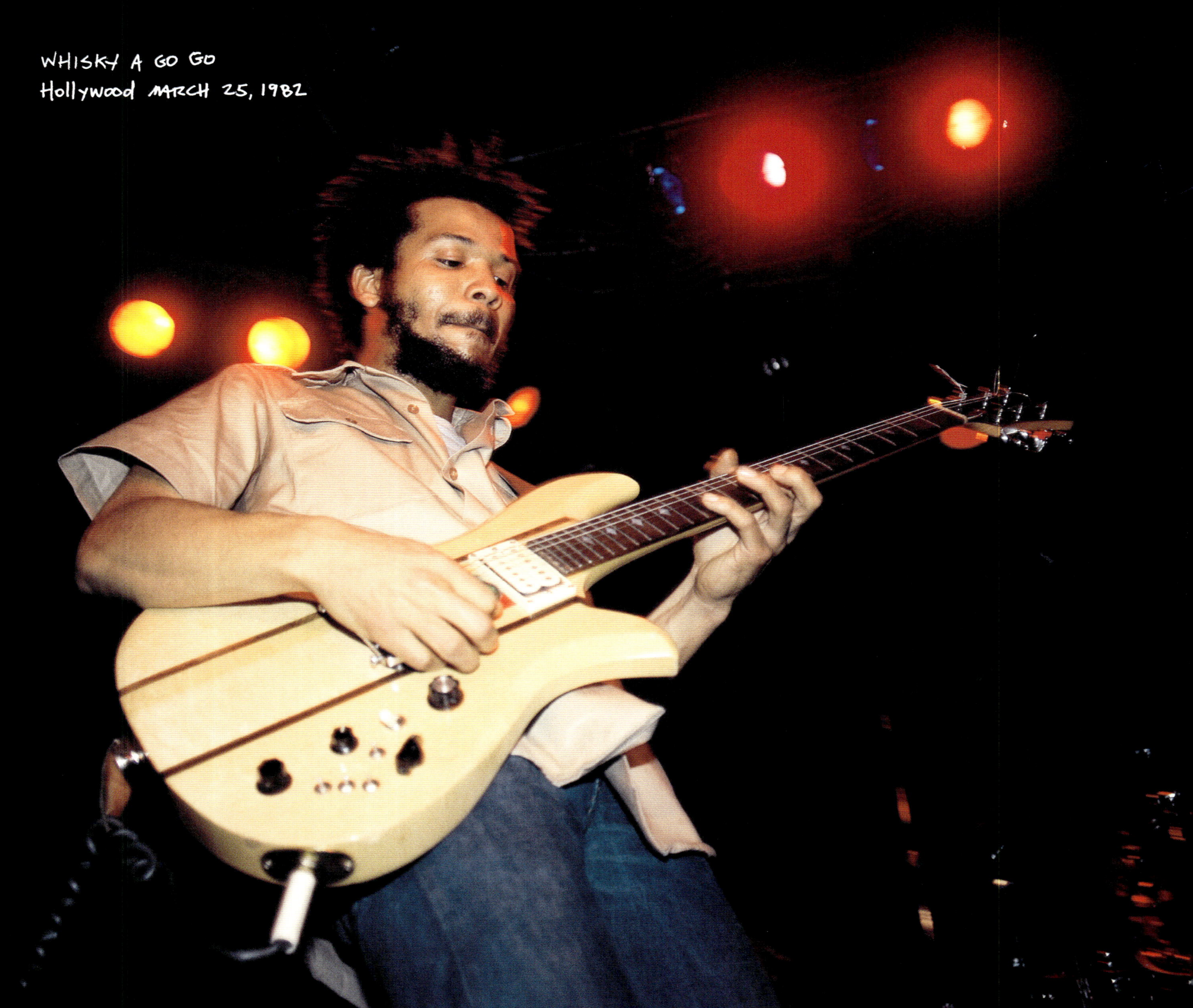
WHISKY A GO GO
Hollywood MARCH 25, 1982

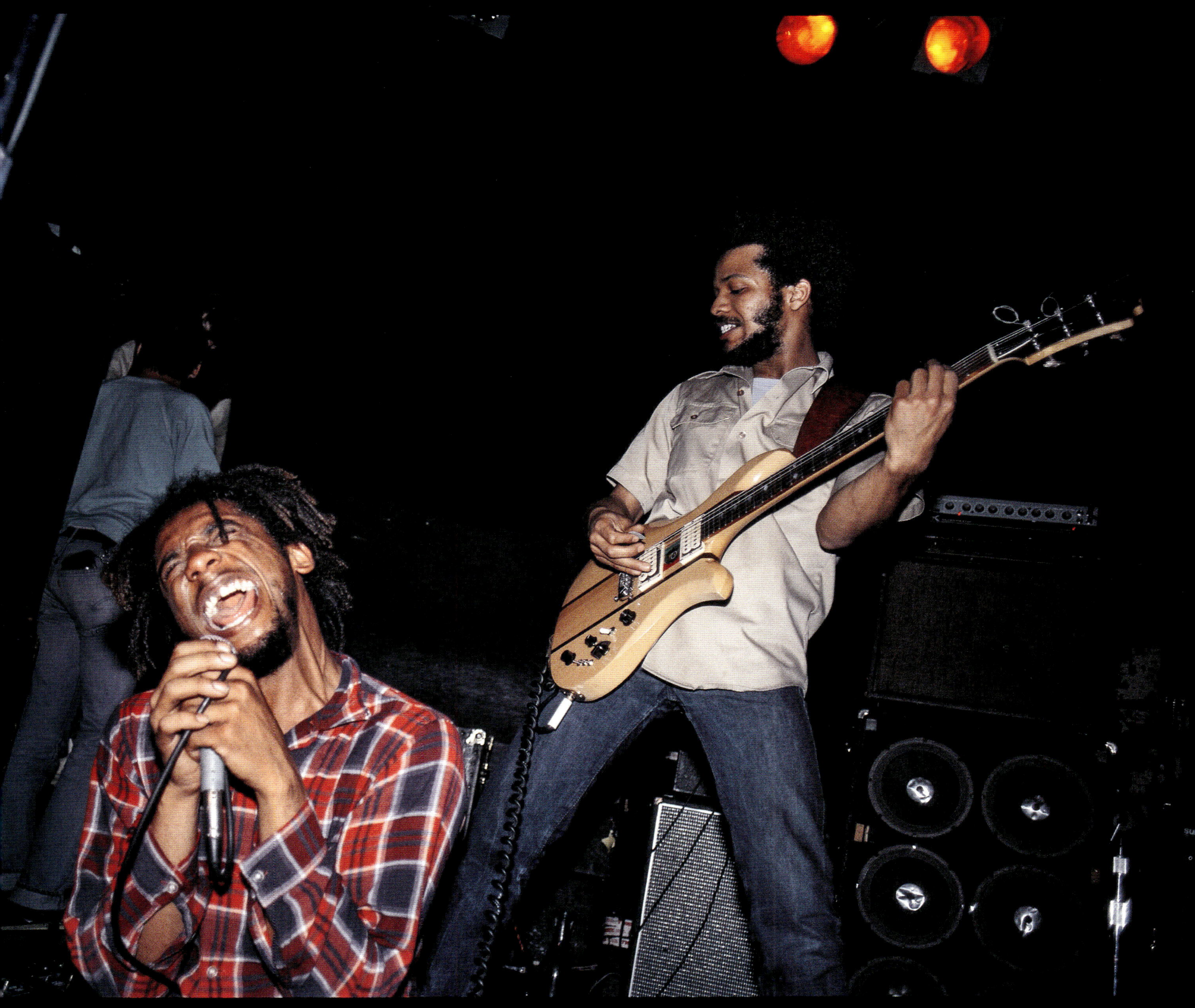

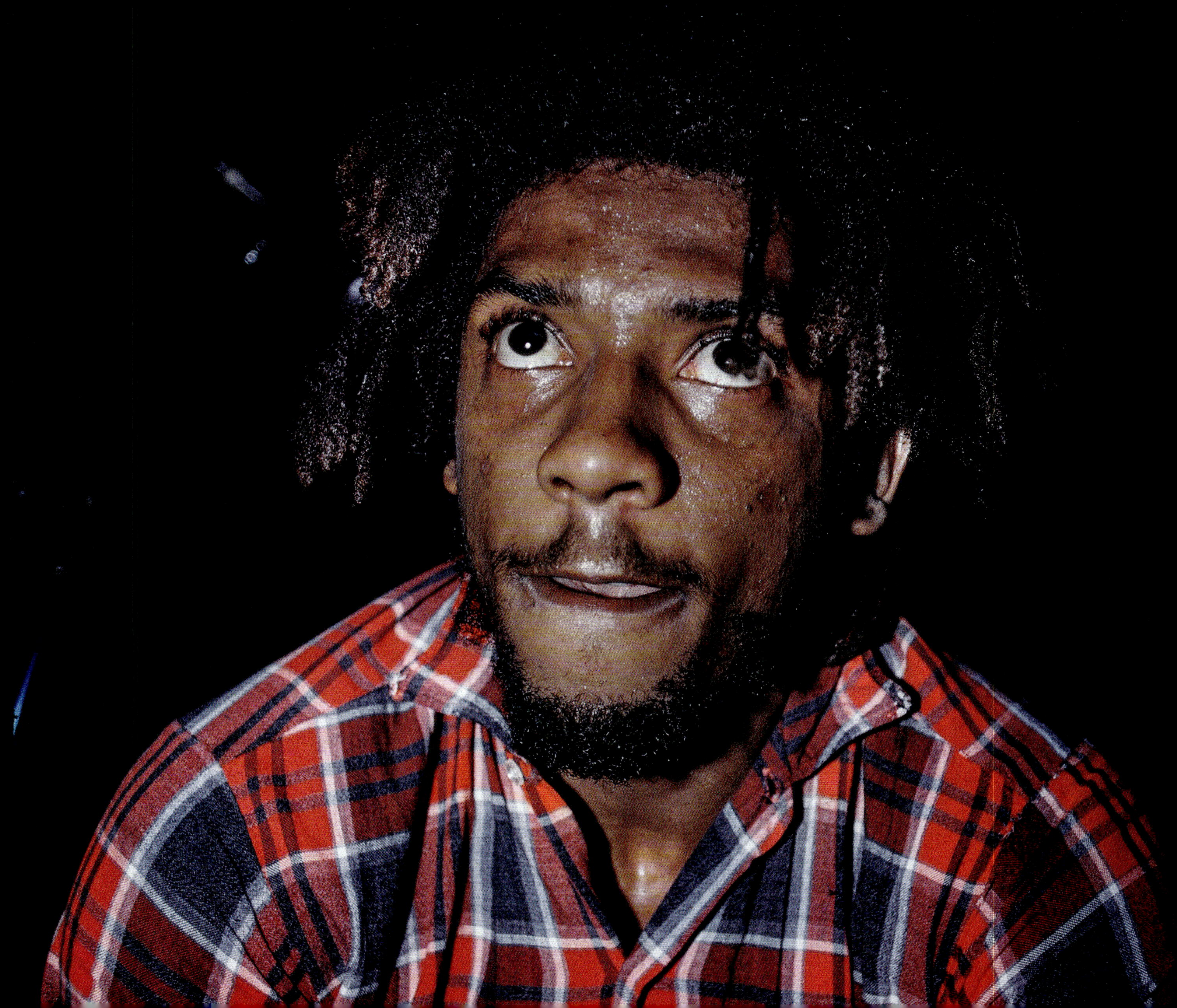

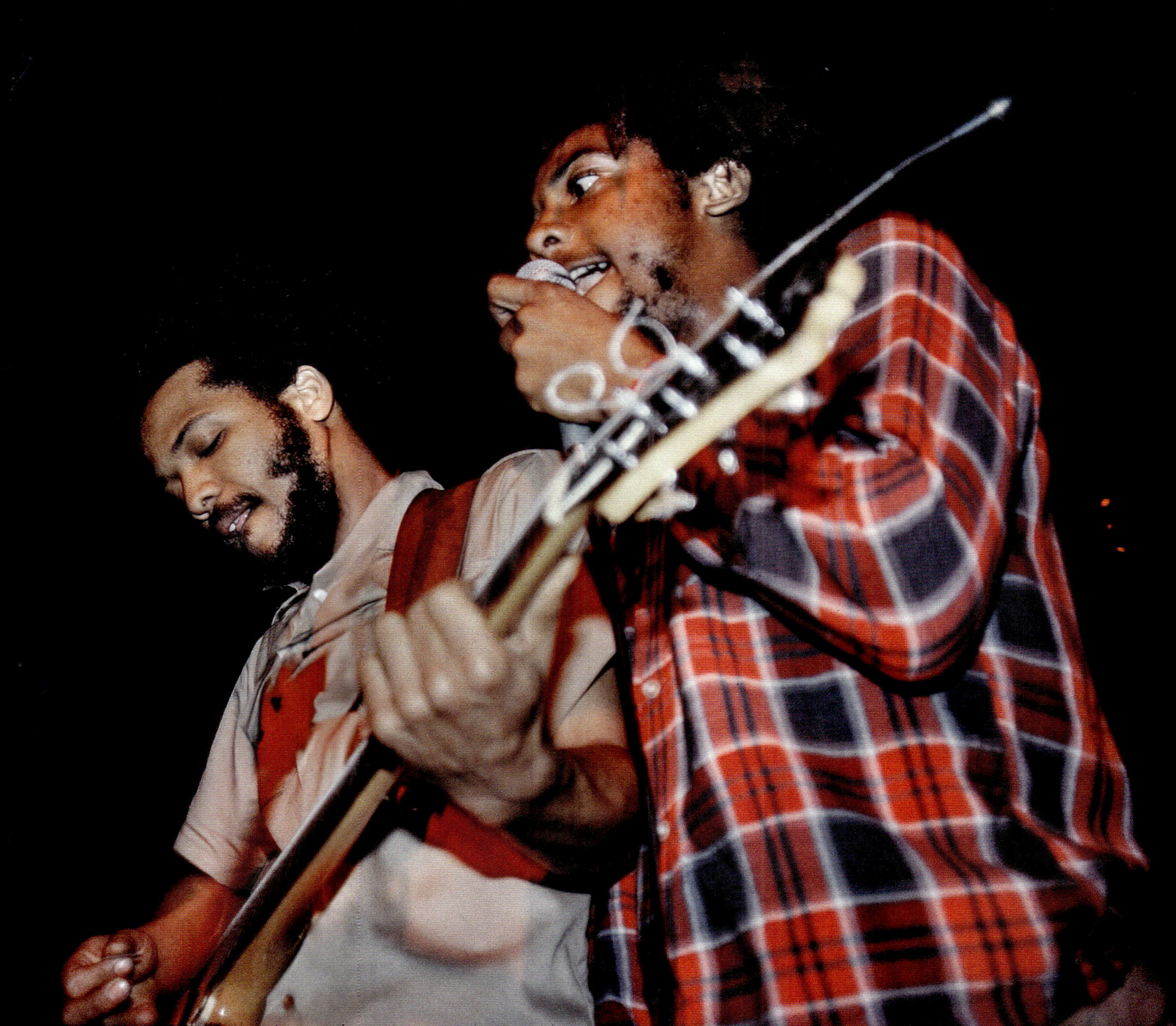

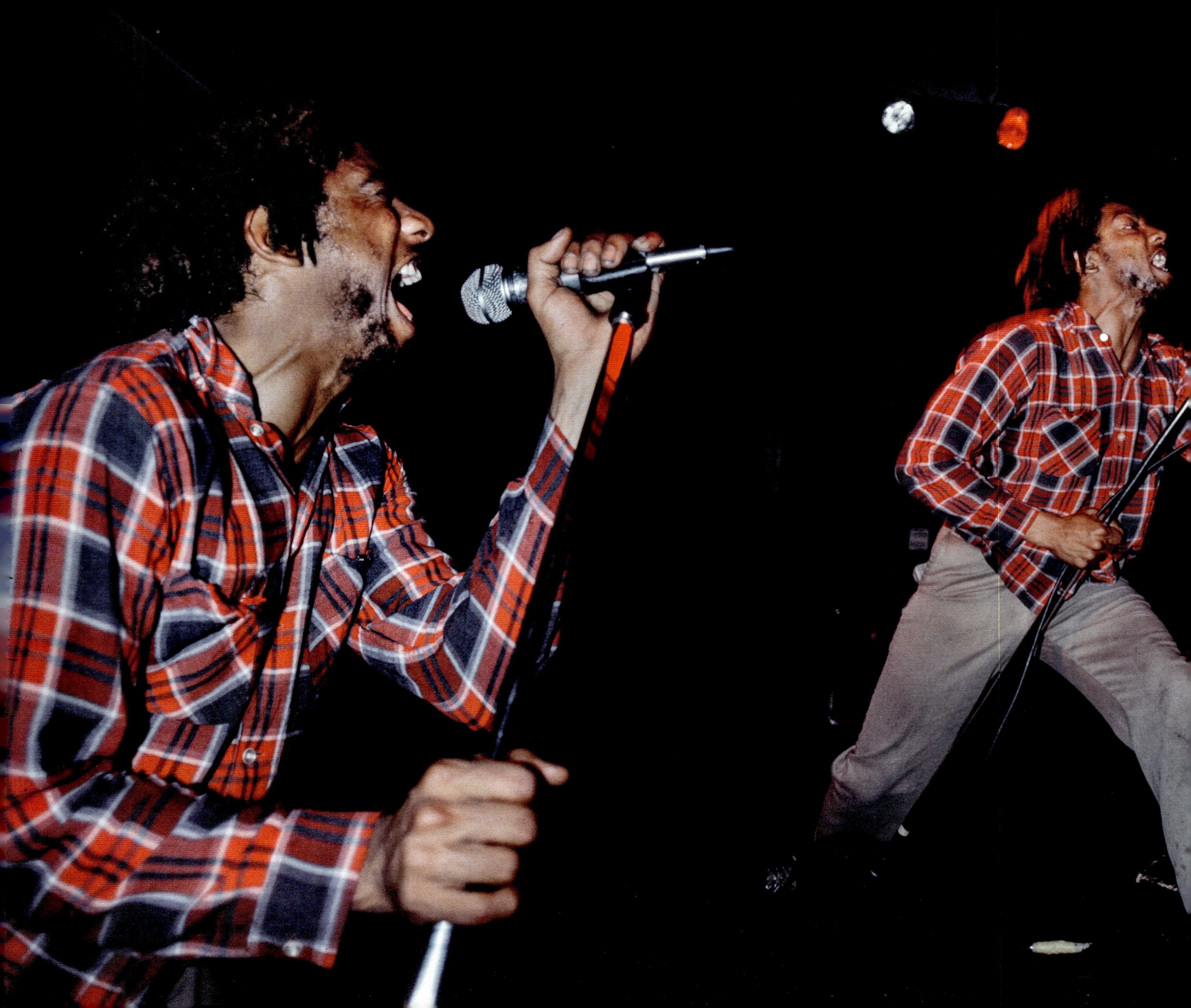

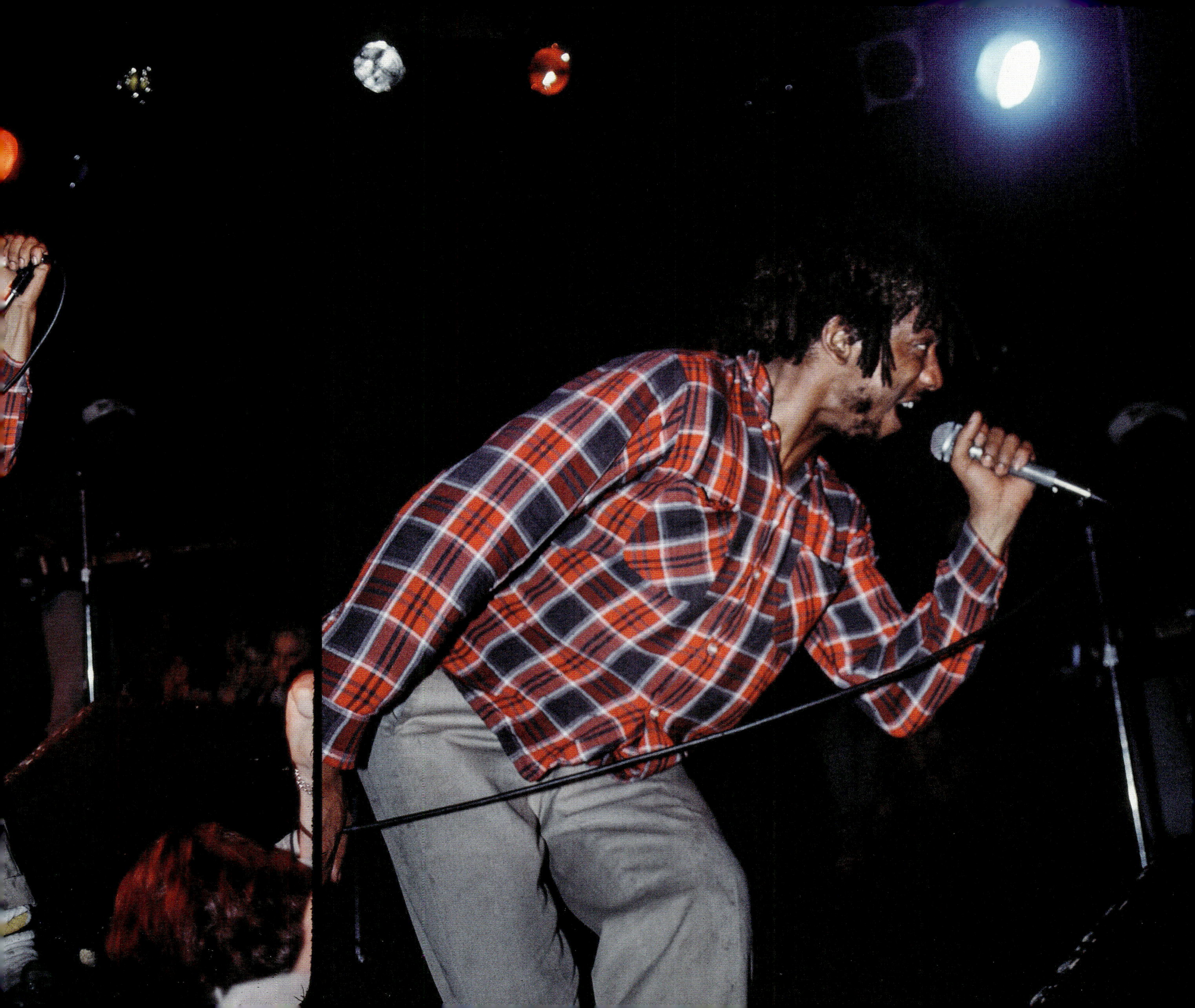

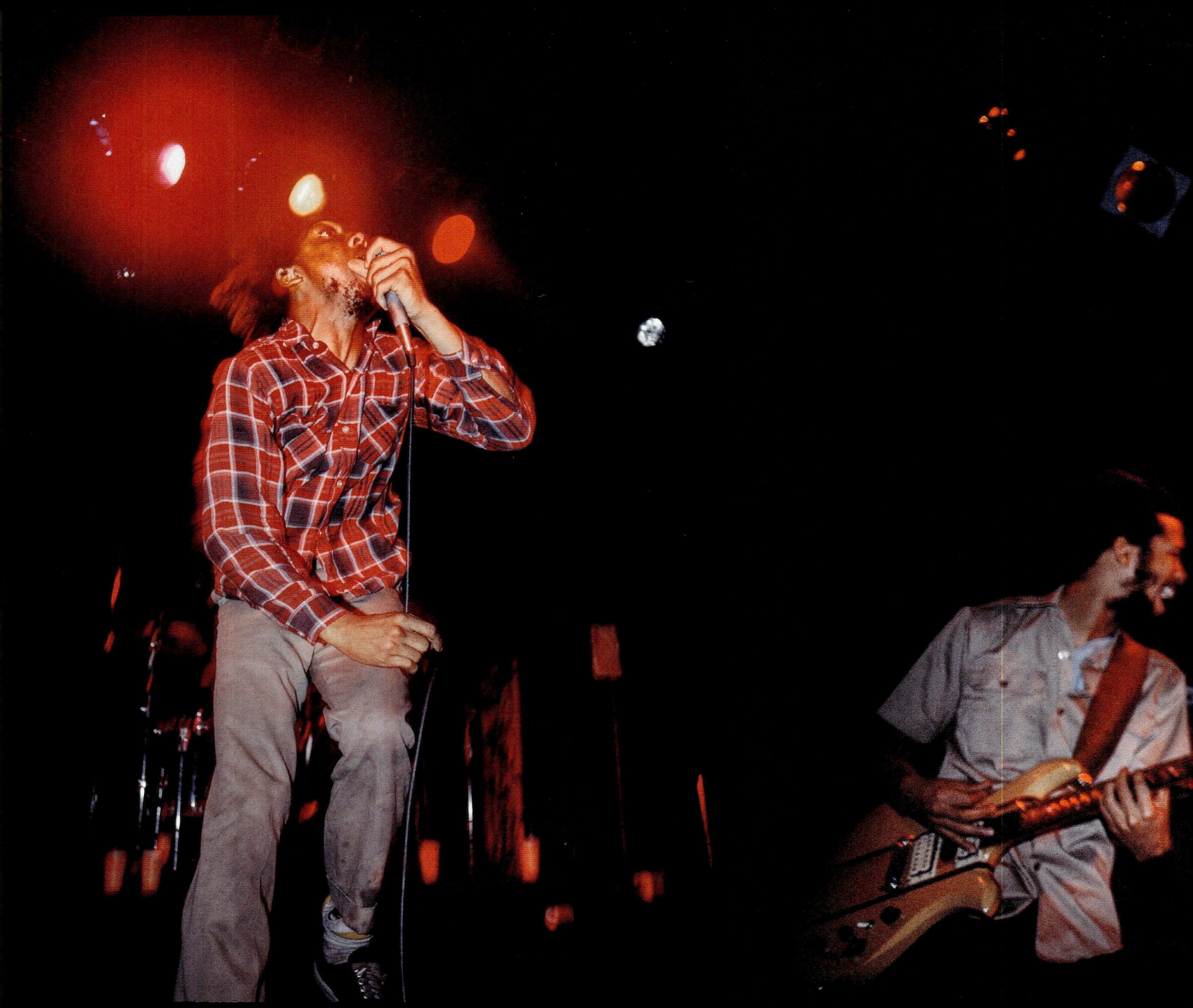

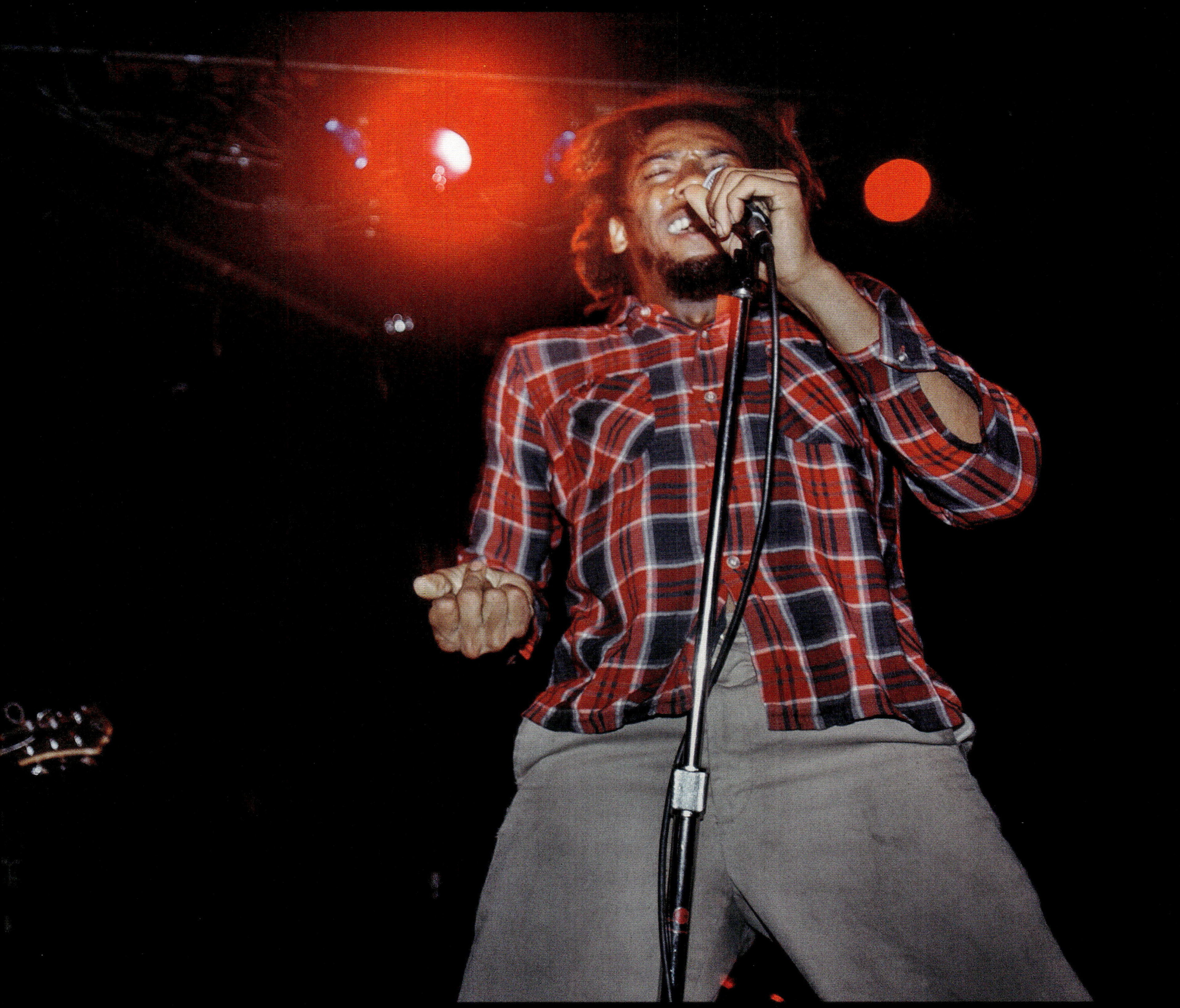

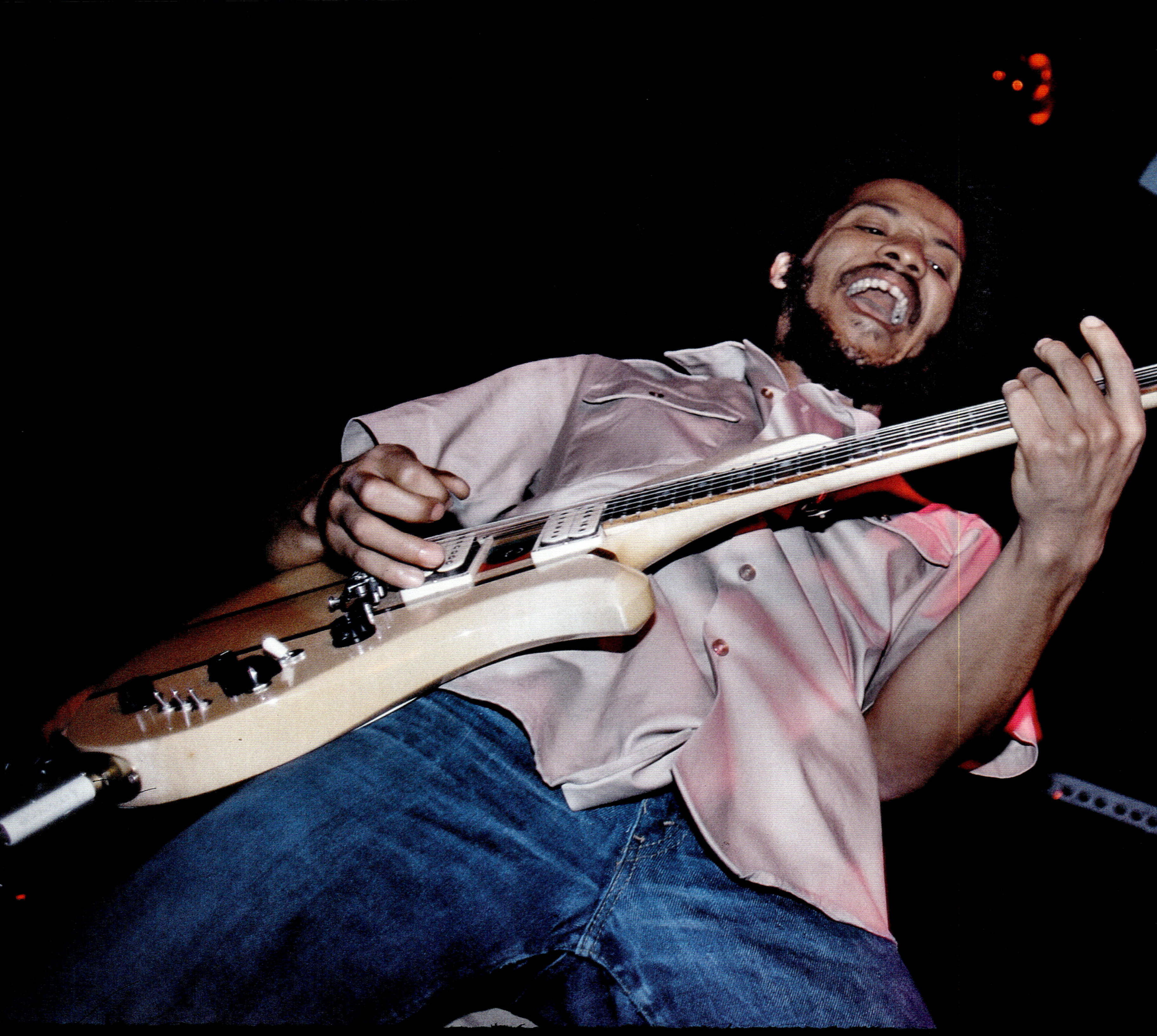

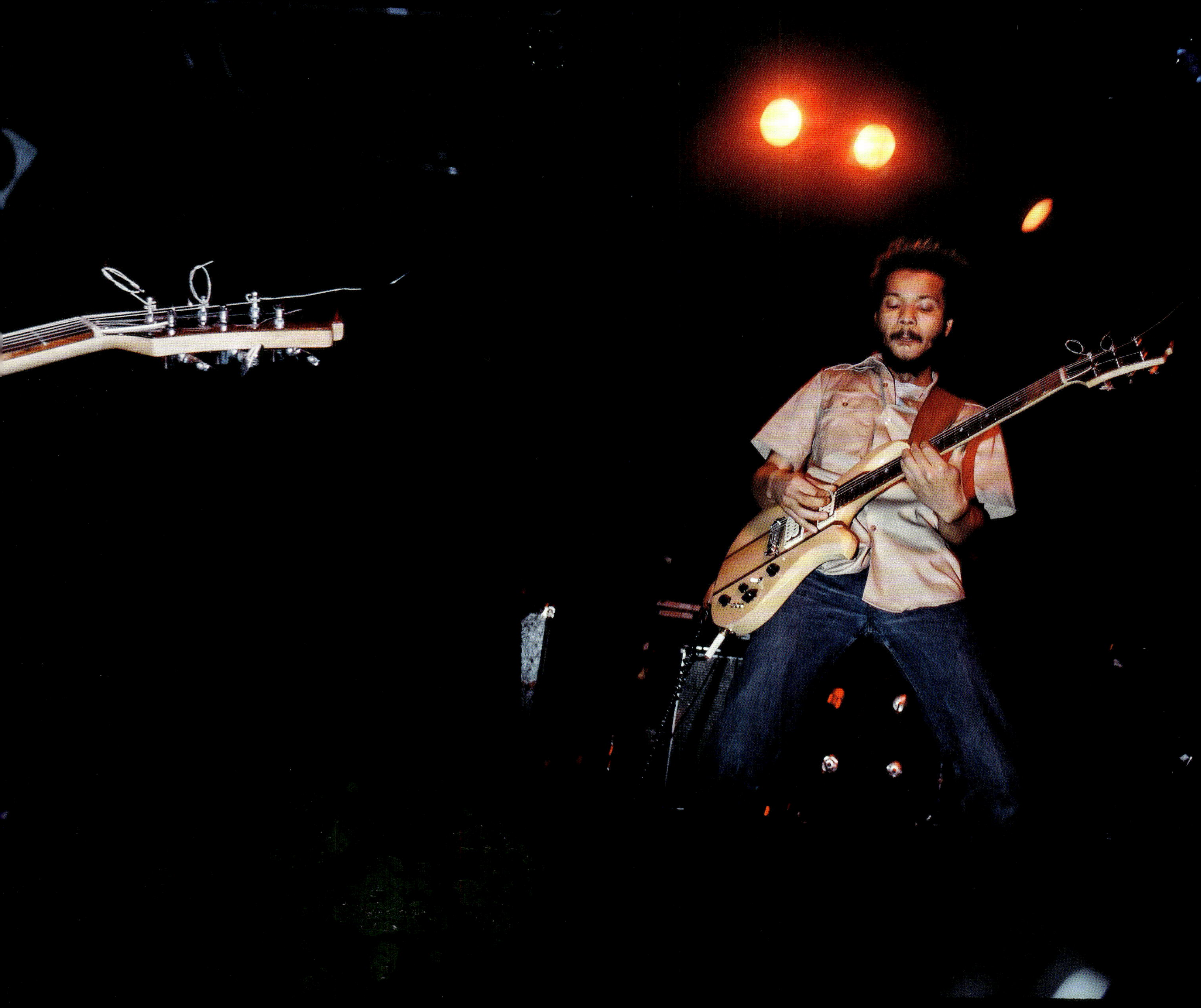

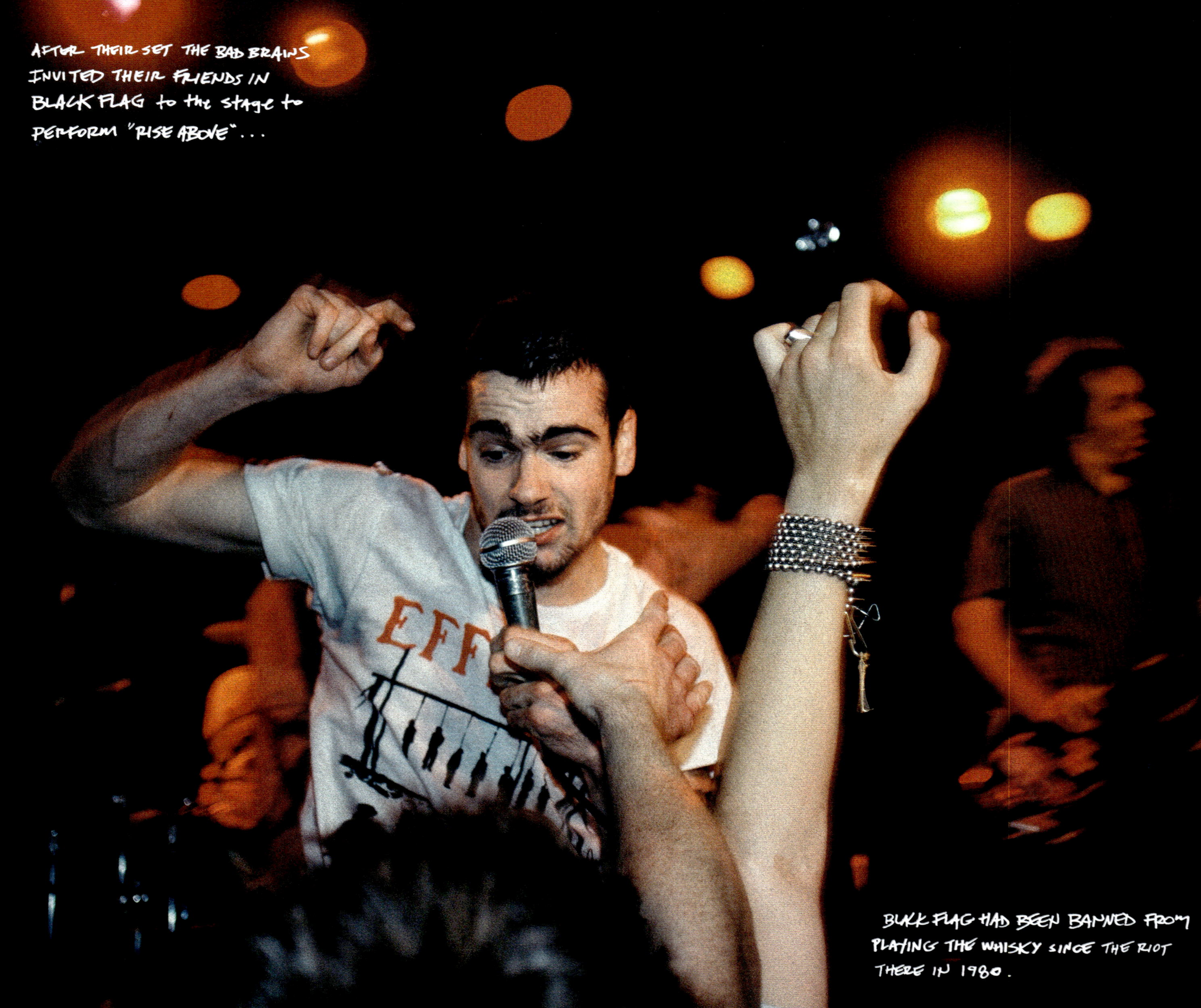
AFTER THEIR SET THE BAD BRAINS
INVITED THEIR FRIENDS IN
BLACK FLAG to the stage to
PERFORM "RISE ABOVE"...
BLACK FLAG HAD BEEN BANNED FROM
PLAYING THE WHISKY SINCE THE RIOT
THERE IN 1980.

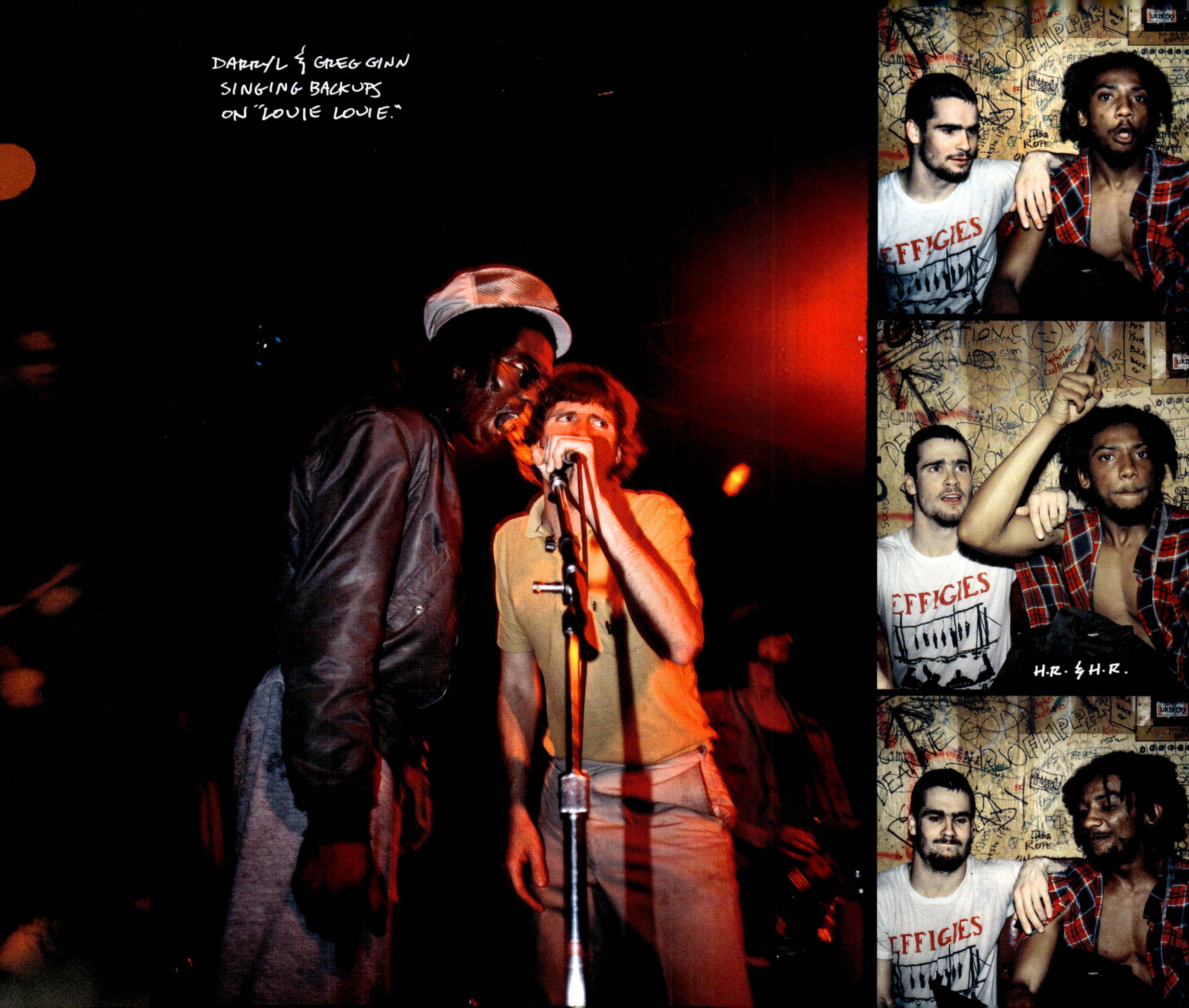
DARRYL & GREG GINN
SINGING BACKUPS
ON "LOUIE LOUIE."
H.R. & H.R.

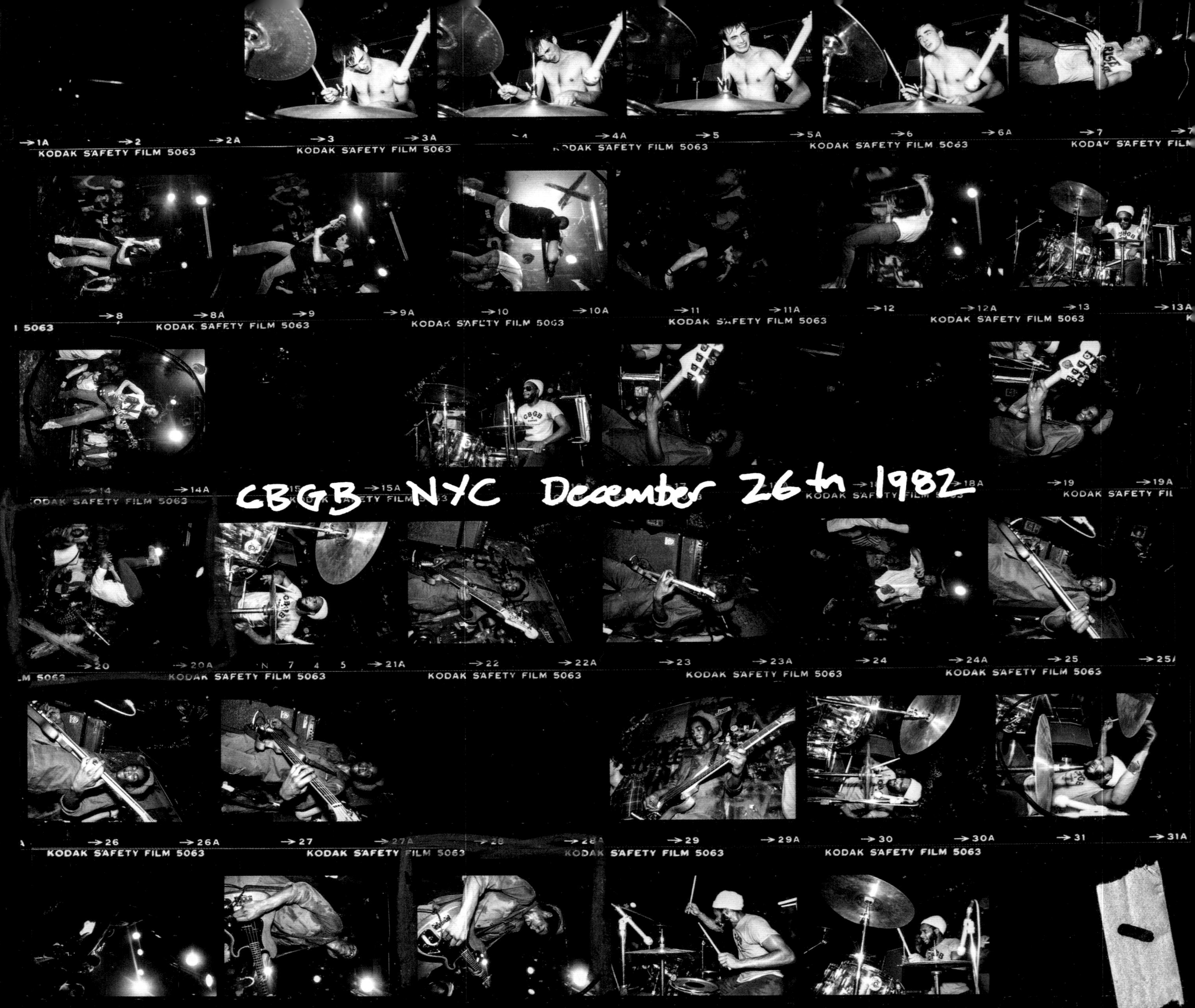
CBGB NYC December 26th 1982

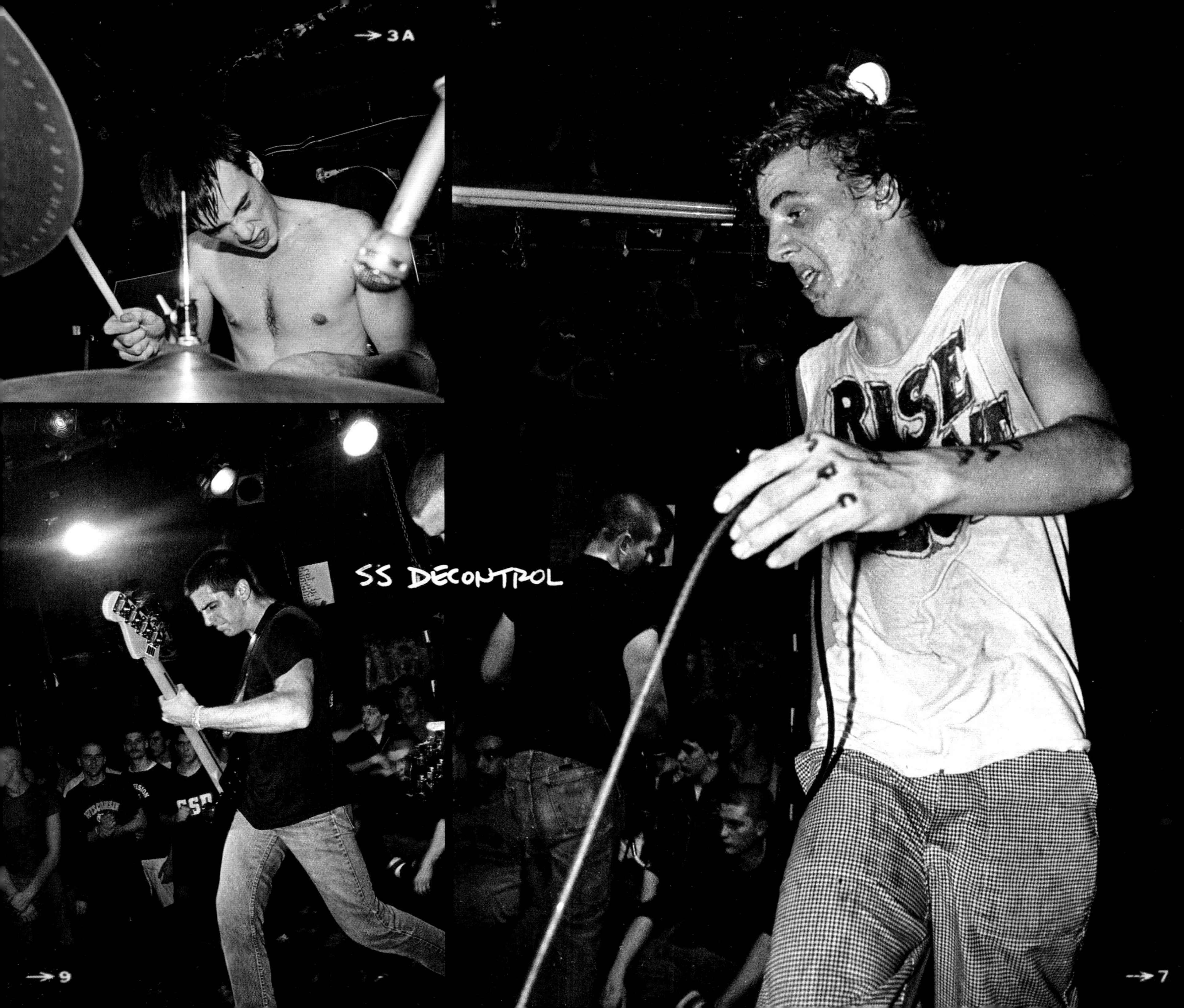
→ 3A
SS DECONTROL
RISE
→ 9
→ 7

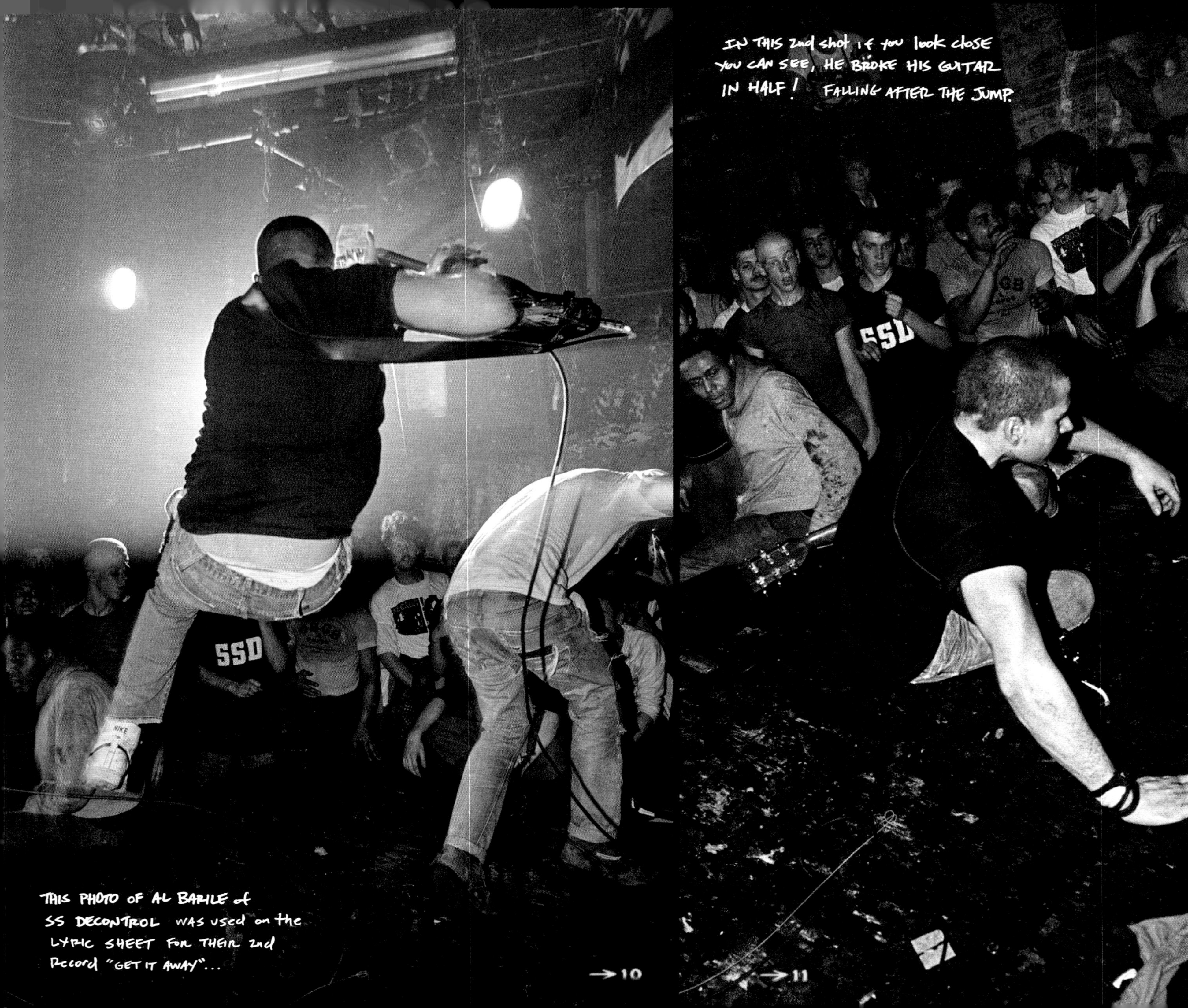
IN THIS 2nd SHOT IF YOU LOOK CLOSE
YOU CAN SEE, HE BROKE HIS GUITAR
IN HALF!   FALLING AFTER THE JUMP.
THIS PHOTO OF AL BARILE of
SS DECONTROL WAS USED ON THE
LYRIC SHEET FOR THEIR 2nd
RECORD "GET IT AWAY"...
→10
→11

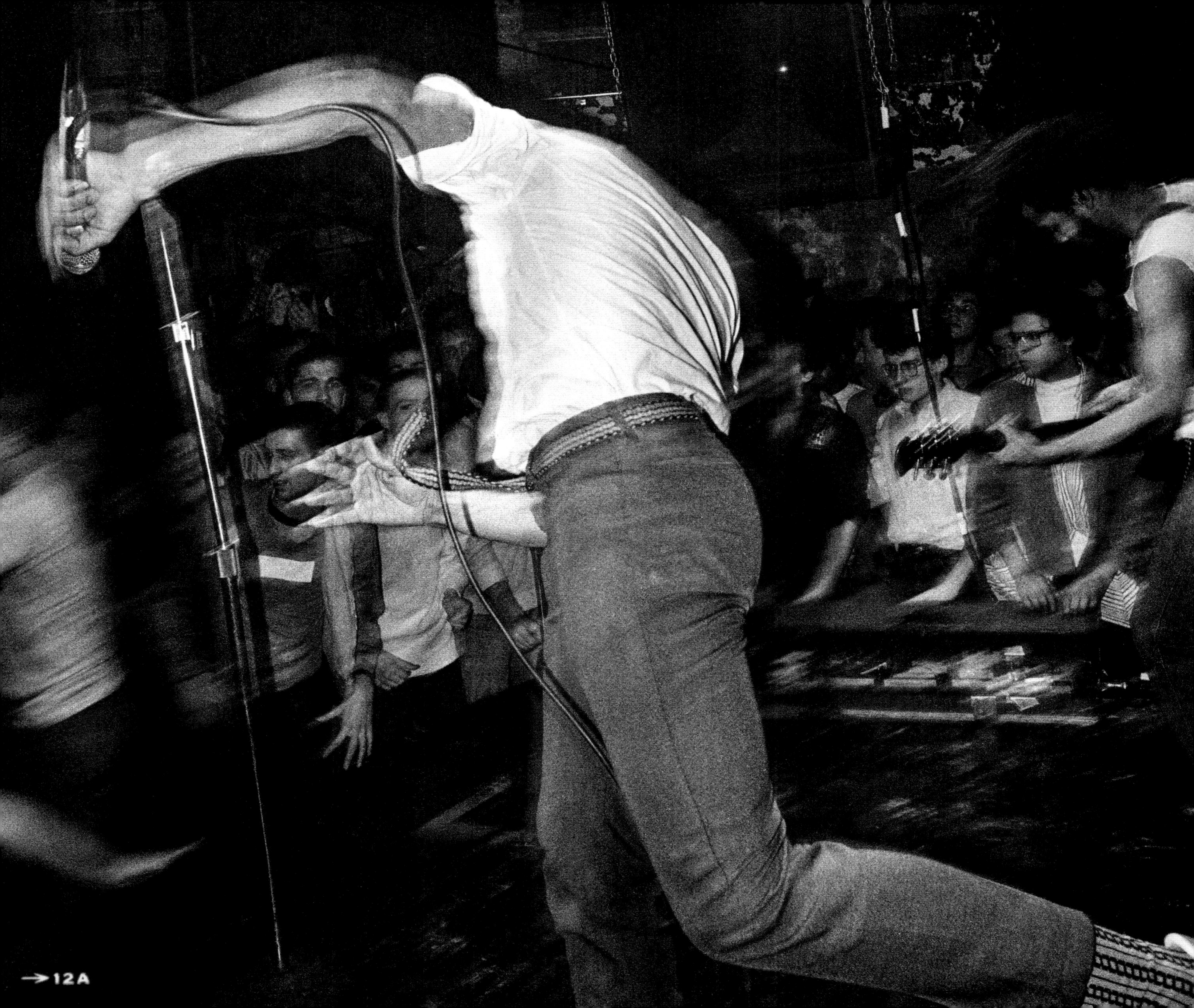

12A

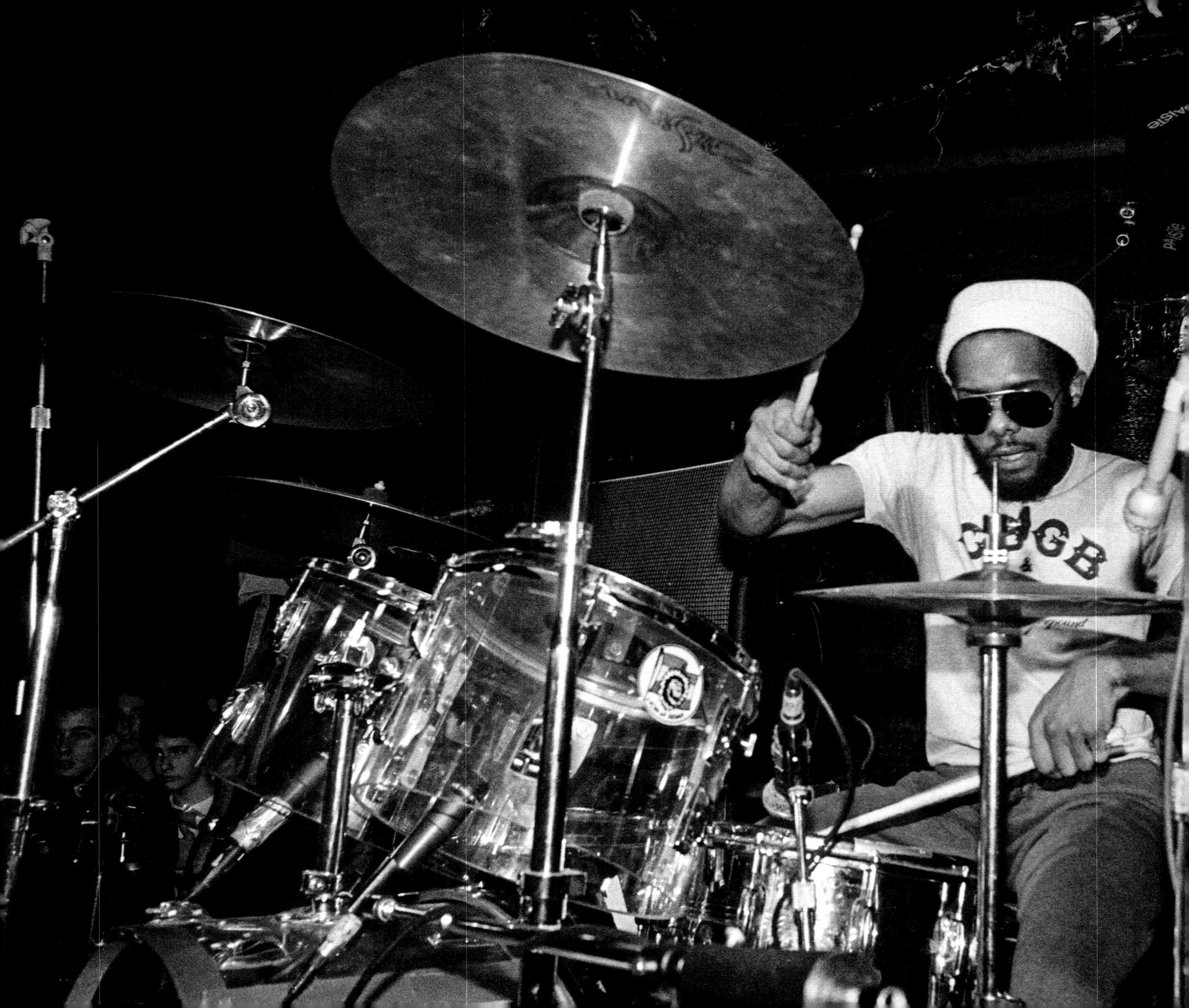

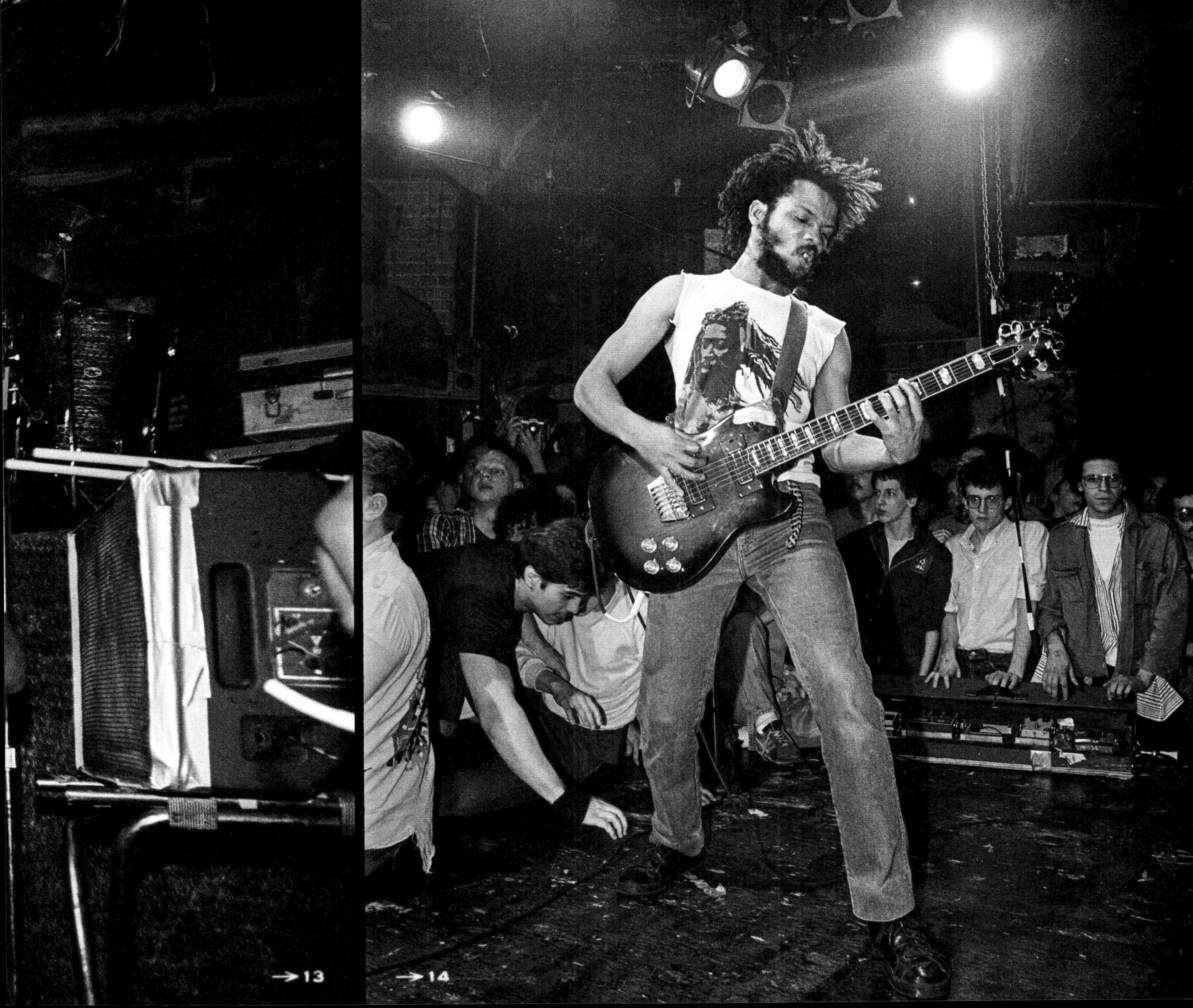
13
14

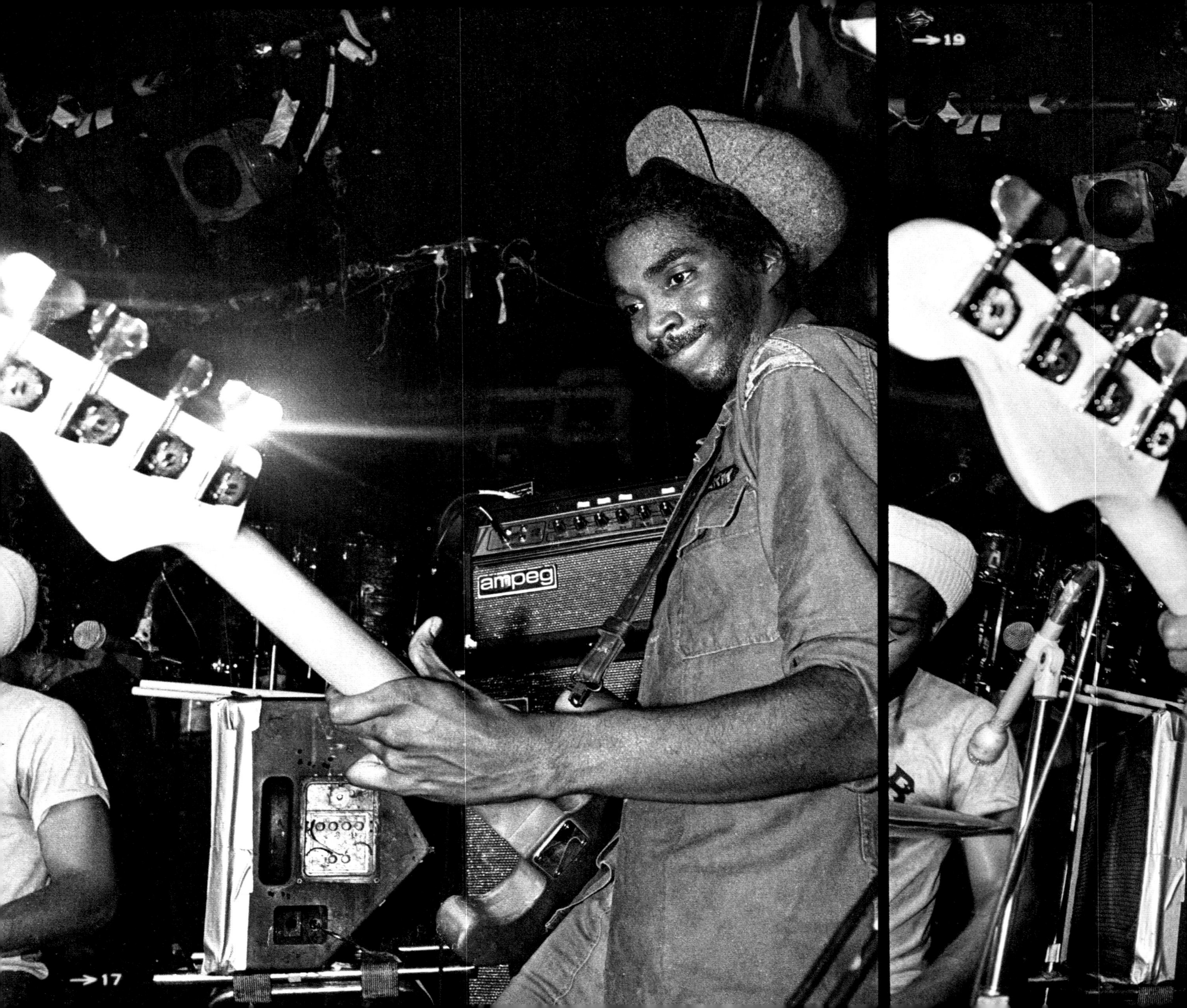
ampeg

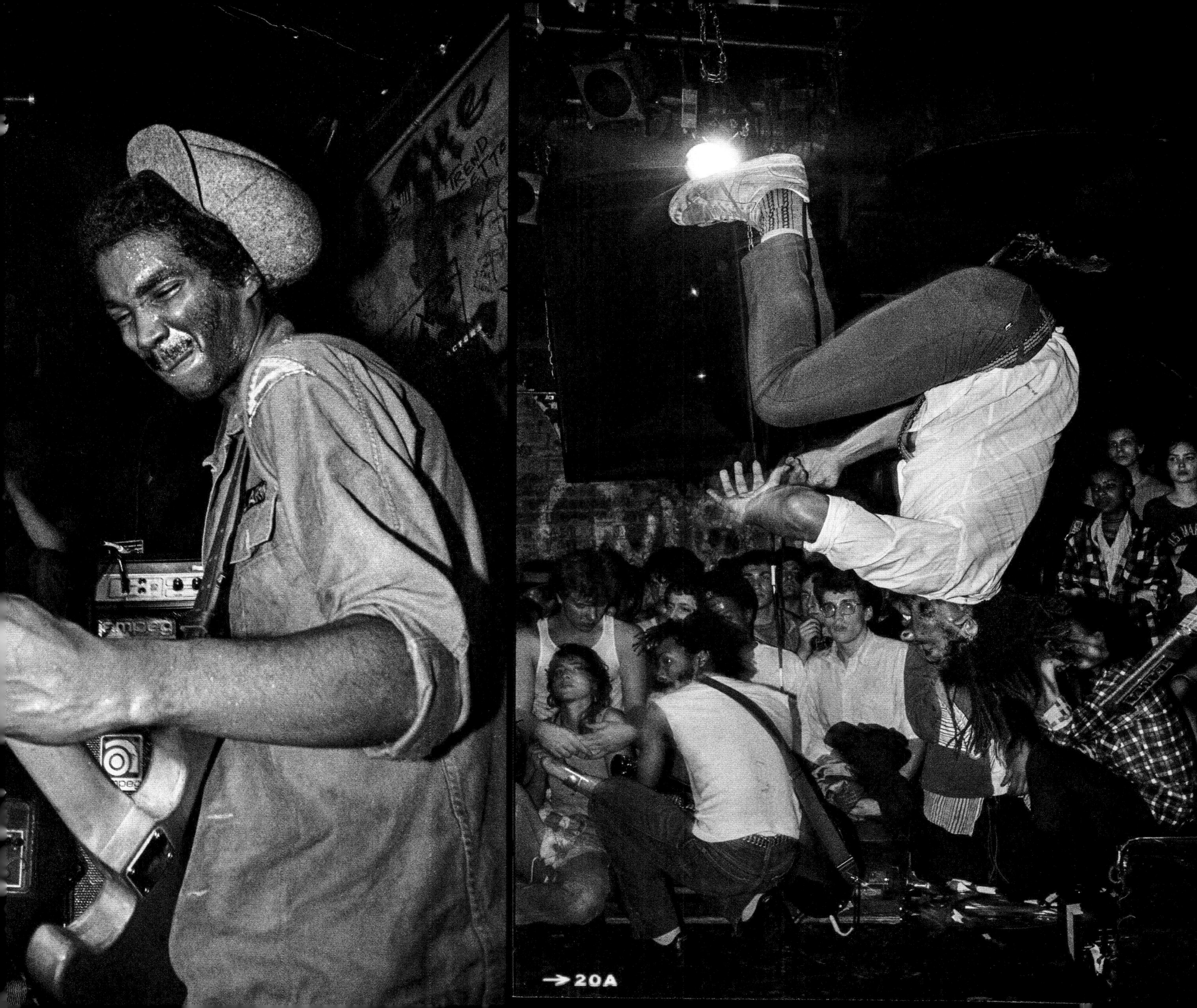
20A

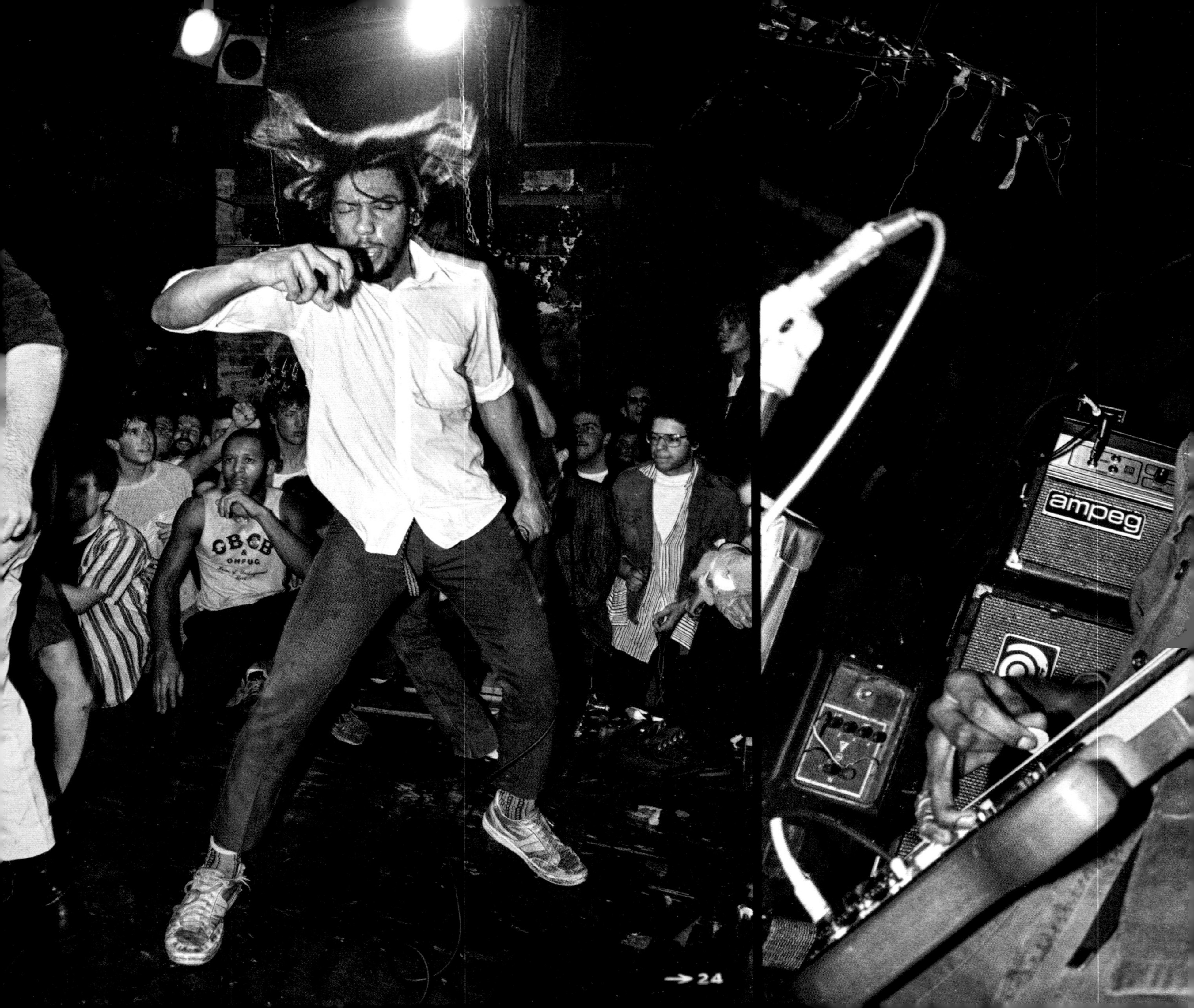
CBGB
& OMFUG
ampeg

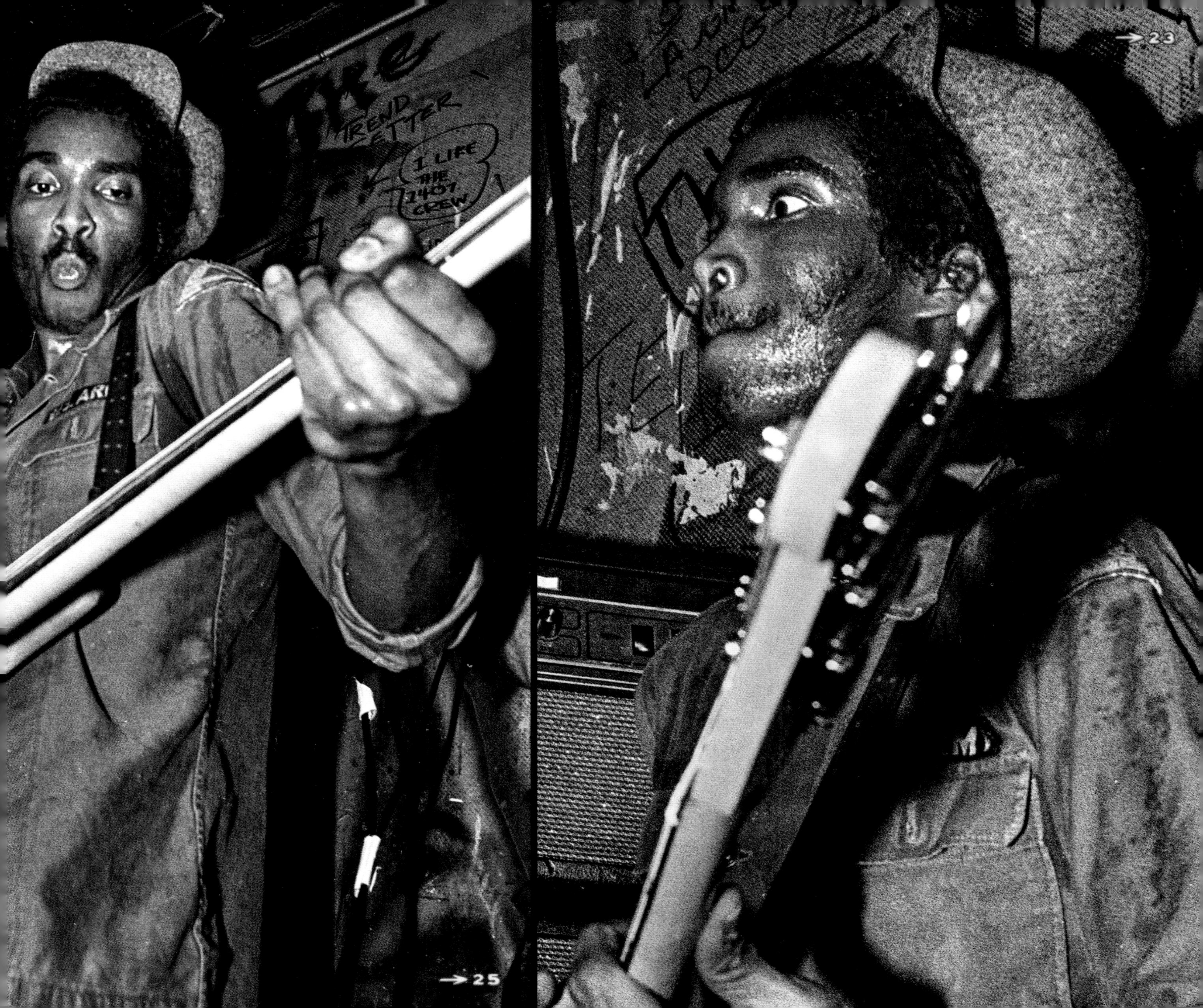
FIRE
TREND SETTER
I LIFE
THE
1407
CREW
23
25

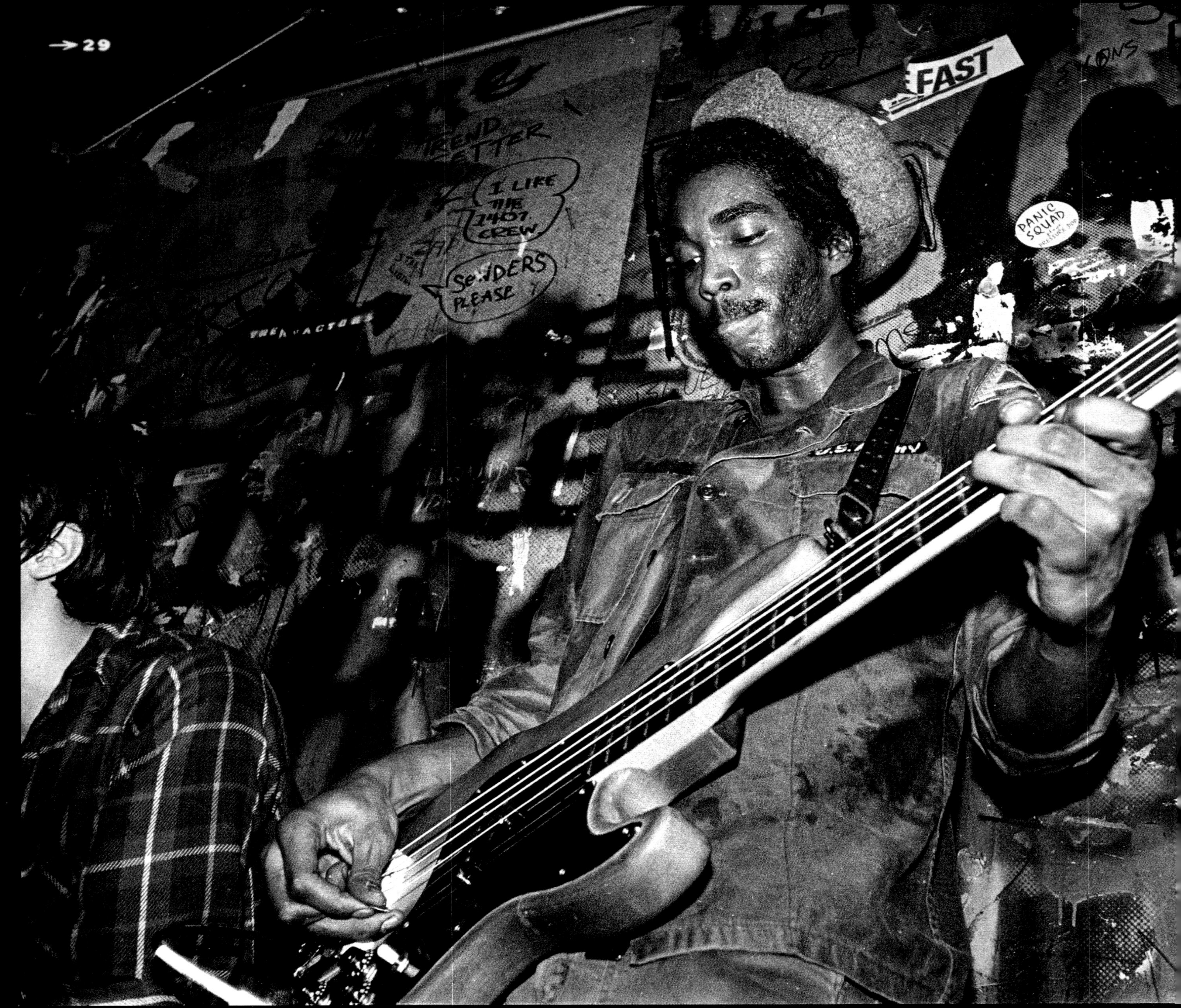
FAST
PANIC SQUAD
I LIKE THE 2407 CREW
SENDERS PLEASE
U.S. ARMY

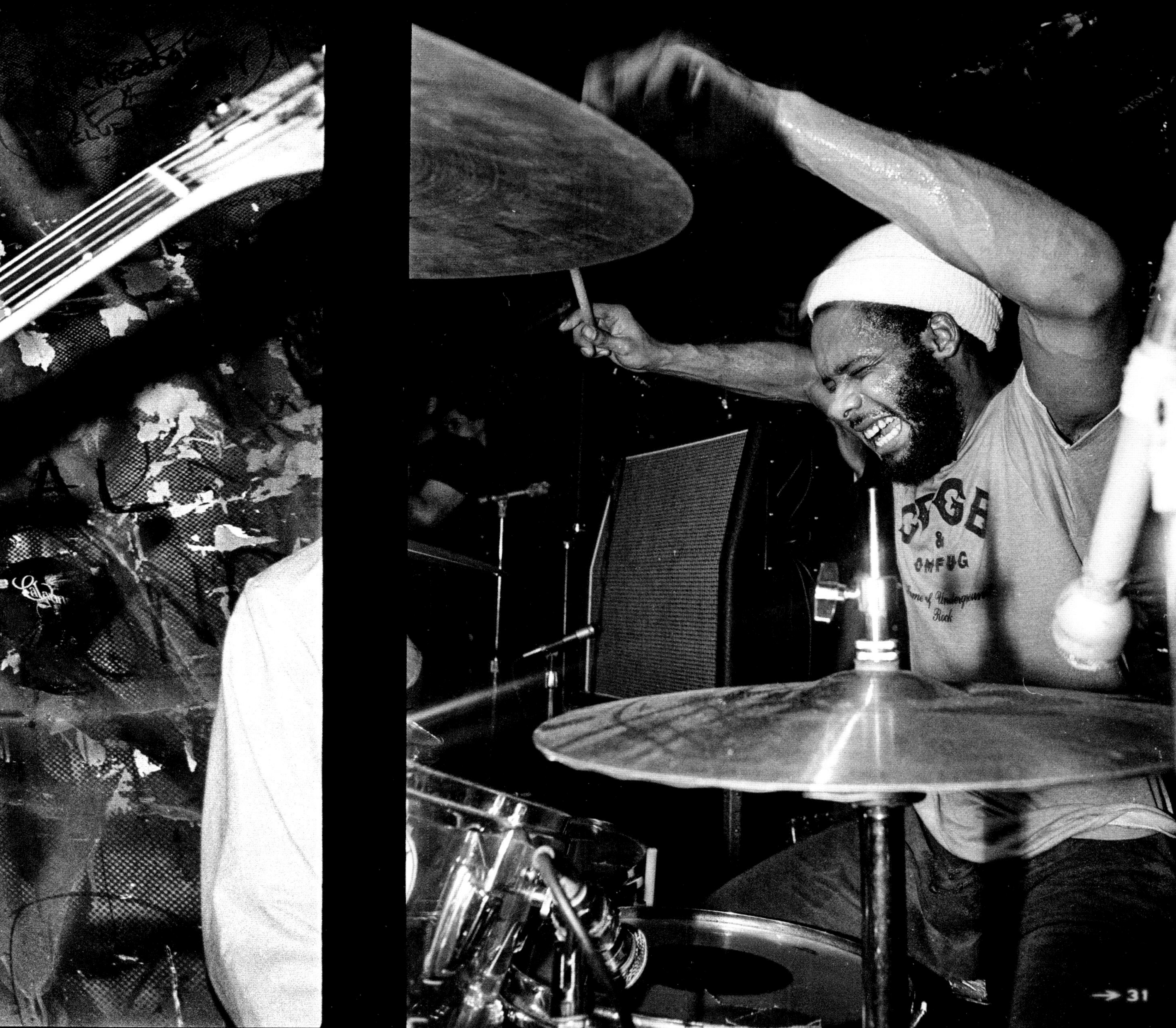
CBGB
&
OMFUG
Home of Underground
Rock

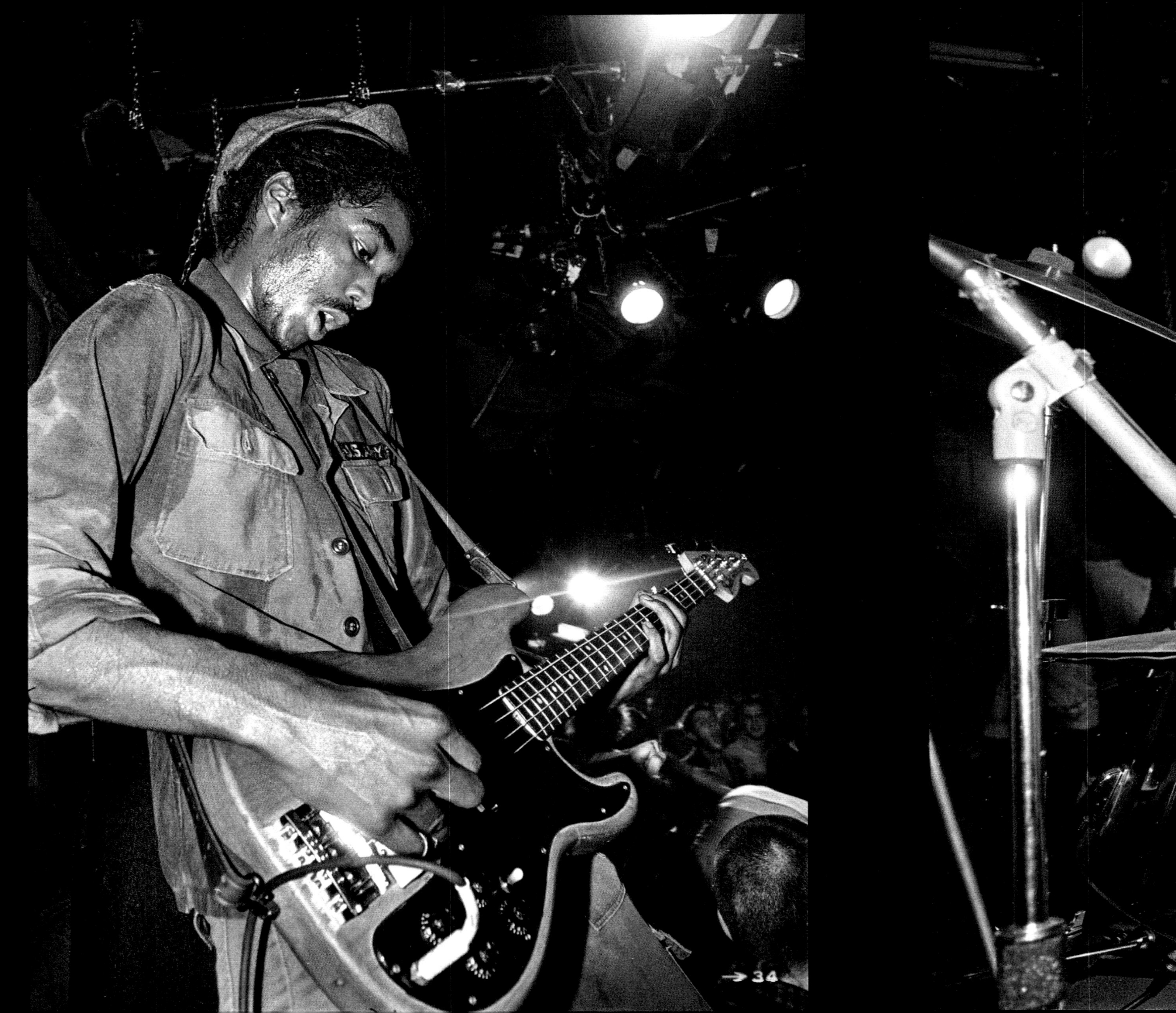
34

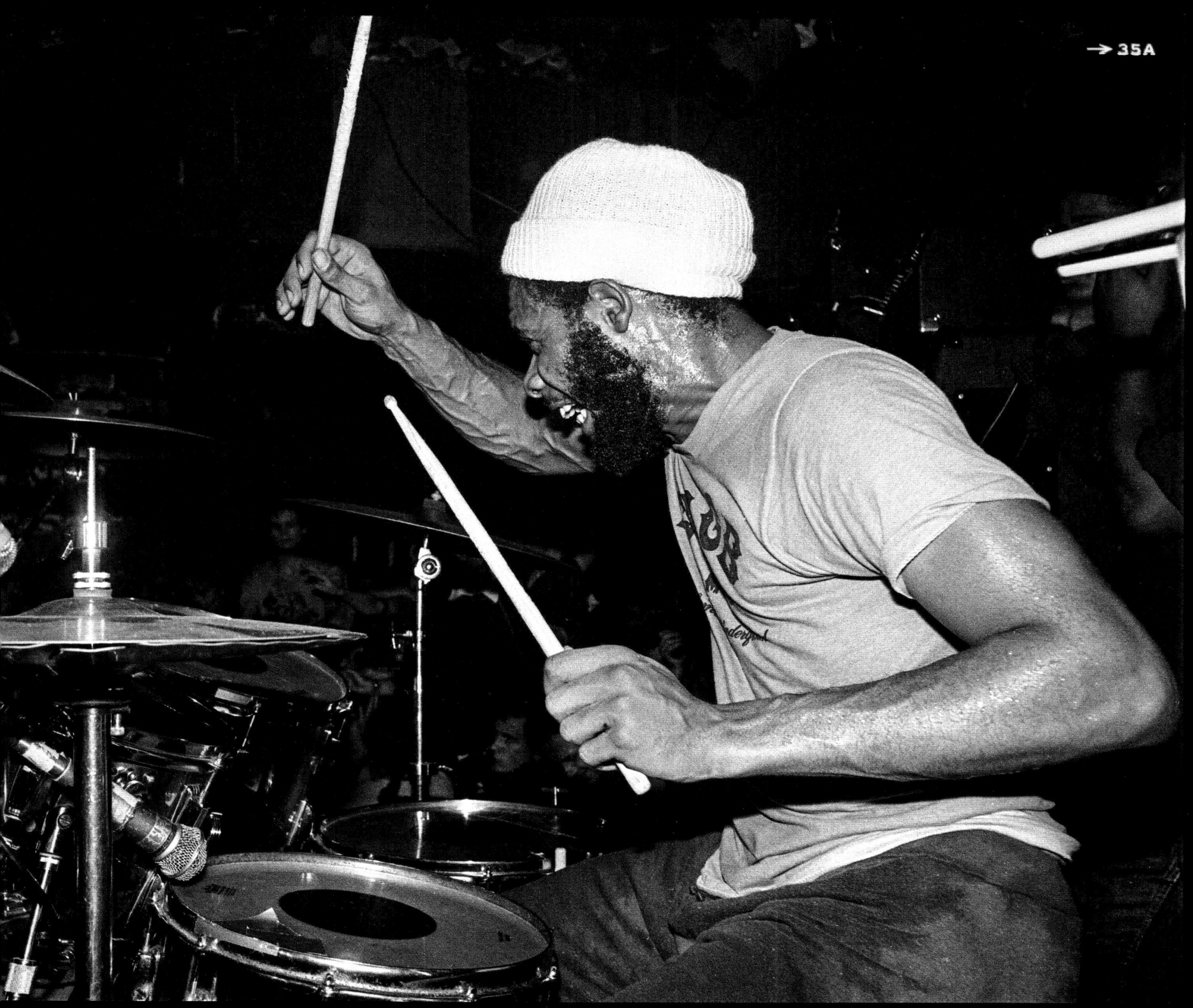
→ 35A

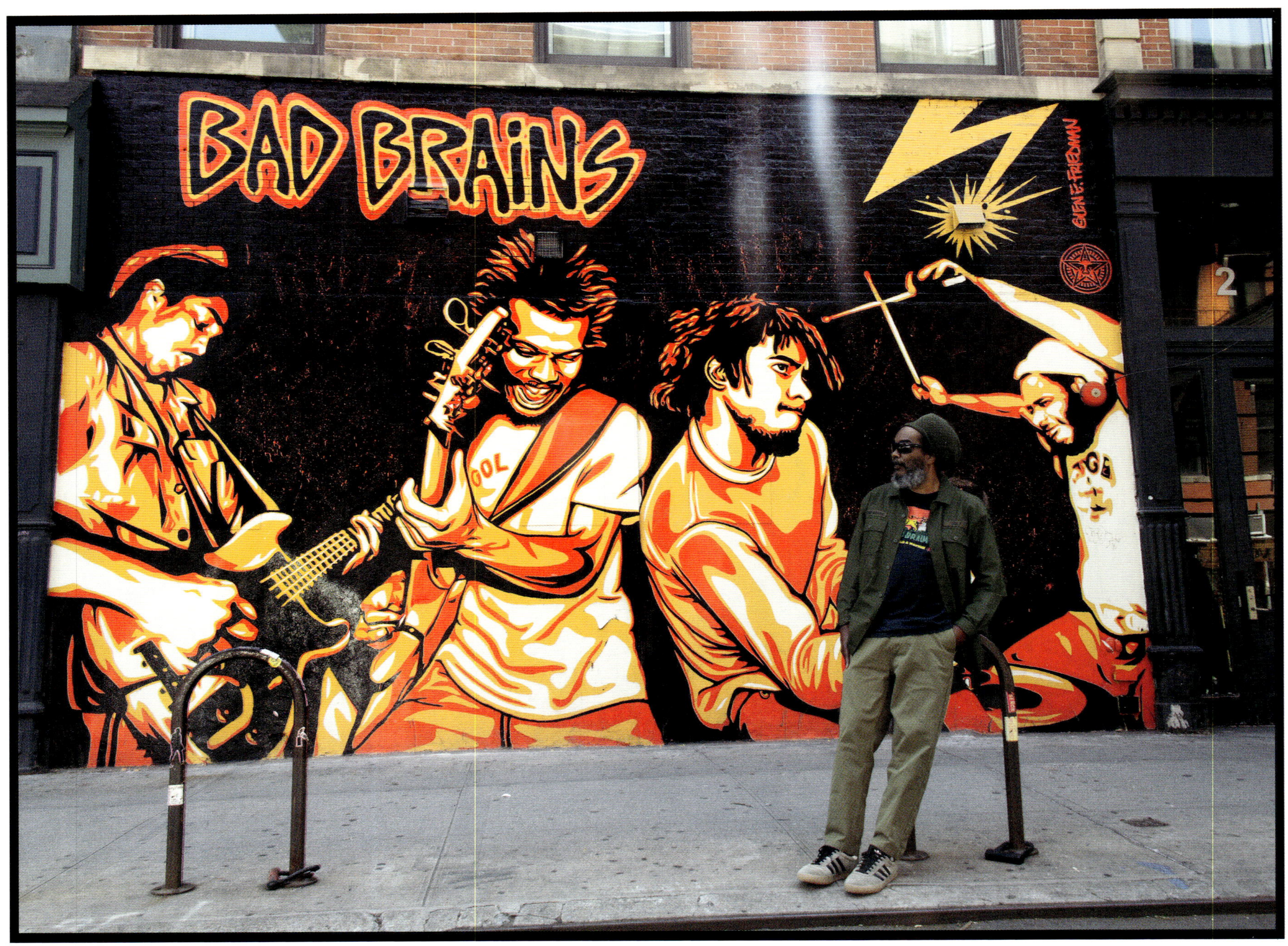



*Darryl on Bleecker Street, NYC, in front of the Shepard Fairey mural,
looking across the intersection toward the original CBGB. May 21, 2024.*

A few more words                                          by Darryl Jenifer

Once the Bad Brains got out of Washington, DC, and started to play New York City frequently, our goal was to conquer New York the same way we conquered DC with our style of punk rock music. 1980–81–82 was a very special time for us all.

PMA (Positive Mental Attitude) had taught us never to settle. CBGB in New York was the center of the "big city" universe and the punk mecca of the era. For me personally it was all about playing that place and mashing out a set that destroyed everything prior. Bad Brains were on a PMA mission to the extreme.

These early days were FUN. The journey was also filled with struggle, every struggle one goes through when arriving in New York City . . . Talking about being in a band, looking for places to sleep, hustling loose joints for mac & cheese and 40s, and getting into CBGB for free. This was PUNK ROCK before hardcore—the only HARDCORE at this time was up on 42nd Street in the XXX district.

I'm so glad G.E.F. was there and cared enough to photograph us. Back in the day I was a rebel against photographers and journalists, kinda like a punk rock Peter Tosh. I seem to have a funny memory of telling Glen not to interfere with the performance, getting too close. Evidence over the years proves Glen is the man. When I look at the photos, they remind me of how serious we were with this "band shit" and how I used to buy shoes off 9th Street. His photos are THE photos of Bad Brains and they are incredible, awesome photos. And I'm glad they exist.

The G.E.F./Obey mural across from CBGB is the pinnacle for me. It's sooo dope. It's all the recognition I need . . . Fuck platinum plaques and Rock & Roll Hall of Fame inductions!

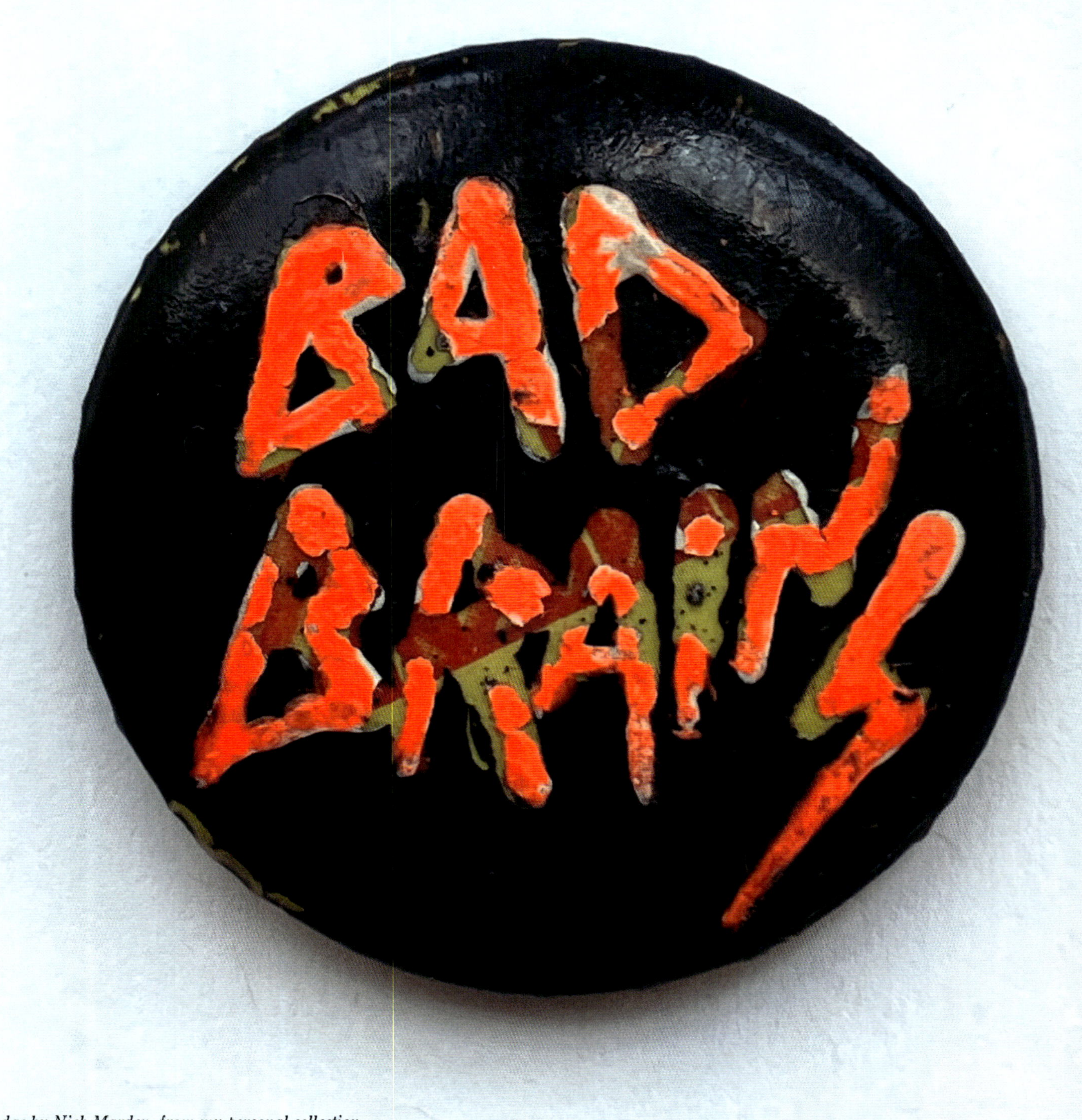


*1980 hand-painted badge by Nick Marden, from my personal collection.*

Everything Explodes on the One                                    by Zack de la Rocha

I was fourteen years old and it would be a full year before I would have what I consider to be a historical encounter. To call this event just a show somehow puts a ceiling on the experience. Limits its weight and gravity as a life-altering event which without question it was, and its force continues to inform my present days. An event that still triggers joy, and exhilaration. One that still grounds my days with a sense of purpose and meaning despite the fact that it happened almost forty years ago. An experience that I'm afraid more and more could become an anomaly amid the psychologically violent expansion of the digital realm, and the interactive public sphere it intrinsically seeks to decimate. It was four musicians who would ascend to the stage in front of me, in both the literal and historical sense, to stand at a place where sound, fury, and Black resilience intersect.

And in that year their presence was looming. They had already acquired mythological status as their name alone sent the imagination running. The slivers of information darting half-cooked into conversations, crews of outsiders attempting to separate truth from fiction, self-appointed underground afficionados disputing or affirming, pulling from scrappy clues of ephemera, xeroxed zine photos, rumors, and third-generation cassette recordings already beginning to wear thin. Mentioned in passing as the greatest punk band who originally played jazz fusion. Rastafarians who thrashed harder than any of my disposable cult heroes thus far; and any link between their Pan-Africanist vision and the antiauthoritarian impulses of a young Chicano punk was at that point beyond me. But was soon to be permanently etched in memory when confronted with the wailing, the prophetic articulation, the sonic upheaval, the naked revolutionary fury of the Bad Brains from Washington, DC.

Fender's Ballroom in downtown Long Beach, California wasn't so much a club as it was a powder keg. A social combustion point of no return. Going to shows there more often than not defied reason. The question you're asking from wherever you found parking on 1st Street until you laid down your cash at the ticket window is, *Why on earth am I paying to see bands in the punk equivalent of a Vacaville prison yard?* Blood will be drawn. By fist or by knife. It's not if, it's *when.* And because of its violent unpredictability, every time I approached its doors, without fail or exception, the fear rose to the level I assume would accompany walking into a burning building.

Upon entering, it wasn't clear that the shit wasn't actually on fire. A thick smoke rose through the crowd of about 1,200 people mashed into a space that held 900 like it was a Tokyo subway stop at rush hour. It reeked of gunpowder and it was inescapable. The origin of the smoke couldn't be placed until you pushed your way forward toward the stage. Because Fender's was a lot of things to a lot of people. To punks, it was the venue of consequence after many LA clubs essentially closed their doors due to police intimidation and violence. To the promoters who will remain nameless here, the shows at Fender's were a convenient way to clean up some drug money. To local punk gangs like the LADS (Los Angeles Death Squad) or Circle One, Fender's had little to do with catching a show, and more about catching the fade. The space for them was solely somewhere to exact pain on a rival for some line crossed, or some perceived broken code. Then there were the skins. Not the Motown-oldies-rocking, Trojan Records–collecting, working-class, moon-stomping friends in the fight. The other kind. The fucking fuckers. The Nazis' version of Fender's typically envisioned the dance floor as being some kind of territory to hold. Some kind of private Idaho to keep pure, which was masking a senseless excuse to see someone bleed. But on this night, they were intent on playing the role of saboteurs. Bringing us back to the origin of the smoke.

It was the fuckers who thought they could put a wrench in the works by sneaking in bags of fireworks, and hurling packs of firecrackers, ground flowers, and Piccolo Petes, lit on the edges and thrown into the center of the floor. While trying to catch a breath through air so dense, smoke-filled, and foul, with sparks and fire ripping through the crowd, it dawned on me that there was a rapidly growing number of reasons to turn around and get the fuck out of there. But we didn't come to get mellow. And nothing was gonna deter us from bearing witness to who we thought was the greatest band on earth, who a year prior seemed like nothing more than an amalgamation of powerful rumors—enigmatic and unconfirmed.

The crowd was moving from restless to hostile and started to resemble a drunken rugby scrum, unable to maintain its footing, swaying in several directions at once, and in sections collectively stumbling to a collapse. The weight of the bodies shifted my vantage randomly in those moments before the band appeared, and suddenly I was shoved from just left of center and pressed directly against the PA that lined the right side of the stage, and with the firecrackers snapping at our heads, the swaying scrum, the sweat-drenched air, and a sense of drowning setting in, I watched from the corner of my eye the gods enter the building, and the feedback began to howl.

It didn't register as a warning because it came first in the form of a miraculous storm of sound. Exhilarated shock set in once the opening guitar passage of "F.V.K." was met in a brutal exchange by drum fills that defied my young sense of timing. Thrown like a flurry of jabs, as fast and as unpredictable as Ali, until the chords hit, blunt like body punches, forceful. Joe Frazier forceful; Doc, Earl, and Darryl in unison, swinging in what sounded like a fight for their lives, and most certainly a fight for ours. Along with H.R.'s freight-train determination, comfortably assuming the role of lightning conductor. Then, in rhythm with one swing of his arm, the storm broke, the feedback returned, and for a fleeting moment the gods rested. Then they re-armed. Two snare hits, unrecognizable as such. They were too thin to be gunfire, but with equal effect. And now everyone in the room was officially warned.

Everything explodes on the one. The speed and the precision of the storm intensified, with its own surging inertia producing swells that literally flooded the stage with bodies, in a scene that was as joyful as it was dangerous and unsettling. The first phrase from H.R.'s throat, drawn from the depths of what seemed like a life of conflict, unable to be repressed for another second, in gospel-like exuberance and fury, with the swagger of knowing that history would soon absolve him, the raison d'être laid bare, in tandem now; the storm and the meaning, the target defined and the next warning issued: *"The bourgeoisie had better watch out for me / All throughout this so-called nation / We don't need your filthy money / We don't need your innocent bloodshed / We just wanna end your world."*

Everything exploded on the one as the otherworldly sonic force from DC reclaimed and reinvented a genre right in front of my eyes in real time, and in an instant the possibilities widened. Everything. Songs were no longer just songs but bursts of truth uncontainable, confrontational, dangerous— from which new realities emerge. Explodes. The fifteen-year-old who felt powerless, or lesser than, being lifted by this beautiful fury to raise my head and stare the world in its eyes. Everything I knew was shifting as the band surged like it was hardwired into the sun. Explodes, and my burgeoning cynicism melted away, transformed by what I read in the performance and fearless intent over the next hour.

It was in Dr. Know's smile as if he was privy to a divine presence that he was channeling into the room through his guitar. It was in Earl's hands, a constant fiery blur stealing back time from the enemy. It was in Darryl's poised, determined anchor rhythms and chords amid the chaos. And it was in H.R.'s swagger and unflinching eyes—piercing through the glare and scorching heat, piercing right through the crowd, through the walls of the club, into the streets beyond and into the night, transfixed on a distant calling—as they thrashed unscathed through the hatred and tribulation, dead set upon a place in heaven, undeterred by this American hell.

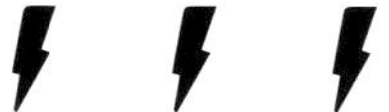

This collection of G.E.F.'s images of the Bad Brains registers as something far beyond a group of photos. Each time I pore over them, another window to a period so reflective of the current one gets opened. The layers of meaning thicken. There is no staging to disguise the reality they impose. Spontaneity and instinct are in the driver's seat here, pulling two progenitors of their respective fields together into an exchange that gathers more gravity from one frame to the next. Unlike the beautiful abstractions of Glen's book *The Idealist* and the fertile proven ground of his *Fuck You Heroes* collection, these sequenced shots bang like RZA beats, allowing their imperfections to carry their power in a conscious refutation of past forms. In turn, Glen's approach here more accurately reflects the jagged, raw technicality of the Bad Brains sound. Which is what makes this exchange such a conversation of consequence; Glen manages to pull off what seems like an impossible feat by delivering a collection that matches the intensity of arguably the most powerful and dynamic band that has ever graced a stage. This volume transcends reminiscence and posits itself as living memory that intentionally informs the present. Because fuck nostalgia.

These are critical moments of music history. They are not simply documents of a couple encounters that the band and Glen had in the early eighties. These are of a ferocious form and movement that speak with precision upon the immense tension and antagonism lying just beneath the surface of our current condition. And in the context of daily life under late capitalism, they read like a visual precursor to a coming collective boiling point.

These images enable the uninitiated to stand as close as possible to the explosion. And that detonation reaches its end point in its most direct and unfiltered state. In a manner that grants no quarter from its social-realist implications. In a form that offers no novocaine for the wounds.

What the Bad Brains challenge us to recognize in no uncertain terms is that the organized sadism posing as Western civilization will not come to reckoning with its nature on its own, for it is steeped in blindness while it simultaneously regenerates itself through violence.

Their music enables us to see more clearly the forces of oppression which made their jubilant confrontation so necessary. The miraculous storm of sound which demands our attentiveness, our recognition, our humility, and fundamentally our action. We must become louder than the gunshots, more determined than the state gendarmes who are firing them, we must become the chords, become the unrelenting fury of bass and drums, stare deeply, painfully at the cause, in order to ensure a more human effect. We must become the defiant poetry, and we must never give in, never give in . . .

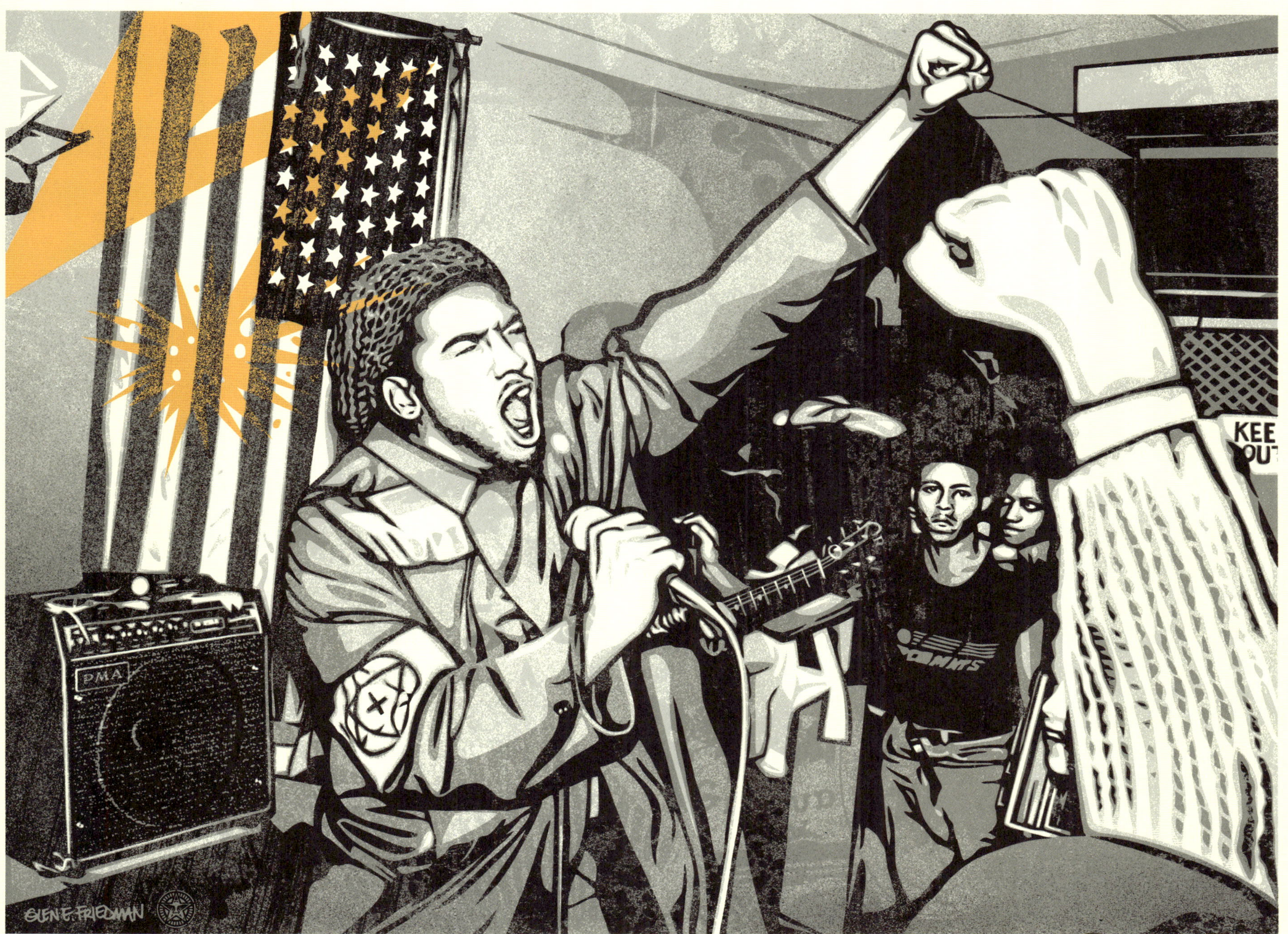

PMA
GLEN E. FRIEDMAN
KEE
OUT

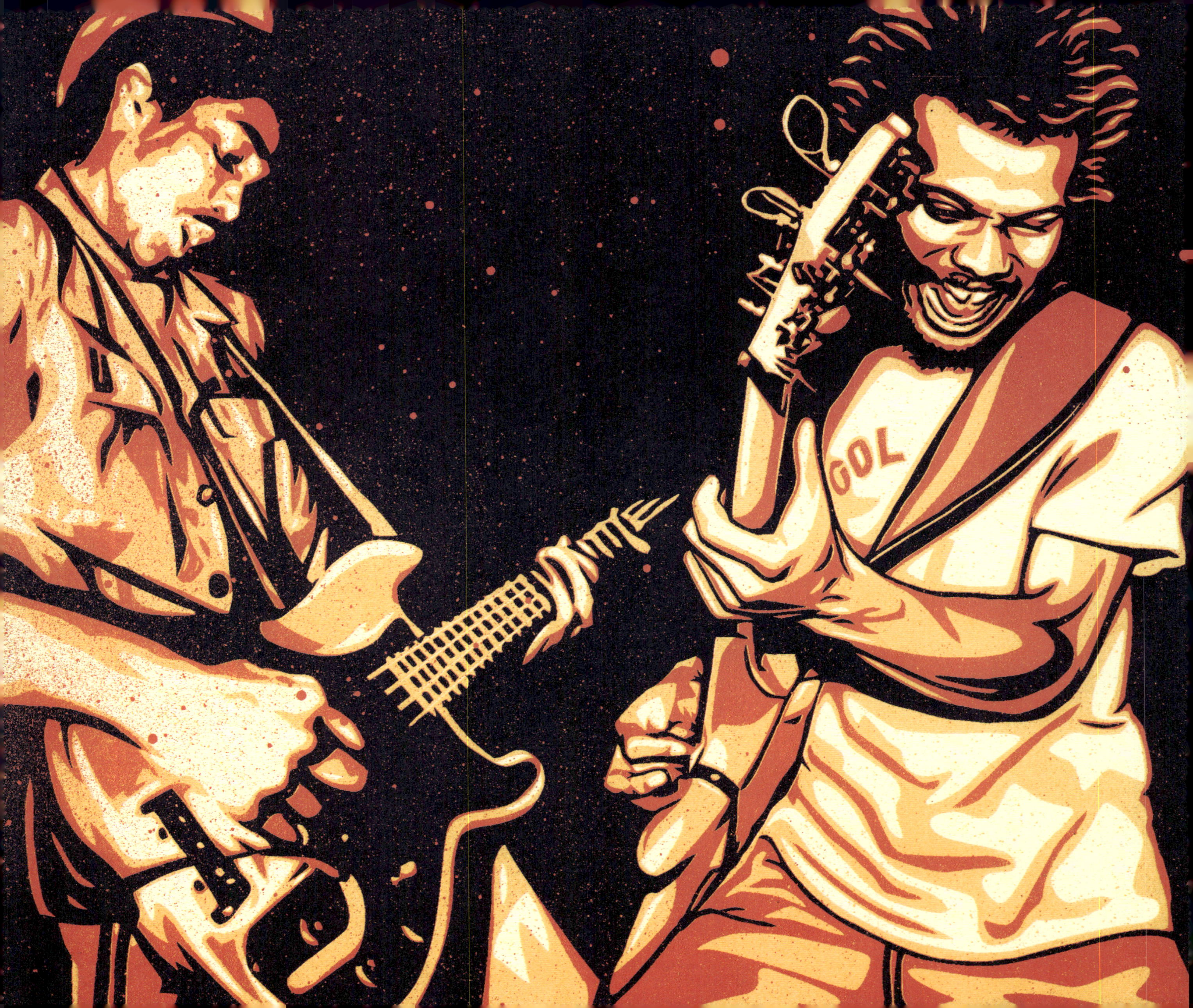
OOL